SAME-SEX MATTERS

SAME-SEX MATTERS

The Challenge of Homosexuality

Edited by

CHRISTOPHER WOLFE

SPENCE PUBLISHING COMPANY · DALLAS
2000

Published in the United States by
Spence Publishing Company
111 Cole Street
Dallas, Texas 75207

Library of Congress Cataloging-in-Publication Data

Same-sex matters : the challenge of homosexuality / edited by Christopher Wolfe
    p. cm.
    Includes bibliographical references and index.
    ISBN 1-890626-30-9
        1. Homosexuality—United States. 2. Homosexuality—Government policy—United States. 3. Homosexuality—United States—Psychological aspects. 4. Homosexuality—United States—Religious aspects. I. Wolfe, Christopher.
HQ76.3.U5 S34 2000
306.76'6'0973—ddc21   00-056351

Printed in the United States of America

*With admiration and gratitude
for those who have courageously struggled
with the affliction of same-sex attraction,
and for those who have dedicated their lives
to helping them.*

Contents

V
The Homosexual Experience

The Challenge of Homosexuality

Christopher Wolfe

S*ame-Sex Matters: The Challenge of Homosexuality* is the second of two volumes on the question of how the American people should understand and respond to problems regarding the phenomenon of homosexuality. Like the first volume, *Homosexuality and American Public Life*, its goal is to advance an understanding of the truth about homosexuality, so that we may respond intelligently, prudently, and compassionately to current efforts to legitimize homosexual acts and ways of life of which they are an integral part.

The basic stance of both volumes is that same-sex attractions are fundamentally disordered and that homosexual acts are intrinsically immoral; that, while they are not usually *chosen*, same-sex attractions are neither genetically or biologically *determined*; that change of such "sexual orientation," while difficult, is sometimes possible; that, in cases where change does not occur, the people who experience same-sex attractions can and should live good and fulfilling lives without acting on those feelings, and deserve our admiration and support as they strive to do so; that society should publicly recognize the disorder of homosexuality, the better to reinforce individuals in their personal struggles, and also to protect very important social interests, especially the recognition of the family—husband, wife, and children-as the essential foundation for individual and communal well-being.

The contributions to *Homosexuality and American Public Life* reviewed the current state of scientific and medical knowledge about homosexuality, examined moral arguments regarding the immorality of homosexual acts, and explained why homosexuality is a proper concern not just of individuals but also of the common good and law.

Same-Sex Matters: The Challenge of Homosexuality, building on these earlier contributions, discusses difficult questions regarding the appropriate arguments to make in public discourse, provides guidance on a number of important public policy issues, surveys some of the participants and fields of battle in the ongoing "culture war," describes a number of orthodox Christian and Jewish theological responses to homosexuality, and concludes with accounts of people who have lived the homosexual life and then come out of it.

Part one takes up questions of how the case against legitimizing active homosexuality can be made in public discourse. I begin by offering suggestions for some lines of arguments. A first line of argument takes advantage of numerous similarities between alcoholism and homosexuality. Beyond that, it is necessary to work out arguments identifying the harms of homosexuality, moving from more direct harms, such as those involving disease, to less tangible but more important harms, such as the undermining of the family.

Patrick Fagan follows with an argument that homosexual sex is a kind of inverted sex, focused on the self, and he maintains that the increasing acceptance of homosexuality is not surprising, given the inversion of heterosexual sex in the form of widespread contraception. Most of "heterosexual America" is now pretty close in its attitudes to the very heart of the homosexual affective disorder: the inversion unto the self. These attitudes have had increasingly deleterious effects on children and created for them a culture of rejection that is incapable of providing the antidote to the challenge of homosexual culture.

While recognizing that the question of contraception is a serious one, Lawrence Burtoft respectfully disagrees, on theological and philosophical grounds, and also on rhetorical grounds: the way to win the battle of public opinion on homosexuality is not to invoke arguments (such as those against contraception) that are themselves even more controversial. He stresses, instead, the importance of countering the false notion, echoed throughout the major media, that homosexuality is somehow innate in some people. Americans—especially those struggling with same-sex attractions—need to know the truth that homosexuality is preventable and treatable. It is this message that will bring hope, healing, and freedom.

Michael Pakaluk introduces part two, which deals with public policy, with a chapter on homosexuality and the principle of "nondiscrimination." He argues that there are strong grounds for retaining anti-sodomy laws, that it would be wrong to enact blanket prohibitions against discrimination on grounds of sexual orientation (for example, in employment and housing) and that homosexual couples should not be treated as heterosexual couples, for purposes of marriage, foster-parenting, and adoption.

Joseph Broadus describes some of the key legal and legislative battles of the "culture war." He analyzes the Supreme Court case *Romer v. Evans,* finding in it a deplorable absence of sound legal principles and an extraordinary judicial claim to power incompatible with democracy. He describes the Defense of Marriage Act, an effort to thwart judicial imposition of gay marriage through the Full Faith and Credit Clause of the Constitution, but notes threats to it from arguments based on *Romer.* Finally, he contends that the Employment Non-Discrimination Act, which would forbid discrimination based on sexual orientation, is both unnecessary and dangerous to freedom of speech and religion.

Melissa Wells-Petry describes the impact on the military of the adoption of a philosophy of "pansexualism," a philosophy of radical sexual individualism. This philosophy generates three key notions undermining the effectiveness of the military: that the individual's wants and needs are more important than the military mission, that soldiering is not a special calling and the military is not a separate, specialized society, and that tolerating sexual license is a *moral* imperative. Moreover, the harmful effects of these notions can be seen in other institutions, for example, churches, marriages, and families.

Mary Beth Style contributes a thoughtful chapter on homosexuality and adoption. Her key point is that adoption should always be governed by the criterion of the best interest of the child, and that sound adoption policy is distorted by a shift to a focus on the "rights" of would-be parents. Lessons can be learned from the harms occasioned by recent changes in the areas of putative fathers' rights and family preservation policies. While there may be cases in which a homosexual should be permitted to adopt a child, because in that case it is in the child's best interests, there should not be "adoption rights" for homosexuals, and adoption policy should recognize heterosexual marriage as the norm for adopted children's best interests.

Shepherd Smith concludes this section with a discussion of HIV-AIDS policy, arguing that "perhaps no disease in history has become so politicized . . . and certainly none other has so challenged the process of translating fundamental tenets of science and medicine into sound policy, as HIV-AIDS." He describes the early history and distorted policy development of this serious public health problem and emphasizes the importance of dealing with it according to established principles of sound medicine.

Part three begins with Michael Medved's analysis of homosexuality and the entertainment media. He explicitly rejects the contention that the entertainment media are sympathetic to the gay agenda because gays are overrepresented in the media. Social and communal pressure within the Hollywood community, from heterosexuals no less than homosexuals, is the key. He also rejects the notion that increasing and sympathetic treatment of gay themes in Hollywood is motivated by the desire for profit. While some gay-themed movies are successful, a large number are not. The best explanation, Medved argues, is a carefully thought-out and well-executed plan, spelled out in the gay press years ago, to change Americans' attitudes on homosexuality. The only way to resist the trend is a similar effort to defend marriage and the family.

Robert Knight describes some of the different ways in which advocates of the legitimization of homosexuality have pursued their goals and catalogues many of the groups that have participated in this effort. He points out that this effort often goes well beyond simple demands for tolerance and includes active legal efforts that threaten freedom of religion, speech, and association.

David Wagner looks specifically at the activities of the homosexual movement in certain key institutions of our society: churches, schools, and libraries. He describes efforts within churches either to deny the authority of Scripture on this subject or to reinterpret it to remove its clear condemnations of homosexual acts. He gives examples of various programs and clubs within schools that attempt to delegitimate resistance to the goals of the homosexual movement (relying especially on themes of rejecting hate and of safety). And he identifies key library policies, such as book selection (whether of gay-affirmative or gay-negative books), as a battleground, providing evidence that groups like the American Library Association have a strong, left-wing ideological agenda.

Part four begins with Robert Wilken's analysis of the historical scholarship of John Boswell, which is often cited on behalf of the proposition that early Christians did not consider homosexual acts to be always sinful. Professor Wilken shows that Boswell's arguments are unpersuasive and generally recognized by scholars as such, despite the uncritical acceptance of them by many in the media.

Rabbi Barry Freundel describes Judaism's understanding of homosexuality, according to which there are no "homosexuals," but only those who engage in homosexual acts, and who, though sinful, should still be welcomed by the community as full-fledged Jews. He provides an analysis of why homosexual acts are condemned as immoral (one which accounts for the greater condemnation of male homosexual acts) and describes the practical prescriptions that flow from Jewish thought: above all, that homosexuals can and should change their sexual orientation, within a supportive enviromnent of the Jewish community.

Bishop Fabian Bruskewitz gives a presentation of the Catholic Church's teaching on homosexuality, explaining that the absence of complementarity in homosexual acts makes impossible both the reciprocal gift of self, despite the illusion of a false intimacy, and the procreative meaning of the bodily act of mutual self-giving in the marital act. Charity toward sinners is an obligation, but cannot obscure the immorality of the act, the disorder of the orientation, the justice of some discrimination, and the need to defend monogamous heterosexual marriage.

In the fifth and last part of the book, Jane Boyer gives compelling personal testimony to the powerful grip of homosexual attractions, the depth of the pain to which they are a response, the anguish of the struggle to overcome them, the joy and hope that come from experiencing liberation from them through faith, and the urgency of the need to share this message with others. Fr. John Harvey describes the principles of Courage, a program based on prayer and friendship for Catholics who experience same-sex attractions but strive to live interior chastity, and the theological and ethical foundations on which it is built.

In a brief Afterword, I comment on some aspects of the current public debate on homosexuality, and especially the striking tendency of gay activists to substitute *ad hominem* arguments for rational discussion.

This book, like its predecessor, is based on papers delivered at a conference sponsored by the American Public Philosophy Institute at Georgetown University Conference Center in June 1997. The reason for both conference and books is the APPI's conviction that our nation's answer to the question of the public status of homosexuality will greatly affect fundamental aspects of its public philosophy. The ultimate question here is whether the nature and ends of marriage, the family, and sexuality are to be *defined by* personal choice or to be regarded as objective realities that should *direct* personal choice. Or, to rephrase that question: is human freedom realized by defending individual *autonomy* in such matters, or is freedom achieved by means of our capacity to know and to act in accord with some intelligible *truth* about human life?

Contributors

Jane Boyer, founder of Amazing Grace Ministries in Portland, Maine, is a registered nurse currently working on an advanced degree in medicine.

Joseph Broadus is an assistant professor of law at George Mason University School of Law.

Bishop Fabian Bruskewitz is the Catholic bishop of Lincoln, Nebraska.

Lawrence Burtoft is a senior fellow in Family, Church, and Society at the Focus on the Family Institute.

Patrick Fagan is the William H. G. FitzGerald Research Fellow in Family and Cultural Issues at The Heritage Foundation.

Rabbi Barry Freundel serves the Kesher Israel Congregation of the Georgetown Synagogue in Washington, D.C.

Father John Harvey, OSFS, is the founder of Courage.

Robert H. Knight is Senior Director of Cultural Studies at the Family Research Council.

Michael Medved is a film critic, bestselling author, and nationally syndicated radio talk show host.

Michael Pakaluk is an associate professor of philosophy at Clark University.

Shepherd Smith is co-founder of the Children's AIDS Fund. He served previously as president of Americans for a Sound AIDS/HIV Policy.

Mary Beth Style is the former vice president of the National Council for Adoption.

Melissa Wells-Petry, a former Army major and member of the JAG Corps, serves as legal counsel for the Family Research Council's Military Readiness Project.

David M. Wagner is an associate professor at Regent University School of Law.

Robert Louis Wilken is the William R. Kenan Jr. Professor of Early Christian History at the University of Virginia.

Christopher Wolfe is a professor of political science at Marquette University and president of the American Public Philosophy Institute.

I

Making the Case

Homosexuality in American Public Life

Christopher Wolfe

THE STATUS OF HOMOSEXUALITY IN AMERICAN PUBLIC LIFE is one of the broad cultural, political, and legal questions of the day. Traditional understandings of a homosexual orientation as "unnatural" and of homosexual acts as "immoral" have been under attack for the last two decades and have lost much of their coherence for many Americans. The major remaining opposition to the acceptance of homosexuality as a legitimate lifestyle comes from more "conservative" religious groups, especially Catholics, evangelical Protestants, and Orthodox Jews. This opposition is unlikely to be successful because the "public square" is "naked" enough these days that many Americans, especially so-called opinion makers, are deeply suspicious of religious arguments—that is, arguments based on specifically religious grounds, most obviously the Bible.[1]

I will outline what I think is a reasonable position for policy makers on homosexuality in American public life.[2] I believe that most Americans still privately consider homosexuality a disorder and that many view it specifically as a moral disorder. Unfortunately, relatively few can defend their intuitions on the subject. What is much needed is an effective argument that will explain the reasonableness of their instinctive resistance to the legitimization of active homosexuality.[3]

It cannot be denied that a powerful emotional argument can be made on behalf of active homosexuality. Andrew Sullivan, a homosexual and former editor of the *New Republic*, has done so in *Virtually Normal: An Argument About Homosexuality*. He often draws with great rhetorical effectiveness on an analogy between homosexuals and other previously oppressed groups, most obviously racial minorities. Sullivan also evokes the confusion, discomfort, fears, unfair treatment, contempt, anguish, and suffering that many homosexuals have experienced in coming to grips with their homosexual orientation in a world that until recently was dominated by traditional views very hostile to homosexuality and often unwilling to distinguish between the orientation and the act.[4]

Nevertheless, I believe that the careful analysis of important distinctions undermines Sullivan's position. I will try to get at some of these distinctions by starting with an analogy between homosexuality and an issue on which public opinion has gone in the other direction, alcoholism. I will then try to put forward an argument about the harms of homosexuality (where the analogy of alcoholism is not very useful), looking at both personal and social dimensions of harm. I will rely on, without repeating, certain arguments made in this volume and its predecessor, *Homosexuality and American Public Life*, for key elements of the best public argument against legitimizing homosexuality. These include: that a homosexual orientation is not genetically or biologically determined, that environmental factors (especially developmental and psychological factors) play a large role in creating same-sex attractions, that counseling and support can in many cases lead to a shift from a homosexual to a heterosexual orientation, and that homosexual acts are immoral.[5]

The Analogy to Alcoholism

The parallels between alcoholism and active homosexuality are striking, particularly on points that have been an effective part of the rhetoric of the homosexual movement. After making a few points, rather briefly, about alcoholism, I will elaborate these parallels.

First, the root causes of alcoholism are not simple. Certainly they involve more than just the simple moral choice to engage habitually in the morally dubious activity of excessive alcohol consumption. Rather, there is evidence to support the position that the roots of alcoholism are a complicated mix of physical predisposition, psychological problems, and moral choices.

Second, even if there is a genetic or biological contribution to the causes of alcoholism, and even if that contribution is great, we would still not think of alcoholism as an acceptable way of life. We might consider the alcoholic not fully culpable for falling into his lifestyle, but we would still actively work to preserve him from it. Moreover, even if an alcoholic told us that we were causing him great frustration and unhappiness, we would not feel that we must, or should, indulge his alleged compulsion.

Third, alcoholism is not always an "obvious" or easily identifiable condition. Though some people may "look" or "act" like alcoholics, it is also true that many very "ordinary" people we live and work around are alcoholics. They have many attractive personal qualities and virtues—they are often friendly, hard working, decent, and quite "functional" in everyday life. Only as time passes do we discover how many people around us are subject to alcoholism.

Fourth, the status of being an alcoholic is not an appropriate one for either moral or political judgments. For one thing, it is very difficult to judge culpability in the matter, since the element of free will in the "choice" to be an alcoholic is often unclear. Moreover, many alcoholics recognize their problem and struggle against it, some with great success, and they deserve our support and often our deep admiration. (Keep in mind that those who are dominated by the inclination to drink excessively are still "alcoholics," even when they win in their difficult struggle to live a sober life.)

Fifth, at the same time, the lifestyle of an "active" alcoholic (one who denies that there is something wrong with his lifestyle) is one that appropriately elicits moral disapproval and pity. It is harmful to the person himself and in varying degrees to those with whom he is socially linked. We would not be persuaded if someone said to us, "If you don't like alcoholism, don't be an alcoholic—but leave me alone!"

Sixth, alcoholics, like all human beings, find it difficult to sustain the dissonance between the way they feel and act and the way they think. Their powerful desires, then, if not subject to the control of reason, will themselves direct the use of reason in the form of rationalizations. This leads to the phenomenon known as "denial," in which the alcoholic refuses to accept that his excessive drinking is a problem and which is not uncommonly accompanied by anger and resentment and striking out against people who are trying to help him.

Seventh, there are people with close social relationships to alcoholics who facilitate the alcoholic's activity, sometimes out of a false compassion, sometimes due to various problems they themselves experience. These people are called "enablers," and their conduct, even when well-intentioned, is rightly subject to criticism.

Eighth, overcoming alcoholism is very difficult, and many people who try to do so fail, but general efforts and specific programs to encourage and help alcoholics to live a sober life are not only worthwhile but essential.

Ninth, when alcoholism leads to harmful acts, such acts are clearly a fit subject for the action of the criminal law. For example, drunk driving has increasingly been recognized by society as a terrible evil that results in numerous tragedies each year.

Tenth, in general, in a society that values (and sometimes overvalues) liberty as much as ours, the criminal law will not ordinarily act directly to punish the acts of an alcoholic that have little effect on anybody but him (for instance, private drunkenness). Nonetheless, social disapproval can still be necessary and appropriate. Alcoholism undermines the common good not only in direct ways, through injuries caused by drunk driving, but also in more indirect ways, perhaps especially through the suffering visited on so many families of alcoholics. Efforts by society to prevent or reduce the incidence of alcoholism or control its effects are fully justified. In fact, the failure to cooperate in these efforts—especially the indirect support of alcoholics by enablers—is rightly subject to moral disapprobation.

Eleventh, even if the role of criminal law is limited, this does not mean that law and public authorities must be neutral. Besides social disapproval of different kinds, other action by society is justified. In particular, given the substantially public character of much of our educational system, the law must still, in its more positive dimensions (such as public education), be allowed to identify the orientation toward excessive use of alcohol as a "disordered" one that is undesirable, one whose causes ought to be resisted and whose effects should be controlled. Efforts toward the prevention of alcoholism and counseling for those who fall into it are very important and highly desirable.

Twelfth, and finally, this position on alcoholism should be put forward in such a manner that it is clearly not a punitive crusade against or an attack on the minority of alcoholics in society, but rather a simple recognition of the facts (including the "moral facts") of life, a recognition that is completely compatible with, and indeed rooted in and intertwined with, charity toward alcoholics. At the same time, it will not be surprising if many alcoholics we try to help (and some of their enablers) react with bitterness and accusations of hatred.

Having made these basic points about alcoholism, let me now try to show why I think that there are substantial—though, of course, not perfect—parallels between alcoholism and homosexuality.[6]

First, the root causes of homosexuality are still difficult to discern, but it seems likely that they are a complex mix of physical (including genetic) predisposition, psychological events (especially in infancy, early childhood, and first sexual experiences), and moral choices (especially in the case of homosexuality that is ideologically inspired). The best literature on the subject suggests strongly that of these three, the second (psychological) is the predominant cause, but it also seems that there is much to learn.[7] At any rate, the disposition to homosexuality is generally involuntary.[8]

Second, even if there is a genetic or biological contribution to the causes of homosexual orientation, and even if that contribution is great, that would not in itself demonstrate that homosexuality is an acceptable way of life. We might consider the homosexual not fully culpable for falling into his lifestyle, but we should still actively work to preserve him from it. Moreover, even if a homosexual told us that we were causing him great frustration and unhappiness, we need not feel that we must, or should, indulge his alleged compulsion.

Third, homosexuals are not an easily identifiable minority—the old stereotypes of lisping and limp wrists obscure the reality that ordinary people are homosexuals. They are people who, like the rest of us, have many attractive personal qualities and virtues, who have the right to live a decent life and make their own distinctive contributions to society.

Fourth, the status of being a homosexual should not be the basis for negative moral and political judgments. The degree of personal responsibility involved in being a homosexual is typically very unclear, so that it is very difficult to make judgments of culpability. Moreover, it is a fact that some homosexuals recognize that their inclination is disordered and try to struggle against it. Homosexuals who make the effort to live continence (not acting on their same-sex attractions) deserve our support and admiration.

Fifth, at the same time, the lifestyle of an active homosexual is one that appropriately elicits moral disapprobation and pity. It is harmful to the person himself and in varying degrees those with whom he is socially linked. (This point is central to my argument, and the actual substantive harms are sufficiently different from those associated with alcoholism that I discuss this point separately below.) For this reason, we would not be persuaded if someone said to us, "if you don't like homosexuality, don't be a homosexual—but leave me alone!"

Sixth, homosexuals, like all of us, find it difficult to sustain tension between the way they feel and act and the way they think. Their powerful desires, then, if not subject to the control of reason, will dominate and direct the use of reason. This leads to the rationalization of those desires and to denial that they constitute a problem. Such desires are a powerful stimulus to the formation of a "gay pride" ideology.

Seventh, people with close social relationships to homosexuals may facilitate active homosexuality, especially by providing moral support. This may perhaps be the case especially with parents, but also with many others who fail to see the harmful effects of their good intentions and false compassion.

Eighth, overcoming a disposition toward same-sex attraction is extremely difficult, and many people who try to do so fail, but general efforts and specific programs to encourage and help homosexuals to overcome their disposition and to live a chaste life are not only worthwhile, but essential.

Ninth, when homosexuality leads to acts that harm others, such acts are a fit subject for the criminal law. Our society's laws cannot prevent alcoholism, and not all traffic fatalities are caused by alcoholics, but it is still imperative that the law treat drunk driving with severity. Likewise, our laws cannot do much about private homosexual acts, and not all AIDS cases are caused by homosexual acts, but it is still imperative for the law to treat the transmission of HIV by means of homosexual acts (as well as in other ways) seriously, as it would any public health problem. So, for example, AIDS partner notification should be a matter of common sense, not controversy.

Tenth, in a society like the United States that greatly values, and sometimes overvalues, liberty, the criminal law will typically be of limited use in dealing with the problem of active homosexuality. One might even make plausible arguments for removing antisodomy laws from our books, under current conditions, on the grounds that they are virtually unenforced and unenforceable, and—just as important— they seem to lack the support of social mores in our culture of tolerance. In their obvious irrelevance, they may accomplish nothing more than to undermine respect for the law. Moreover, their occasional enforcement may do more to undermine than to support what popular disapproval there is of homosexuality by providing an opportunity for opinion makers (who are generally very sympathetic to a relativistic sexual morality) to agitate against traditional moral attitudes. Even an unenforced law can be used as a focal point for organizing opposition and currying sympathy.

On the other hand, there is a powerful argument for keeping such laws on the books without making efforts to enforce them (except perhaps in extreme cases where they are deliberately and publicly flouted —just as private drunkenness is not sought out and punished, but public drunkenness is punishable), on the grounds that they serve an essential educative function in our society, representing society's judgment that such acts are wrong.[9]

Eleventh, even if the role of the criminal law is quite limited, this does not mean that the law must be neutral on homosexuality. Especially given the public character of much of our educational system, it is imperative that society be able to identify the homosexual orientation as a disordered one that is undesirable, one whose causes and effects ought as far as possible to be resisted or minimized. Efforts at prevention of homosexuality and counseling for those who have been afflicted by it are very important and highly desirable.

Twelfth, society ought not in any way to engage in a punitive crusade against homosexuals (including active homosexuals). The recognition of a simple fact of moral life—the disorder of homosexuality —is perfectly compatible with, indeed, is rooted in and intertwined with, charity for those who are subject to this unfortunate condition. In fact, it is precisely those who give the impression that they have contempt and hatred for homosexuals who give credence to the otherwise silly neologism "homophobia." Nonetheless, we will not be surprised if those who try to offer hope and healing to homosexuals are often attacked by those whom they are trying to help (and their supporters) and accused of hatred and intolerance.

As this brief set of parallels suggests, if those who are trying to articulate a reasonable public stance on homosexuality are asked why they take the stance they do, they can often find a good answer by asking themselves how they would respond if the question were about alcoholism.[10] At the same time, this analogy does have its limits, and I want to turn to points where different kinds of arguments have to be made. In particular, I want to turn to the question of the public harm of active or legitimized homosexuality. Here we will have to shift to a different line of argument, since the analogy to alcoholism is much less useful.

The Harm of Homosexuality

What is the harm of homosexual acts that should lead to our disapprobation and pity (and the maintenance, though not aggressive enforcement, of criminal laws) and also to a public stand in education on the disordered character of homosexual orientation, and to a public denial of the status of marriage to homosexual couples?

Starting with a relatively simple argument, we can note the very substantial costs that are often, though not always, associated with living as a homosexual, especially the physical costs. It is not only HIV and AIDS, but a wide variety of other serious illnesses that are found disproportionately among active homosexuals, which include:

- a very dramatic decrease in life expectancy—in some studies, for male homosexuals, on the order of twenty-five to thirty years;

- chronic, potentially fatal, liver disease—infectious hepatitis, with increased risk of liver cancer;

- immune diseases and associated cancers;

- rectal cancer;

- multiple bowel and other infectious diseases;

- higher rates of suicide.[11]

On the basis of health considerations alone, is it unreasonable to ask if it is better not to be an active homosexual? At the very least, don't the facts suggest that it is desirable to prevent the formation of a homosexual orientation and to bring people out of it when we can?

A second argument, leading to the same conclusion, is that homosexuals will never have the opportunity to experience a very fundamental human good: conceiving and bearing children in the normal course of a stable marriage. Some will respond that we ought to facilitate for homosexuals experiences that are as similar as possible to marriage (for example, artificial insemination for lesbians and adoption for homosexual couples). Whatever the value of that argument, however—and I think it is not persuasive—our first, and more important, response should be that, if it is possible, we should try to prevent homosexuality and, where it exists, try to treat it and overcome it, in order to make the very great human good of procreation available to those who might otherwise not be able to achieve it.

Accordingly, we should try to promote policies that prevent the formation of a homosexual orientation. In most cases, a heterosexual or homosexual orientation is well established very early in life and will not be significantly affected by social norms, laws, or public policy. But there are some cases in which policy can have an effect, cases in which other factors (for example, the personal relationship of the child with his father and mother) have left the child's gender identity weak but not settled—the case of so-called "waverers." In such cases, the social approval of homosexuality may encourage attitudes and experiences (such as sexual experimentation) that undermine the normal and proper formation of gender identity.

The legitimization of active homosexuality would authorize homosexuals to compete with heterosexuals for influence in forming the gender identity of young people in broader educational activities (such as school sex education programs) and in more personal efforts to guide adolescents into an active homosexual life as a way of "finding themselves." Some of these latter efforts would be with older, more "mature" adolescents who, although they have not reached their majority, have been held by courts to have "privacy" rights against their parents.[12]

And some efforts, to be entirely frank, would be with younger children, as the activities of the North American Man-Boy Love Association (NAMBLA) suggest.[13] While seductions of young children could still be criminal in a legal order that had legitimized active homosexuality and homosexual marriage, that does not mean that the new legal order would not provide new opportunities for homosexual predators. And while there are many heterosexual predators who ought to be equally subject to legal constraint, there is a considerable body of evidence that promiscuity and lack of sexual restraint is more serious a problem for homosexuals than for heterosexuals. It is true that there are more heterosexual molesters than homosexual molesters, but homosexuals constitute a higher *proportion* of molesters relative to their percentage of the population. And there is evidence to suggest that perhaps 30 percent of homosexuals have been subject to some form of childhood sexual abuse.[14]

We should be clear that many homosexual activists are opposed to such behavior (and that some heterosexuals are not). I mention this sensitive issue not because it is the most common problem but because it is an important problem even if it occurs only in a limited number of cases. And, in this regard, the prominence of NAMBLA, even as a fringe group in the gay rights movement, cannot be ignored.

At the same time, I want to make it clear that my main concern is not with the relatively fewer—though tragic—cases of abuse of pre-pubescent children but rather with the facilitation of homosexual activity in freely-chosen encounters as young people confront their first decisions about what forms of sexual conduct to engage in, especially for those young people who, for varied reasons, may be "at-risk" of falling into homosexual activity. The point is that, in many cases, prevention of the formation of a settled homosexual orientation is possible, with appropriate counseling, therapy, and support.[15]

So far my concern has been primarily with the harm of homosexuality for individuals. I will turn now to the broader social harms.

The Meaning and Purpose of Sex

The most important social harm of homosexuality lies in its indirect but substantial effect on the family. There is a growing consensus that—to cite the title of a now-famous article—"Dan Quayle was right."[16] What Quayle was saying—what he was "right" about—is that the best community for human beings to be born and grow up in is a family based on the stable bond between a husband and wife. The relationship between a husband and a wife is complementary, one in which the union is solidified by the distinctive contributions of masculinity and femininity (not necessarily in their exaggerated stereotypical forms). The husband and wife each contribute something to the union, providing something without which the other party would perceive himself or herself as "lacking" something.

The formation of gender identity and of moral ideas regarding sexuality, and the actions based on them—indeed the whole realm of sexuality—is therefore not a merely "private" matter: it is replete with profound implications for the individual and society. In a society where men and women are puzzled and ambivalent about what it means to be a man or a woman and about the nature and purpose of sexuality, it would be logical to expect greater difficulty in maintaining the stable union between man and woman that we call marriage.

The simple existence of homosexuality, by itself, is not an obstacle to the recognition of the nature and purpose of sexuality any more than the existence of people who have physical deformities necessarily impedes our recognition that such deformities are unfortunate. But a social commitment to the normality of homosexuality—its moral equivalence to heterosexuality, or at least its full moral acceptability—will certainly be one factor among others in the formation of social norms of sexuality.

The most significant harm of legitimizing active homosexuality—the way it would harm the family most—would be the educative impact on the formation of people's ideas regarding the nature and purpose of sex, marriage, and family. Most important, the legitimization of active homosexuality would be the most straightforward and comprehensive attempt to separate the essential connection between sex and children that society has ever proclaimed. In so doing, society would be undermining one of its most fundamental institutions, marriage.

Marriage between a man and a woman is the institution that provides the framework for conceiving, bearing, and educating children. It is irreplaceable. No other way of having and raising children has been successful in general for highly developed societies. (There have been various "experiments" in childbearing and childrearing, but these have either been in exceptional circumstances—for example, the Israeli kibbutz—rather than across the whole of society, or in much less developed societies.) By providing for a father and mother who have deep personal attachments and incentives to perform, in complementary ways, vital roles in the upbringing of children, the family serves as the basic cell, as the foundation of society.[17] Marriage is thus a profoundly "natural" institution in the sense that it is the ordinary mechanism for human beings to be provided with essential conditions for achieving the development of their natural capacities.

What many people fail to realize is that the "naturalness" of marriage is fully compatible with its being very fragile. One of the reasons that marriage is fragile is that men's commitment to the family is much less guaranteed by "merely natural urges" than women's is. Men need "civilizing" or "taming" to play their proper role within the family and society, and so we can say that marriage is natural in the sense that agriculture is: it requires cultivation. This cultivation occurs when society promotes the institution of marriage. The male sex drive is refined and civilized and ultimately rendered much more satisfying by being embedded within a permanent and exclusive personal relationship with one woman, a wife.

Many of our current social pathologies arise from the fact that our society has not been successful in handing on the heritage of social norms supporting a strong, intact family. The instability of family life is a contributing factor to almost any significant social problem today. Rather than weaken the institution of marriage further by establishing a new form of social union essentially divorced from children and the elevated meaning of the sexual urge that children represent, we should reinforce traditional notions of sexuality in which sex is legitimate only within the perspective of family life. Among other things, this would involve resisting the pressure to legitimize homosexual marriage.

One of the explanations for current family problems is intertwined with a likely objection to my argument here. Isn't it true, one might ask, that the issue of the connection between sex and children has already been resolved by our society—and in a way that is profoundly opposed to the position that I have been elaborating? Isn't it true that society's positions on questions such as contraception, premarital sex, cohabitation, and divorce have already undermined the social norm connecting sex and children that I claim is being undermined by the legitimization of homosexuality?

The answer is, simply, "yes." I think there is no question that our current family instability—and the growing acceptance of homosexuality—reflects, among other factors, the influence of changing social mores on contraception, premarital sex, cohabitation, and no-fault divorce. Moral relativism promotes a certain form of sexual morality: the principle that whatever is pleasant and does not immediately harm others in some relatively tangible way is at least tolerable. This (by now) conventional sexual morality starts out by justifying masturbation, premarital sex, and contraception, and having done so, it jeopardizes the strongest arguments for opposing homosexual acts. If sex simply for pleasure or for a sense of personal intimacy really is unobjectionable, and if everyone has a right to sexual self-fulfillment or gratification, then homosexuality is no better or worse than more conventional sexual acts. In the first place, then, it is important for those who wish to resist the legitimization of homosexuality to try to undo the acceptance of the central principles of the "sexual revolution": that all consensual sex is legitimate and that everyone has a "right" to sexual gratification.

Despite the increasing acceptance of the principle that all consensual sex is legitimate, most people have not really confronted the implications of this principle, and when forced to, may hesitate to accept it. Concrete examples of consensual sex that most people would hesitate to accept are polygamy, bestiality, and "consensual" incest. People tend to misunderstand this argument, thinking that it is meant to imply that homosexual acts are just "like" polygamy, bestiality, and incest. Hence, many will regard it as an adequate response to say that

homosexual sex is (or at least can be) different: monogamous and between unrelated human beings.[18]

But the structure of the argument is not as they suppose. In the
case of homosexual acts, it goes something like this: 1) traditionalists
say that heterosexual acts can be morally legitimate and homosexual
acts cannot be so; 2) defenders of homosexual acts ask why homosexual
acts cannot be moral; 3) traditionalists respond with some sort of argument about the nature of sex or practical reason laying down certain requirements for good and acceptable sex; and 4) defenders of
homosexual acts respond by saying that traditionalists' sex is acceptable, but that there is no reason why sex cannot be acceptable when it
is different.

Now take the structure of this argument and apply it to the cases
of polygamy, bestiality, and consensual incest: 1) the (moderate) defender of homosexual sex says that heterosexual and homosexual acts
are legitimate, but polygamy, bestiality, and consensual incest cannot
be so; 2) defenders of polygamy, bestiality, and consensual incest respond by asking why the only legitimate sex is between two unrelated
people; 3) their opponents respond with some sort of argument about
the nature of sex or practical reason implying certain requirements for
good and acceptable sex (that it be monogamous and between two unrelated human beings); and 4) defenders of polygamy, bestiality, and
consensual sex respond by saying that monogamous sex between unrelated human beings is acceptable, but that there is no reason why
sex cannot be acceptable when it is between three or more people,
between a person and an animal, or between father and daughter.[19]
The key here is that, once we turn people's attention to the nature of
sex or practical reason as implying limits on acceptable forms of sex—
once traditionalists show that even defenders of homosexual acts acknowledge that there are some limits on sex besides mere consent—we
improve the chances that people will take seriously the idea that homosexual sex might also be problematic.

The underlying problem for traditionalists is that defenders of the morality of homosexual acts often benefit from the corrosive contemporary scepticism about moral arguments in general—from the powerful strains of moral relativism in our society. But relatively few people are consistent moral relativists, and it is good to make those who adopt a relativist line on the distinction between heterosexual and homosexual sex confront the moral question of the lines between monogamous and polygamous sex, human sex and sex with animals, and sex between unrelated people and sex between father and daughter. In these cases, they are more likely than not to say that there is something about the nature and purpose of sex that makes sex between two people—but not three or more—good, sex with another human being—but not with an animal—good, and sex between unrelated people—but not between father and daughter—good. Of course, there are some consistent relativists who will accept the consequences—who will defend polygamy, bestiality, and consensual incest. But if it can thereby be made clear that accepting homosexual sex involves accepting these other acts, then the arguments for homosexual sex are much less likely to prevail in public opinion.

These arguments only take us so far, of course. It remains necessary to talk about the nature and purpose of sex and why it imposes limits—on polygamy, on bestiality, on consensual incest, and on homosexual acts. Ultimately, that argument has to do with what is truly distinctive about sex, what sex does that nothing else can do so well: it unites two people in one flesh as a sign of a mutually exclusive and permanent commitment, in a way that is ordered to bringing new human beings into existence. This unique and permanent relation is marriage, which provides the necessary context for sex within which its unitive and procreative dimensions are fully realized, precisely by their mutually reinforcing interpenetration.[20]

As I suggested above, a variety of contemporary phenomena undermine a sexual morality rooted in this view of the nature and reason of sex, especially contraception, premarital sex, cohabitation, and divorce. But is it true that the acceptance of these new heterosexual moral norms requires that we carry the process further by legitimizing homosexuality? I think the answer to that question is "no."

An argument justifying something that has harmful consequences cannot rest on the observation that we are already suffering those harmful consequences from other sources. On the simplest level, we might ask how we will better off if we follow a line of logic to even greater harm? Those of us who oppose the legitimization of homosexual conduct can and do fairly agree that the appropriate response is to backpedal on the expanding tolerance of heterosexual norms that undermine the family. Moreover, it is also possible to argue that there is at least some plausible distinction between legitimization of homosexuality and the changing norms of heterosexual activity (divorced from childbearing and childrearing) to which I have referred. This argument is that those heterosexual activities still tend to be understood in a larger natural context that includes children as an important element. If the change in heterosexual mores attenuates the connection between sex and children, it is not widely understood as annihilating it. Homosexual sex does.[21]

Compassion for Homosexuals

Does this argument imply that homosexuals' sexual desires must simply be sacrificed on the altar of society's needs? This is not an indefensible position, since one might argue that everyone has a moral obligation to support the essential requirements of the common good. I would argue just as readily, for example, that unmarried heterosexuals' sexual desires do not justify permarital sexual activity. And all those who restrain their own sexual desires, homosexuals and heterosexuals alike, would, in this view, be benefitting not only society but themselves, for "acting morally" is one of the essential goods for all human beings. In the same way, an alcoholic's desires for drink should be "sacrificed" for greater goods.

At the same time, there are more direct arguments that homosexuals themselves benefit from mores that condemn homosexual acts. Even apart from the relatively straightforward argument that male homosexuals in particular have much shorter life expectancy, there is a broader argument about sexual satisfaction. There is substantial evidence that homosexual activity intrinsically tends toward promiscuity.[22] Insofar as homosexuality may be the result of psychological causes related to "arrested development," homosexual sex may never provide an adequate means of achieving the kind of fruition that monogamous heterosexual sex can provide.[23] The absence of one-flesh communion between a man and a woman, intrinsically oriented toward children as a single reproductive unit, as the natural end and meaning of sex to which sexual pleasure is ultimately subordinated in heterosexual sex, leaves homosexual sex—which is not capable of one-flesh communion, since it involves no complementary beings who together form a single reproductive unit—facing an endless striving for the inherently unattainable goal of genuine personal communion. This requires, of course, the recognition of a distinction between genuine personal fulfillment and mutual sexual gratification, even the gratification of a genuine personal relationship that spuriously mimics the deeper interpersonal communion of marriage.

One of the striking aspects of Andrew Sullivan's book—on the whole, a moderate and even "traditional" defense of homosexual marriage—is precisely that, after a carefully nuanced argument portraying homosexuality as an involuntary condition and homosexuals as "virtually normal" people who seek the same ends in sex as heterosexuals do, he ends his book by making surprising assertions about homosexual sex—assertions that undercut the earlier arguments dramatically: among "gay male relationships, the openness of the contract makes it more likely to survive than many heterosexual bonds"; "there is more likely to be greater understanding of the need for extramarital outlets between two men than between a man and a woman"; "there is something baleful about the attempt of some gay conservatives to educate homosexuals and lesbians into an uncritical acceptance of a stifling model [that is, because truly monogamous] of heterosexual normality"; "to flatten their varied and complicated lives into a single, moralistic model [that is, the model of complete fidelity] is to miss what is essential and exhilarating about their otherness." In the end, it seems that exclusiveness is simply not a feature of homosexual sex. Sullivan characterizes this as "exhilarating," but I believe that it is, rather, an indication of the inability of homosexual sex (and promiscuous heterosexual sex) to satisfy human beings in the way that ordinary conjugal heterosexual sexual relationships, based on genuine fidelity, can.

Responding to the Challenge of Homosexuality

What, then, are we to do? Society should firmly adhere to social norms according to which homosexuality is a disordered, unnatural form of sex. That message should be conveyed by people within the institutions of civil society through social disapproval of active homosexuality. The object of social action, above all, should be the prevention of homosexuality and the facilitation of its treatment by refusing to legitimize homosexual activity (which would undermine any incentive to seek treatment) and educating homosexuals on the availability of support. Government can contribute to the maintenance of the social norms in definite but limited ways, especially by the stand it takes in public education, and by the firm refusal to legitimize homosexual marriage.[24]

What should homosexuals themselves do? First, young homosexuals in particular should seek out counseling to explore the possibility of therapy to reverse their orientation. The fact that, in the given concrete circumstances of their lives, only a minority of homosexuals will likely find it in themselves to accomplish this (for no one would argue that it is an easy task) should not obscure the fact that a significant minority may find it possible. After all, no one rejects the idea of encouraging alcoholics or drug abusers to seek aid in reforming their lives, merely on the grounds that, more often than not, such treatment is not successful. They owe it to themselves at least to explore this possibility seriously. It is unfortunate that the effort to legitimize active homosexuality will prevent many homosexuals from even recognizing that their orientation is a "problem" and from seeking help to deal with it.

Second, homosexuals who do not succeed in changing their same-sex attractions should live good and meaningful lives that do not include homosexual acts. When they fail to live up to this ideal, they should—like heterosexuals who experience similar failures—return to the struggle, knowing that such moral struggle, with its ups and downs, is an important part of everyone's moral life—though the specifics of that struggle will vary from person to person.

What about the sexual frustration they will experience, the personal anguish that continence will entail? It will be a difficult struggle for many of them, of course, but this does not mean that the exhortation to live such a life bespeaks a lack of compassion or an insensitivity to suffering. It is the same exhortation that ought to be addressed to unmarried (many of them never-to-be-married) heterosexuals. It is an exhortation similar to the one that ought to be addressed to alcoholics, to those whose impulses to anger are difficult to control, to drug addicts, and so on. It is similar to the exhortations that are addressed to those with physical disabilities, to face up to the difficulties that are beyond their control and to live a good life in spite of them. These exhortations do not deny suffering, but they do, I think, help people to ennoble it. It is not a celebration of disabilities, but of heroic efforts to deal with them, which can be an occasion for personal growth and happiness even in the face of difficult circumstances. It is not an altogether pleasant or comforting truth that a life which involves some suffering can be good and meaningful, and it is understandably difficult for those who suffer to accept such exhortations cheerfully when they come from those who do not share their suffering. But it is, nonetheless, an important truth about life—one that our modern, affluent, secularized society has great difficulty acknowledging.

Coping with the difficulties that people face has a social dimension of course: suffering alone is harder than suffering within a supportive community. The need for support is one reason why it is important for those who oppose active homosexuality to make it very clear that the homosexual orientation itself does not relieve people of their dignity. In fact, it is imperative that defenders of "traditional" norms regarding homosexual acts convey their admiration and affection for homosexuals who strive to live lives of sexual self-control.

But, inevitably, the most important and credible source of exhortations to live according to right moral norms will have to be homosexuals themselves, who can provide support and friendship to each other in these efforts. Groups such as Courage, Exodus International, and Homosexuals Anonymous, for example, serve as essential, institutionalized forms of moral support for many homosexuals in these difficult circumstances.

In the long run, legitimization of active homosexuality is not true compassion. It would be destructive for both homosexuals themselves and for society at large. Creating a world in which it is possible for those with same-sex attractions to live with pride and dignity and according to right moral norms will not be easy. It certainly will involve something other than "returning" to some traditional form of society, since the mechanisms for enforcing social norms against active homosexuality in the past were too blunt, failing to recognize the extent to which homosexual orientation is not always simply a choice and all too often subjecting homosexuals to condemnation. But the effort to create that better world will also avoid the easy way out of legitimizing the pursuit of sexual gratification. Legitimizing homosexuality is wrong because it denies the truth about homosexuality. It is wrong because it is a false form of compassion—a kind of "enabling." It is wrong because it holds out a false hope, rooted in an underlying despair that it is possible to subordinate sexual desires to more profoundly fulfilling aspects of human life. The ultimate message of those who oppose legitimizing homosexuality must be the positive one of genuine compassion and respect, hope and healing, and dignity in truth.

2

The Inversion of Heterosexual Sex

Patrick Fagan

I T IS IMPOSSIBLE to look at our culture over the last few decades without realizing the extent of the changes in our sexual mores. The strength of the contemporary homosexual movement is rooted in these changes, which began in the latter part of the nineteenth century, gathered steam in the early part of the twentieth century, and by 1930 had caused a significant rupture in the unified tradition of Christian religious and moral teaching on the nature of the sexual act.

By the late 1940s American married couples were contracepting in growing numbers. In the 1960s the children of these contracepting couples led the sexual revolution, logically rejecting the need for marriage as the context for the sexual act. By the 1970s the next generation enshrined the "woman's right to choose" abortion, the elimination of the natural fruit of the sexual act. A generation later, in the 1990s, we have the rise of homosexual rights.

All of these gradual slouchings towards Gomorrah[1] are the inevitable by-product of the severing of the sexual act from its prime end, its fundamental natural function: the begetting of children. This severance changes the focus of the sexual act: from being ultimately "other focused," sex becomes "self-focused." This introverted sex changes, both psychologically and interpersonally, those who engage in it.

If one no longer considers childbearing part of the nature of the sexual act, and if married heterosexuals claim childless sex as a "right"—they have and the Supreme Court long ago upheld it[2]—then it is difficult to deny this "right" to those whose sexual acts always preclude children—that is, homosexuals. Our sexual mores—changed solely for the sake of sexual pleasure—leave no response to the argument that homosexuals receive no pleasure from the heterosexual sexual act and are therefore deprived of an equal right to the pursuit of pleasure by laws that discourage or forbid a homosexual lifestyle. Their position, in our current culture, is unassailable.

Sexual Inversion

Few will deny that contraception has radically changed the social function of the sexual act or that the whole of society has, in its turn, been transformed. After decades of legalized contraception, the social data on heterosexual culture are massively disturbing. The heterosexual disorder at the heart of contraception is related to, and is more dangerous than, the inner psychological structure of the homosexual orientation.

One psychoanalytic description of homosexuality as a psychological phenomenon states:

> Homosexuality is regarded as one of the systems developed by individuals to organize experiences and expressions of conflicting and painful feeling, and the system serves as a containment of deeper anxieties, and offers for the individual a modus vivendi. The system is not just an object choice, but a long standing way of relating, is part of a person's character development and far more complex than the notion of it being part of object choice. It is important to distinguish homosexual identity and homosexual behavior. The presence of homosexuality, if conflictual or repressed could give rise to symptoms such as anxiety, social in-

hibitions, or to sexual dysfunction such as impotence or frigid-
ity.[3]

This definition can be recast to describe the majority of married
couples in the United States today, as well as a huge proportion of
unmarried heterosexuals:

> [Contraception] may be regarded as one of the systems devel-
> oped by individuals to organize experiences and expressions of
> conflicting feelings and desires. The [contraceptive] system serves
> as a containment of deeper anxieties, and offers for the individual
> a modus vivendi. The system is not an object choice [the choice
> of the one to be loved] but is a long standing way of relating,
> and is part of a person's character development. It is important
> to distinguish heterosexual identity and this form of heterosexual
> behavior. The presence of heterosexuality, if conflicted or re-
> pressed, as is the case in habitual contraception, could give rise
> to symptoms such as anxiety, marital inhibitions, or to sexual
> dysfunction such as divorce, child rejection and abortion.

In the psychological conflict experienced by homosexuals, the threat
to the integrity of the self stems from the demands of intimacy with
one of the opposite sex. In the conflict caused by contraception, the
threat to the self is the intimate attention demanded by the child.

Ismond Rosen, a leading British therapist and the editor of *The
Oxford Book of Sexual Deviations*, writes: "According to my observation the homosexual lifestyle is learned, and if this becomes incorporated as part of the individual's sense of identity or self, the chances
of that person changing to a heterosexual orientation become much
more remote, due to the unconscious resistance aroused by the threat
of an actual loss of identity or sense of self."[4] These insights on the
development of the homosexual orientation can be transposed validly
to the contraceptive orientation and be reconstructed thus: "The contraceptive life-style is learned, [it takes a lot of repeated teaching, and

now has a massive educational and medical infrastructure devoted to attaining that end] and when it becomes incorporated as part of the individual's sense of sexual identity and habitual practice the chances of that person changing to a 'giving sense of self' become much more remote, due to the anxiety aroused by the threat or fear of a loss of self in the sacrifice involved in bringing a child into existence."

Early Views on Contraception

My thesis is not new and is not anchored in a religious doctrine but rather in a natural law understanding of the power of the sexual act to fundamentally orient or disorient not only the life of an individual but also the whole of society. This present disorientation and dysfunction of our society, and of those who live in it, was predicted by many in anticipation of the widespread practice of contraception. The accuracy of their predictions give their underlying insights a serious claim to validity.

From very different quarters we find similar opinions. Sigmund Freud—no friend of religion—pointed out in "The Sexual Life of Human Beings" that the separation of procreation and sexual activity is the most basic of perversions, and that all other sexual perversions are rooted in it: "The abandonment of the reproductive function is the common feature of all perversions. We actually describe a sexual activity as perverse if it has given up the aim of reproduction and pursues the attainment of pleasure as an aim independent of it. So, as you will see, the breach and turning point in the development of sexual life lies in becoming subordinate to the purpose of reproduction. Everything that happens before this turn of events and equally everything that disregards it and that aims solely at obtaining pleasure is given the uncomplimentary name of 'perverse' and as such is proscribed."[5]

In the face of vigorous lobbying by Margaret Sanger, founder of

Planned Parenthood, Mahatma Ghandi insisted on the inevitable deleterious impacts of artificial contraception:

> Artificial methods [of contraception] are like putting a premium on vice. They make men and women reckless . . . Nature is relentless and will have full revenge for any such violation of her laws. Moral results can only be produced by moral restraints. All other restraints defeat the very purpose for which they are intended. If artificial [birth control] methods become the order of the day, nothing but moral degradation can be the result. A society that has already become enervated through a variety of causes will still become further enervated by the adoption of artificial [birth control] methods . . . As it is, man has sufficiently degraded women for his lust, and artificial [birth control] methods, no matter how well-meaning the advocates may be, will still further degrade her.[6]

From Contraception to Rejection

In the course of the twentieth century, contraception has become widespread and habitual (figures 1 and 2). Sterilization has become an increasingly popular form of birth control, especially for parents who have had one or more children (figure 3). If we assume that there is but one partner sterilized in each marriage, an assumption open to question but which helps put the data in perspective, a clear picture of our contraceptive culture emerges (figure 4).[7]

The sex education industry, which includes most of our large foundations, their educational and social science counterparts in the universities, and their allies in the medical and nursing professions, has all put massive efforts into changing the ideas that we, and especially young people, have about the nature of the sexual act. They have made massive inroads into the ordinary culture on teenage contraceptive use (figure 5). Nevertheless, their success has come with a price. Corresponding to the time, money, and efforts of these groups is a change

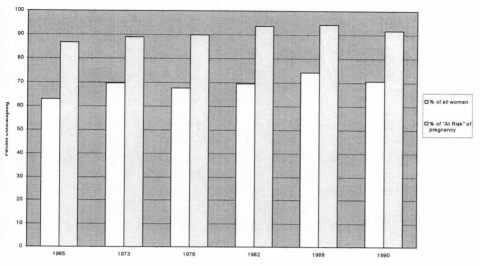

figure 1

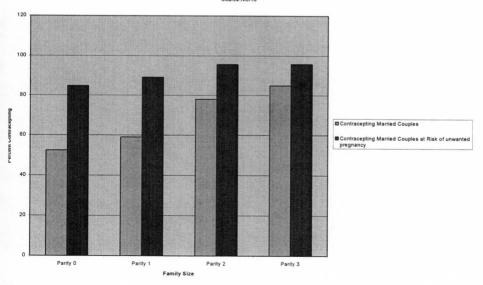

figure 2

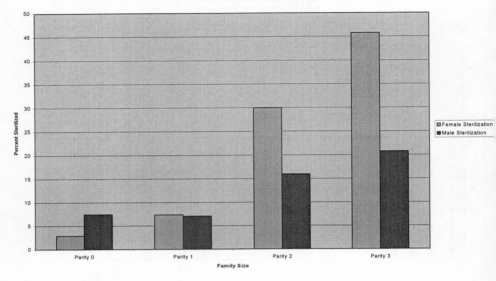

figure 3

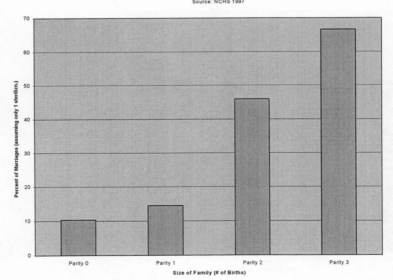

figure 4

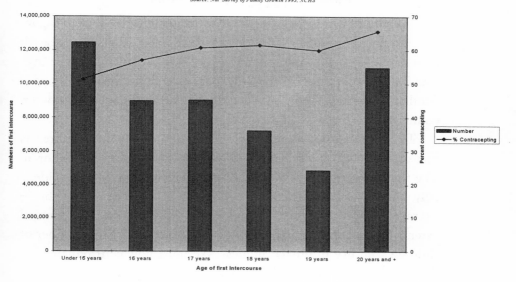

figure 5

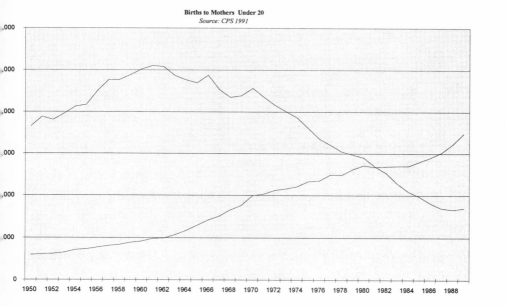

figure 6

in a most fundamental behavior of young adults during these same years (figure 6). This pattern parallels a wider societal change (figure 7). Among the poorest families, marriage has all but disappeared; corresponding to this disappearance is an increase in child abuse (figures 8 and 9). But this correspondence is present not just among poor families. A British study casts clear light on the connection between family structure and child abuse (figure 10).[8]

The fundamental result of the separation of sex and children is that our society has increasingly become a hostile place for children. The trend toward out-of-wedlock births—which has, not coincidentally, only accelerated as contraception has become more available— aggravated by the divorces which leave children without married parents living at home, has led to a steady increase in the number of children who live in broken homes. We must now confront the fact that for the young our culture is predominantly a culture of rejection (figure 11).

The effects of these changes are incontrovertibly negative. Broken homes increase the risk of:

- health problems;
- retarded cognitive, especially verbal, development;
- low educational achievement;
- low job attainment;
- behavior problems;
- low impulse control;
- warped social development;
- physical and sexual abuse;
- crime in the local community.

As broken homes become more numerous, the results are still more devastating. Charles Murray has determined that when the proportion of broken homes in a given community reaches about 30 percent, the community itself becomes a source of additional risks, rather than of support, for children and the family.[9]

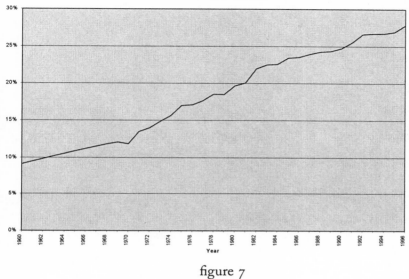

figure 7

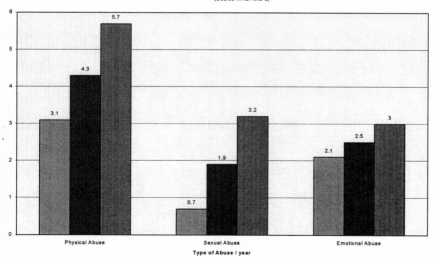

figure 8

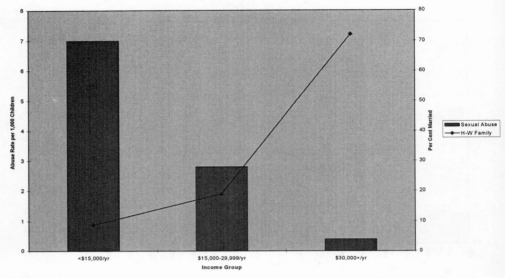

figure 9

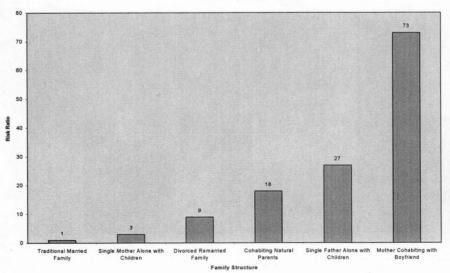

figure 10

Rejection Ratio: Number of Children Entering a Broken Family Each Year for Every 100 Children Born that year.
Sources: Derived from MVSR on births, and Children in Divorce

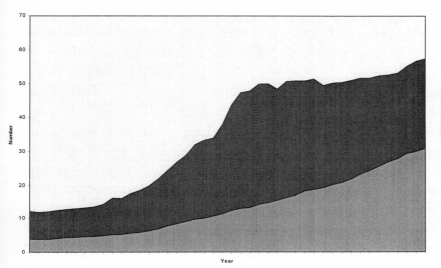

figure 11

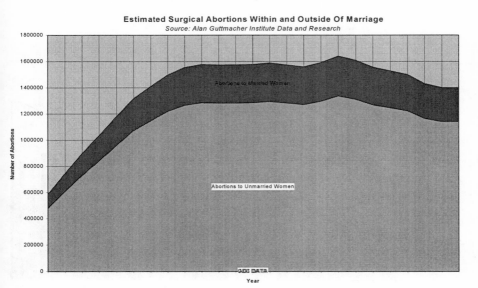

figure 12

From Rejection to Abortion

The ultimate rejection, of course, is abortion. "It is apparent that nothing short of contraceptives can put an end to the horrors of abortion and infanticide" promised Margaret Sanger and many others.[10] But most abortions now take place outside of marriage, that is among those who claim the right to the inverted sexual act (figure 12). Moreover, a National Abortion Rights Action League pamphlet argues that though "contraceptives should be more widely available and promoted, in the present state of contraceptive technology, given the continuing possibility of human error in the use of even the best methods, abortion is needed as a recourse. Its use is not preferable to contraception, but once a pregnancy occurs, it is the only means of birth prevention."[11] When we combine the ratios to live births of children in broken homes, out-of-wedlock births, and abortions a staggering picture emerges of our cultural rejection of children (figure 13).

All of the social and psychological disorders I have described are disorders of "heterosexual culture." Once we severed the child from

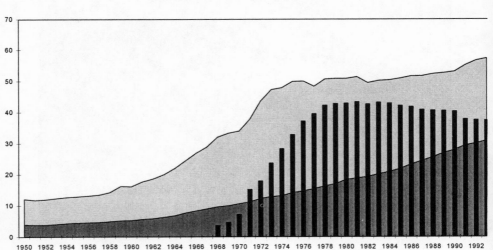

Annual "Rejection Ratio" for Every 100 Live Births
Source: NCHS data and Alan Guttmacher data

Children born our of Wedlock Children of Divorce Children Aborted

figure 13

the sexual act, we altered the relationship of marriage to sex. This naturally led to the altering of the relation of sex to marriage. Having disposed of marriage, we needed to dispose of unwanted children. Having disposed of the child and marriage, we increasingly view the homosexual act as just another variant of this new, modern sexual act.

In a traditional society, adults assume the burdens and accept the blows of life so their children may grow and develop in peace. Today, it is children who bear the burdens while parents seek their own pleasure. Society exists to raise children: "People do not live together merely to be together. They live together to do something together ... No social group will long survive its chief reason for being," writes Ortega y Gasset.[12] Europe—in particular Italy, Spain, and Portugal, whose population growth rates are negative—illustrates this observation only too well. The United States is not far behind.

Defining Deviancy Down

One of the functions of religion is to shore up society's adherence to the natural moral law. When the institution of religion caves on a moral issue, other institutions (family, education, government, and the marketplace) cannot be expected to maintain their defense of society on the issue in question. When the institutions of religion "define deviancy down," in the words of Daniel Patrick Moynihan, other institutions are likely to follow. And that is what has happened on the issue of contraception.

The birth control movement, the vehicle of the practice of contraception, has its roots not only outside of Christianity but among groups that were quite hostile to Christianity. The official beginning of the religious severing of the sexual act from the procreative was the Lambeth Conference of 1930, but the attack on traditional moral principles had been going on for some time, as the following observation from an Anglican divine in 1919 illustrates: "Although many Malthusians are rationalists, they are well aware that without some religious sanction their policy could never emerge from the dim underworld of unmentioned and unrespected things and could never be advocated openly in the light of day. To this end birth control is camouflaged by pseudo-poetic and pseudo-religious phraseology, and the Anglican Church is asked to alter her teaching. Birth controllers realise that it is useless to ask this of the Catholic Church but as regards the Church of England, which makes no claim to infallibility, the case is different, and discussion is possible."[13]

In the Lambeth conferences immediately preceding 1930—those of 1908, 1914, and 1920—the Anglican Church felt itself under pressure to change its moral teaching and saw the need to reiterate the traditional moral law:

> We utter an emphatic warning against the use of unnatural means for the avoidance of conception, together with the grave dangers—physical, moral and religious—thereby incurred, and against the evils with which the extension of such use threatens the race. In opposition to the teaching which in the name of science and religion encourages married people in the deliberate cultivation of sexual union as an end in itself, we steadfastly uphold what must always be regarded as the governing consideration of Christian marriage. One is the primary purpose for which marriage exists—namely, the continuation of the race through the gift and heritage of children; the other is the paramount importance in married life of deliberate and thoughtful self-control.[14]

If a single date could be identified as the historical break with traditional natural law principles of sexual morality—if one desired to highlight the West's very first official step down the slippery slope—it would be August 15, 1930, when, by a vote of 193 to 67, the Lambeth Conference passed Anglican Bishops' Resolution 15, which read in part:

> Where there is a clearly felt moral obligation to limit or avoid parenthood, the method must be decided on Christian principles.

The primary and obvious method is complete abstinence from intercourse (as far as may be necessary) in a life of discipleship and self-control lived in the power of the Holy Spirit. Nevertheless, in those cases where there is such a clearly felt moral obligation to limit or avoid parenthood, and where there is a morally sound reason for avoiding complete abstinence, *the Conference agrees that other methods may be used, provided that this is done in the light of the same Christian principles.* The Conference records its strong condemnation of the use of any methods of conception-control for motives of selfishness, luxury, or mere convenience. [emphasis added]

Similar debates were underway in many other denominations. Orthodox Jews held to the traditional moral norm, but Reformed Jews had already broken on this issue. The Central Conference of American Rabbis had taken a stand in favor of contraception in 1929. The United States' Federal Council of Churches (now the National Council of Churches) had been waiting for someone else to take the lead in "modernizing" the church's stand on birth control. In March 1931 it endorsed "the careful and restrained use of contraceptives by married people," while at the same time conceding that "serious evils, such as extramarital sex relations, may be increased by general knowledge of contraceptives."

Nevertheless, statements by other churches and by the secular press give an idea of how different the conception of the sexual act was then from what it is today. Condemnations followed quickly on the declarations of Lambeth and the Federal Council of Churches.

Dr. Walter Maier of Concordia Lutheran Theological Seminary: "Birth Control, as popularly understood today and involving the use of contraceptives, is one of the most repugnant of modern aberrations, representing a 20th century renewal of pagan bankruptcy."[15]

Bishop Warren Chandler of the Methodist Episcopal Church South: "The whole disgusting [birth control] movement rests on the assumption of man's sameness with the brutes. . . . Its [the Federal

Council of Churches] deliverance on the matter of birth control has no authorization from any churches representing it, and what it has said I regard as most unfortunate, not to use any stronger words. It certainly does not represent the Methodist Church, and I doubt if it represents any other Protestant Church in what it has said on this subject."[16]

The Presbyterian (April 2, 1931): "[The Federal Council of Churches'] recent pronouncement on birth control should be enough reason, if there were no other, to withdraw from support of that body, which declares that it speaks for the Presbyterian and other Protestant churches in ex cathedra pronouncements.[17]

The Southern Baptist Convention: "The SBC hereby expresses its disapproval of the Hastings Bill, now pending before Congress of the United States, the purpose of which is to make possible and provide for the dissemination of information concerning contraceptives and birth control; whatever the intent and motive of such proposal we cannot but believe that such legislation would be vicious in character and would prove seriously detrimental to the morals of our nation."[18]

Since then, for most of these denominations, the moral teaching on the nature of the sexual act has changed. When asked how this change in doctrine and practice came about, some Christian, non-Catholic theologians from those very denominations that denounced the Lambeth changes but since have come to accept them could only say that it was gradual going with the tide over the years.

In 1931, even secular journalists were shocked by the new teaching. The *Washington Post* reacted to the Federal Council of Churches with a heated editorial: "Carried to its logical conclusion, the committee's report, if carried into effect, would sound the death-knell of marriage as a holy institution by establishing degrading practices which would encourage indiscriminate immorality. The suggestion that the use of legalized contraceptives would be 'careful and restrained' is preposterous."[19] Two days later, the *Post* addressed the matter a second time: "It is the misfortune of the churches that they are too often misused by visionaries for the promotion of 'reforms' in fields foreign to religion. The departures from Christian teachings are astounding in many cases, leaving the beholder aghast at the unwillingness of some churches to teach 'Christ and Him crucified.' If the churches are to become organizations for political and scientific propaganda, they should be honest and reject the Bible, scoff at Christ as an obsolete and unscientific teacher, and strike out boldly as champions of politics and science as modern substitutes for the old-time religion."[20]

To no one's surprise, the Catholic Church remains firm in her condemnation of contraception. Several weeks after the Lambeth resolution, Pope Pius XI explained, in his encyclical *Casti Connubii*: "In order that she [the Catholic Church] may preserve the chastity of the nuptial union from being defiled by this foul stain, she raises her voice in token of her divine ambassadorship and through our mouth proclaims anew: any use whatsoever of matrimony exercised in such a way that the act is deliberately frustrated in its natural power to generate life is an offense against the law of God and of nature, and those who indulge in such are branded with the guilt of a grave sin."[21]

While the doctrinal position of the Catholic Church is clear and frequently reiterated from Rome, the response and practice of most Catholics in the United States seems to be similar to that of most other Americans. The most comprehensive study on the birth control habits of Americans was the 1988 National Survey of Family Growth, which also gathered data on the religious affiliation of the respondents. In 1988, 72 percent of all married Catholic women of childbearing age used artificial contraception; of these, 55 percent said they relied on the pill, 22 percent on tubal ligation, 12 percent on vasectomy, and 11 percent on other methods.[22]

The Consequences of Contraception

The change in the attitudes towards contraception involve a change in man's relationship to God, to the opposite sex, and to himself. As far as reason can know, God's highest creative act is the creation of man. In the sexual act, the Creator makes man his "co-creator," and man and God join in the act that is both man's highest naturally creative act and God greatest creative act: the bringing of another human being into existence for eternity. In the Orthodox Jewish tradition the sexual act is compellingly described as of the order of entering the Holy of Holies in the Temple, meeting God where he is most especially present.[23]

For the resolutely contracepting married person who goes to worship God on the Sabbath an inherent contradiction has crept into his stance before God, for he effectively says: "I worship You as my Creator, but I refuse to join with you as co-creator in exercising our highest acts, in bringing into being that next human creature You want to endow with existence for all eternity." The contradiction is enormous, as are the consequences, as the data show.

The practice of contraception unanchors man. The sexual act, as long as it is open to life, has the effect of keeping us, at a minimum, oriented towards "the other." Otherwise, we become self-centered in that most pleasurable of all activities. This inner psychological rearrangement of mind and heart spills quickly into a changed relationship with our spouses, the opposite sex, and children, resulting in divorce, out of wedlock births, abortions, and abandoned children.

Radical changes for society result: from being ordered to children to being centered on the individual self. One experienced mother put the heart of the test rather graphically: "With my next child I had a choice: to go 'insane' in trying to preserve some piece of my life for myself, or to lose myself in yielding it all up for the foreseeable future in the service of my children."

The future society depends on its producing competent young adults, which in turn depends on loving parents. Loving parents are those who have giving hearts. Contraception inverts these hearts, and this inversion affects first our children, and then all of society.

The present debate on homosexuality is but the latest stage in an old conflict: a gnostic view of man against the natural law view of man. The meaning and purpose of the sexual act is at the core of this conflict. From the Albigensian and Malthusian conceptions of sex to Marx's and especially Engels' view, to Berdeaev's development of the concept of androgyny in this century, down to the more recent feminist redefinition of the nature of women, the same old set of fundamental ideas clash.

If heterosexuals are unwilling to fulfill their responsibilities, how can we ask homosexuals to take on the burden of this struggle? If heterosexuals hold fast to the distortion of the relationship between man and woman at its most intimate level by the decision to avoid new life, how can we ask those who are "organized" differently to resist their particular temptation? Most of "heterosexual America" is now very close in its attitudes about sexuality to the heart of the homosexual affective disorder: the inversion into the self. These attitudes have created for children a culture of rejection that is incapable of providing the antidote to the demands of the homosexual movement.

The massive disorder we see around us is not the making of the "gay community" but of the "heterosexual community." If we want to take the mote out of our "gay" brothers' eyes, maybe we should first remove the beam in our own. If we are to have the compelling attitude of love and affection that is central to helping members of the "gay community" turn from their inversion, then we must first look outwards to those children each of us is individually called to "co-create" and love—those children already existing and those who may yet, if we have the love to grant it to them. If the two inversions continue to compound each other, the future is bleak indeed, especially bleak for children and the society those children will be capable of building.

3

A Rhetoric of Hope

Lawrence Burtoft

T HE BATTLE between competing visions and expressions of human sexuality is fought with ideas in the institutions that propagate them in law and policy. To identify the dominant ideas in a society is to be able to predict, at least to a rough degree, the future of that society's sexual practices and, if history gives any clue, its long-term cultural viability.

For those who have taken upon themselves the burden of cultural and spiritual restoration in our time, few tasks are of more fundamental importance than mastering the ideas at the center of the current conflict regarding human sexuality. This is a formidable challenge, given the multiple fronts of the battle—legal, corporate, educational, ecclesiastical, psychological, scientific, and biblical, to name a few. Formidable, yes, but absolutely necessary if those who hold to the radical sexual ethic represented by the historic Judeo-Christian tradition are to sculpt a rhetoric capable of turning back the tragic tide of disordered desires, human suffering, and social insanity which the sexual revolution perpetuates. While the rhetoric needed to accomplish this is complex, the goal is simply stated: to influence public opinion to support a general social transformation with regard to human sexuality, such that the marital norm is once again the preeminent conviction of the majority of Americans, a conviction that is reflected in social policy and culture.

That this is a goal and not a present reality is due to the fact that we now have a society and a culture deeply influenced by what Patrick Fagan refers to as "the homosexualization of heterosexual sex."[1] By this phrase Fagan points to the general understanding and practice of sex in America today: an inversion upon the self wherein personal pleasure, self-fulfillment, and freedom from social responsibility are the primary standards of expression. In this understanding, whether or not the sexual act takes place between different- or same-sex individuals is of secondary importance.

We can expand Fagan's concept to include the ideology of homosexualism and the culture of homosexualism. By the former, I refer to the belief that all forms of sexual expression, including, but not limited to, homosexual relations, are morally legitimate, on an ethical par with exclusive, lifelong, heterosexual monogamy. By the latter, I refer to the various cultural forms—legal, artistic, educational, ecclesiastical—in which the ideology of homosexualism is expressed. We must respond to this culture and the ideas which animate it, and we must attempt to reverse its advance. For we are dealing with what Norman Podhoretz has referred to as "the terrible distortions of the fundamental realities of life" and all the destruction of human potential that such distortions bring about.[2] Indeed, the senseless waste of human potential through death, disease, and moral decay is the most tragic and damning fruit of all perversions of human sexuality. As Harry Jaffa has pointed out, we have reached a stage where the only norm for sexual expression is not that no harm should be done but only that whatever is done be with mutual consent, as if by some act of moral alchemy consent had the power to transform that which is essentially antilife to life.[3]

Standing behind this whole pitiful mess are ideas about what is moral, about human sexuality, about masculinity and femininity, about freedom and justice, about what constitutes a good life, and, of course, about the nature and value of homosexuality. Ultimately, none of these issues can be avoided; and before this struggle is decided, a majority of Americans will, at least by default, assent to certain ideas about the good and the true.

Our public life flows from our private life. The practices, policies, and laws which govern the public sphere are ultimately rooted in the ideas and values which govern our personal lives. The task, then, of those who are convinced that the future is not best served by embracing a more "progressive" sexuality, is twofold: first, to identify those ideas which have been most influential in affecting public opinion and practice, and second, to develop a strategy for restoring to a place of social respect and institutional sanction the idea that, to put it in biblical language, "the marriage bed alone is undefiled." I will focus primarily upon the first task and attempt to deal with one key aspect of the ideology of homosexualism. I will develop my thoughts in response to the two previous contributions to this volume, by Christopher Wolfe and Patrick Fagan.

The Point of Departure

Fagan has argued in substantial and persuasive detail that the problems of sexual expression in America can be traced to the widespread acceptance of the idea that sex can be legitimately separated from procreation and of the concomitantly widespread practice of contraception, both of which were assisted by the failure of Protestant churches to maintain their traditional opposition to this idea and this practice. Fagan refers to the underlying dynamic which has accompanied this development as the "homosexualization of heterosexual sex," marked by narcissistic inversion. But it is upon the practice of contraception that Fagan places particular blame, seeing in it the practical and technological lubricant which has greased the skids of America's moral decline.

Fagan is clearly concerned that before sexual traditionalists, particularly Christians, cast their stones at those who defend the moral legitimacy of homosexuality, they reflect upon their own practices. Recalling the historic understanding within the Christian tradition that human sexuality is intimately and, in Fagan's view, inseparably connected to the high calling of co-creation with God, he urges a serious reevaluation and soul-searching on the part of Christians: "If heterosexuals are unwilling to fulfill their responsibilities, how can we ask homosexuals to take on the burden of this struggle? If heterosexuals hold fast to the distortion of the relationship between man and woman at its most intimate level by the decision to avoid new life, how can we ask those who are 'organized' differently to resist their particular temptation?"[4]

As an Evangelical Christian whose spiritual homeland, humanly speaking, lies within twentieth-century conservative American Protestantism, I certainly feel the power of Fagan's argument and have often considered it to be a potentially potent rhetorical weapon in the homosexuality debate (not to mention what it means from a spiritual perspective in terms of living a life of faith). His line of thought is primarily sociohistorical, pointing to the ongoing deterioration of sexual mores and practices subsequent to the acceptance of contraception. With this argument there seems little with which to disagree; the truth of it can be seen in both the data and the dire results of the sexual revolution. But Fagan goes beyond mere description to normative judgment—that there is no qualitative difference between homosexual acts and the sexual intercourse of a married heterosexual couple using contraception. From this perspective, these practices share the inversion of the self, a condition in which genuine love of the other is absent. Homosexuality is only one form, albeit a blatant one, of this inversion, different in degree and form, but not in kind. Given this analysis, it follows that, rhetorically speaking, what is required is an educational campaign, primarily within the churches, which will seek to persuade Americans to give up their selfish and shortsighted views

and sexual practices, to abandon themselves into the care of God, and
to express their sexuality only within the context of *contraceptive-free*
heterosexual marriage.

In spite of the persuasive power of Fagan's argument, I have res-
ervations. First, I am not convinced from a theological or philosophical
perspective. I do not find the distinction between artificial birth control and natural family planning (which Fagan, as a Catholic with
integrity, supports) is morally tenable. If procreation is the only good
or end to which the sexual act aims (with the unitive function being
important but secondary), and therefore to which every sexual act
ought to aim, then all forms of intentional control over or prevention
of pregnancy would appear to be illicit. Christians have historically
held that, in judging human action, the intention is more basic than
the action itself. This would seem to render untenable the distinction between natural and artificial birth control, as both share the intention of non-procreation and, thus, would be prohibited on principle.
I fail to see any possible justification for family planning if we insist
that the sexual act is justified only in cases in which procreation is a
possibility.

The more basic issue is whether we are to exercise any control of
any kind—natural or artificial—over the timing and possibility of procreation. If we are, then it seems that method, while certainly important (with certain methods being inherently impermissible—for
example, abortion), is secondary to the issue of intention. The essential issue is permissibility of any form of birth control. If it is permissible for legitimate reasons and the sexual act is taking place within
a legitimate context, that is, heterosexual marriage, it would seem
wholly permissible. Of course, this raises the question of what constitutes a legitimate reason for birth control, a question to which I can
only give a cursory answer. Chief among the reasons would be the
well-thought-through (and, for people of faith, prayerfully considered)
issue of the couple's ability to bear and raise the child.

Other problems with the noncontraception argument include what appears to me to be an arbitrary derogation of the unitive purpose of the sexual act and the problematic nature of sex for those who, for whatever reason, cannot bear children. I realize that there are sophisticated arguments that deal with these difficulties, but this is not the place to enter further into a critical debate regarding contraception per se. Suffice it to say that this is an issue which deserves—indeed, *requires*—serious moral reflection and dialogue by Catholics and Protestants and others who desire to be guided by a biblical sexual ethic. This is particularly true for those who support contraceptive rights while denouncing homosexual acts, or even more important, who have forgotten that marriage does not justify any and all kinds of sexual behavior or attitudes. To remind us, as Fagan does, that sex mirrors the sacrificial and self-giving love of God, is to recall us to first things. He is to be thanked for bringing this issue to the forefront of our attention.

My second difficulty with Fagan's argument is more in keeping with the rhetorical concerns of this paper. If I, as one committed in principle to the biblical norm of sex only within marriage, remain unconvinced regarding the prohibition of contraception, then we must ask serious questions regarding the rhetorical value of this approach. By "rhetorical value" I simply refer to its persuasive power. In other words, setting aside for the moment the question of the soundness of the anticontraception argument, what is the likelihood that such an argument will be effective in convincing a majority of Americans that homosexuality is not a good thing and is not a value that our public institutions ought to support or promote? I have serious doubts about the success of any attempt to convince Americans that homosexuality is wrong by first convincing them that contraception is wrong. Even if it is true that contraception is an evil, it is equally true that there are few ears ready and willing to hear that truth. My point is one of prudence. We are warned in the New Testament against casting our pearls to pigs and giving what is holy to dogs. This is not because Jesus disliked pigs and dogs but because he realized they had no stomach for pearls nor interest in things holy. We must choose our truths carefully in order to wield them effectively, and to avoid a premature and unnecessary negative backlash. Jesus did go on to give his reason: "so that the pigs and dogs don't trample the precious pearls and holy things in the mud and turn and tear you apart." Here I am not referring to those engaged in homosexuality but the far larger heterosexual public. Our task is to persuade, not to cause a stampede.

While Fagan would like to see sex reunited to procreation, it would be a major social and cultural victory simply if it was once again wedded to marriage in policy, public perception, and personal practice. Before we can ever hope to have Americans seriously thinking about contraception, our public moral sensitivities need to be restored to the point that all extramarital sex is once again looked upon as a tragic breach of morality. This is by no means an easily achievable goal, but I believe it is closer to the current sentiments of most Americans than the idea that contraception is intrinsically wrong. As Christopher Wolfe has pointed out, the majority of Americans still recognize intuitively the normative status of heterosexual relations, albeit apart from any tightly reasoned arguments, and certainly without any firm commitment to chastity and marital exclusiveness.[5] This being the case, it would seem that the most hopeful strategy for forming American public thought and policy concerning homosexuality must build upon this intuitive bias toward heterosexuality, supplying it with arguments specifically designed to counter those more immediate ideas that have proven to be influential in creating a social climate increasingly tolerant and accepting of homosexuality. It is these more immediate ideas to which I will now turn my attention.

What, then, are those ideas that have been most influential in increasing public tolerance and acceptance of homosexuality? While Fagan correctly points to our general narcissistic inversion to personal pleasure, Wolfe highlights a fundamental ethical principle which is overlooked in many discussions regarding the causes and conditions which lead to a homosexual orientation. By drawing attention to the many parallels between alcoholism and homosexuality, including the personal and social harms that are associated with these conditions, Wolfe implicitly makes this point: that even if we can identify the factors that may influence one toward homosexuality (or alcoholism), this in no way constitutes a moral justification of homosexual acts.

To point this out can be helpful in clarifying issues in the debate over homosexuality. However, it still requires that we deal with the widespread ethical confusion that characterizes Western culture in general. The loss of a common moral framework beyond pragmatic considerations and, more important, of an ontological context in which a moral framework makes sense, is of incomparable significance. So much of what characterizes the late twentieth century social malaise is attributable to the fact that, in Robert Jensen's phrase, the world has lost its "story" and, with it, any context for making moral distinctions.[6] It is doubtful, therefore, that the conflict over homosexuality will ever be resolved without the recovery of a genuinely transcendent ethic. I agree with Christopher Wolfe's assessment of the social danger of the ideology of homosexualism: "The most significant harm of legitimizing active homosexuality—the way it would harm the family most—would be the educative impact on the formation of people's ideas regarding the nature and purpose of sex, marriage, and family. Most important, the legitimization of active homosexuality would be the most straightforward and comprehensive attempt to separate the essential connection between sex and children that society has ever proclaimed. In so doing, society would be undermining one of its most fundamental institutions, marriage."[7]

Forming Public Opinion

But having said this, I do not believe that this is the place, any more than with the contraception issue, to attempt to counter the ideology of homosexualism. There are other ideas that make up the ideology of homosexualism which can be addressed immediately and which may be countered more easily than questions of a fundamental moral nature. If you are going to peel an onion, you must begin at the first layer, not at the center.

Among the most important of these "surface" ideas is that homosexual orientation is both innate and immutable, that homosexuals are "born that way" and, therefore, cannot change. Though not all homosexuals agree with this understanding, I believe it is has been very persuasive. The change in American public opinion during the last decade regarding the moral status of homosexual relations, illustrated by the University of Chicago's National Opinion Research Center in its General Social Survey Trends 1972-1996, reveals just how persuasive it has been.[8] Beginning in 1972, the survey included as one of its questions the following: "What about sexual relations between two adults of the same sex—do you think it is always wrong, almost always wrong, wrong only sometimes, or not wrong at all?" (I will only give approximate percentages and only for the answers "always wrong" and "not wrong at all.") Public opinion regarding sexual relations between members of the same sex as always wrong remained relatively steady from the early 1970s through 1991, in which year the figure was at 77 percent. By 1993 this had dropped to 66 percent, and then to 61 percent in 1996, the last year for which figures are available. Starting in 1991, we see a corresponding rise in the number of people finding nothing wrong with homosexual relations, going from 13 percent in 1990 to 28 percent in 1996.

If we grant these figures, we see that the percentage of Americans who find homosexual behavior to be always wrong has gone from a high of 78 percent to a low of 61 percent, a loss of 17 percentage points. At the same time, the percentage of those finding nothing wrong with such behavior has risen from a low of 12 percent to a high of 28 percent, a gain of 16 percentage points. Thus it can be said that from 1973 to 1996, the gay rights movement has shown a net gain in public acceptance of about 33 percent. If we are to take these figures as truly indicative of the change in public opinion, then it would seem that

Norman Podhoretz was right in his assessment that the gay rights movement has won, at least in this long first round.[9]

One factor which certainly influenced opinion was the 1973 decision by the American Psychiatric Association to no longer consider homosexuality a pathology. Nevertheless, it took nearly twenty years for the significant change of attitude regarding the moral status (as opposed to the psychological or medical status) to take place, and then not until the American public was exposed to an ever-increasing number of articles discussing various "natural" causes. It will help to document briefly some of this widespread media exposure.

In 1979 sex therapists William H. Masters and Virginia Johnson claimed that homosexuality was a learned behavior which could be unlearned.[10] Within two years, a chorus of dissenting voices began to be heard. In April of 1981, Reuters carried a story on the research of an East German scientist, Guenther Doerner, who believed that homosexuality could be traced to prenatal hormonal imbalances.[11] In August and September of that same year UPI,[12] the *Washington Post*,[13] and *Newsweek*[14] carried stories reporting on research conducted by Alfred Kinsey's Institute for Sex Research suggesting that homosexuality is inborn, possibly as a result of prenatal hormonal influence.[15] Three years later a study conducted by researchers at the State University of New York and the South Beach Psychiatric Center in New York was reported as further suggesting a possible hormonal link to homosexuality,[16] and the *Washington Post* was reporting that "more and more experts think homosexuality has a biological basis."[17]

In 1985 the *New York Times* reported on a panel discussion at the annual convention of the American Psychological Society with the headline, "Panelists Cite Biological Roots of Homosexuality."[18] A year later the PR newswire service[19] carried a story on the possible genetic basis of homosexuality as discussed in a report by Richard C. Pillard and James C. Weinrich of the Boston University School of Medicine.[20] Pillard was quoted as saying of this study of the brothers of gay men that "what we have found in this study is compatible with a genetic component to male homosexuality." What the cautious scientist described with the phrase "is compatible with" is easily misunderstood by the general public to mean "confirms."

By 1988 the idea of biological causation had gained such acceptance that *Parents* magazine ran an article by two Florida Atlantic University researchers debunking parental influence and championing prenatal biological conditions.[21] The following year Judd Marmor, past president of the American Psychiatric Association, who in 1980 clearly agreed with theories focused upon parental influence,[22] wrote a book review for the *Los Angeles Times* in which he referred to "the growing body of research evidence that a significant proportion of male homosexuals are biologically predisposed at birth to become homosexual by virtue of variations in the degree to which they have been exposed to circulating male sex hormones during their intra-uterine development."[23] That same year *USA Today* ran a story with the title, "A Biological Theory for Sexual Preference," which, while it included dissenting voices, gave the general impression that scientific opinion was moving increasingly in the direction of a general recognition of some form of biological causation to sexual orientation.[24] A sociologist, Dr. Lee Evans, is quoted as saying, "I'm certainly open to the idea that [homosexuality] is caused by a combination of things, but I'm inclined to say that all those things happen before someone is born." The same article quotes Richard Pillard, mentioned above, in support: "Most people who really know the issue believe that there's something there of a biological tilt." Again, for the average reader, this "tilt" may be experienced as a landslide.

The 1990s saw a significant increase in the number of articles dealing with the issue of biological causation. A Nexis search for articles on the topic which appeared before 1990 listed thirty-six.[25] The same search parameters for articles from 1990 to the present listed 351. Even though the scientific evidence in support of biological causation has been inconclusive at best, the headlines implied a strong connection. The first significant articles came in 1991, concerning the now-famous brain study by Simon LeVay published in *Science*.[26] Here is a sampling of headlines:

- "Are Men Born That Way? A new study suggest that there is a structural difference between the brains of homosexual and heterosexual men, but that is just part of the story." (*Time*, September 9, 1991)
- "Brain Study: Findings on Differences Between Gays and Heterosexuals Sparks Whirlwind of Recognition" (*Los Angeles Times*, September 8, 1991)
- "Researcher Finds Clue in Brains of Gay Men" (*Boston Globe*, August 30, 1991)
- "Brain Cell Finds Link to Homosexuality. Tissue differs between gay and straight men" (*San Francisco Chronicle*, August 30, 1991)
- "Brain Cells May Affect Sex Choices; Study ties biology to homosexuality" (*Atlanta Journal and Constitution*, August 30, 1991)
- "Brains of Gays, Heterosexuals Differ, Study Shows" (*Orlando Sentinel Tribune*, August 30, 1991)
- "Homosexuality Linked to Difference in Brain" (*St. Petersburg Times*, August 30, 1991)
- "Brain May Determine Sexuality" (*Washington Post*, August 30, 1991)

Early in 1992 *Newsweek* ran a major article with the title, "Born or Bred,"[27] which, though including a number of viewpoints critical of biological causation and a fairly balanced discussion, kept the idea before the public. In August of the same year, *USA Today* published an article with the headline, "Difference Seen in Brains of Gay Men,"[28] reporting a recent study by two UCLA researchers.[29] The *Los Angeles*

Times story on this ran with the headline, "New Homosexuality Link Found in Brain,"[30] and the *Washington Post*'s Associated Press story read "Study Shows Brains Differ in Gay, Heterosexual Men."[31]

A year later stories reporting on the study by Dean Hamer of the National Cancer Institute that suggested a possible genetic basis of homosexuality[32] made the front page of both *USA Today*[33] and the *Wall Street Journal*,[34] with a major article appearing in *Time* under the title, "Born Gay? Studies of Family Trees and DNA Make the Case that Male Homosexuality is in the Genes."[35] Early in 1994 a number of articles discussed the rising concern over the possible ethical problems connected with research into the biological basis of homosexuality—so much so that such well-known researchers as Simon LeVay and Dean Hamer issued statements attempting to assure those concerned that they would do all they could to prevent improper use of such research and any possible test for a gay gene.[36] That such actions were seen as necessary may indicate how widespread the idea of biological causation had become and how many people were convinced of its probable truth.

A Nexis search reveals that, starting in 1990, the number of articles discussing possible natural or biological bases for same-sex attraction increased at a substantial rate through 1993, and though 1994 witnessed a decrease, it has remained relatively steady to the present. It should be noted that it was just after the period of greatest exposure to stories dealing with research into biological connections (1991–1993) that the National Opinion Research Center's poll revealed the biggest change in public attitude.

Interestingly, in 1994 the National Opinion Research Center included for the first time this question: "Do you think being homosexual is something people choose to be, or do you think it is something they cannot change?" Of those who answered the question 41 percent reported believing it was chosen, 14 percent said they did not know, and 45 percent chose "Something they cannot change." It is interesting to note that in spite of this high number, that year still registered a 63 percent negative moral judgment. Unfortunately, the question was not included in the 1996 survey, so we have no idea if the numbers changed; but given the fact that fewer people (down to 56 percent) chose "always wrong," it would be reasonable to hypothesize that the numbers of those believing that the homosexual condition was unchangeable had also increased.

That the correspondence between the public's exposure to the idea of biological causation and its increased acceptance of homosexuality is more than mere coincidence is supported by two journal articles which bear upon this issue. In 1989 two sociologists from Arizona State University conducted a study in which they surveyed 754 people in four societies, looking at the correlation between belief about the origin of homosexuality and tolerance of homosexuals. Their analysis revealed that "those who believe that homosexuals are 'born that way' tend to be significantly more tolerant of homosexuals than people who believe that they 'choose to be that way' or 'learn to be that way.'"[37] A second study, reported in 1992, looked at how their exposure to research dealing with the biological bases of homosexual orientation affected people's attitudes toward homosexuals. The study found that when people are exposed to literature that suggests a biological determination of sexual orientation they are likely to be more positively disposed toward homosexuals than others who either have not been exposed to any literature dealing with the subject at all or to literature suggesting that no biological determinant exists. This was particularly true for women. It is interesting to note that this study involved undergraduate students at a conservative Christian college in Southern California, where one might expect a generally stable negative moral assessment of homosexuality.[38]

What these studies report, and what my comparison of popular media coverage and public opinion polling demonstrates, at least in a preliminary fashion, is what common sense would have suggested and every marketing professional knows: people are extremely susceptible to what they read and hear, and are far more likely to be influenced by the popular media's appearance of objective reporting than by genuine scientific or religious authorities.

There are undoubtedly a number of variables which have aided the advance of the ideology of homosexualism, not the least of which is the neutralizing effect of the public's constant exposure to the issue, the increasing number of "out" gays and gay characters in the media, and the appearance that the truly informed and sophisticated among us all recognize the goodness of being gay or lesbian. A recent article dealing with the public's acceptance of the idea of genetic causation pointed out the relationship between public gullibility and the prevailing political climate: "Popular reactions to genetic claims can be greatly influenced by what is currently politically correct. Consider the hubbub over headlines about a genetic cause for homosexuality and by the book *The Bell Curve*, which suggested a substantial genetic basis for intelligence. Many thought the discovery of a 'gay gene' proved that homosexuality is not a personal choice and should therefore not lead to social disapproval. *The Bell Curve*, on the other hand, was attacked for suggesting differences in IQ measured among the races are inherited."[39]

What people think about the causes of homosexual attraction is of extreme importance. Without a strong and somewhat sophisticated moral sensibility, the idea that homosexuals are born that way and cannot change erodes people's intuitive aversion to homosexuality. Unfortunately, we are not living in a culture that is marked by sophisticated moral sensibilities.

In light of both the steadily shifting tide of public opinion in favor of homosexuality and the fact that this shift seems to be effected in large part by people's perception of the nature of the homosexual condition, Christopher Wolfe's assessment of the importance of communicating two truths about homosexuality deserves repeating. First, regardless of the nature and extent of the conditions which lead some people into homosexuality, these in no way determine the moral worth of the condition or its expression. We study the roots of alcoholism in order to help people escape its destructive hold upon them, not in order to decide whether alcoholism is good or bad. We judge that on a wholly different basis—on what a human being is and is meant to become in the divine design. The same is true with infidelity, breast cancer, obesity, schizophrenia, or manic-depression, all of which have been the object of research as to their possible genetic influence. We cannot do this with homosexuality. Efforts must be undertaken to educate the American public on the truth of this most basic moral insight: what is does not determine what ought to be. If there is no moral standard which transcends empirical reality, then there is no moral standard at all, only tradition and custom, both mutable and transient. We certainly do not decide alcoholism's moral worth by asking alcoholics whether they think their life is just fine, just as we do not confer with criminals to judge the moral value of their behavior.

Secondly, the prevailing idea by which homosexualism has advanced—that homosexuals are born that way and cannot change—must be countered, for it is simply not true. In its place must be the declaration that homosexuality is both preventable and treatable. I cannot here defend the truth of this assertion, but it is true nonetheless.[40] Those who are trained in the appropriate disciplines (biology, genetics, psychology, psychiatry) must bring their expertise to bear upon this issue, helping the public to discern between research that is solid and that which is merely a form of advocacy. Public pressure must be brought to bear upon organizations, such as the American Psychiatric Association, which are currently clearly under the sway of advocates of homosexualism, such that genuine academic and scholarly freedom is once again a reality and therapists working with men and women desiring to rid themselves of unwanted homosexuality are free both to pursue their practices and share their clinical experiences in the appropriate professional journals.[41] Of particular importance in this regard are studies like those of the National Association of Research and Therapy of Homosexuality which document the rate and kind of success experienced in "reparative" or "conversion" therapies and ministries.[42] Those who have access to various forms of popular media (print, broadcast, video, film) must use these avenues for disseminating the truth. In short, extensive efforts are called for so that the falsehoods to which Americans are now being exposed may be shown to be just that, and the thousands of men and women who need and desire help may find it. Those who manage foundation resources or who have access to funding sources must come to the aid of the many struggling organizations and ministries which are seeking not only to put the lie to the claim of "once gay, always gay" but, more important, to bring hope, healing, and freedom to those who experience their homosexuality as unwanted and oppressive.

As it has been considered for millennia by both Jews and Christians, homosexuality is one symptom of the general brokenness of humanity; it is also one of the myriad opportunities for the redemptive power of God to do its work. Our task, in the area of public opinion and policy, is to maximize the opportunities by which those involved in homosexuality, as well as Americans in general, realize that homosexuality is, by the grace of God, both preventable and treatable.

In closing, let me return to the radical analysis that underlies both Fagan's and Wolfe's arguments. Regardless of where one comes down on contraception, it is certainly safe—and necessary—to identify as one of our most pressing needs in America today, and especially in our churches and synagogues, that we demonstrate to those caught in the grips of homosexuality, and all the other forms of sexual and relational futility, the genuine goodness and beauty of the sexual life expressed as God intended it to be—within the liberating bonds of the marital love of a man and a woman. This, it seems to me, is the most effective means of countering the ideology of homosexualism in the long run. And we would do well to reflect on Fagan's observation: "The massive disorder we see around us is not the making of the 'gay community' but of the 'heterosexual community.' If we want to take the mote out of our 'gay' brothers' eyes, maybe we should first remove the beam in our own."[43] It is as we do this that we will see more clearly and be better able to help others in their struggle toward wholeness. In other words, it is time once again, as it always is, for redemptive judgment to begin within the household of God.

II

Public Policy

4

Homosexuality and the Principle of Nondiscrimination

Michael Pakaluk

IT IS UNDENIABLE that homosexuals in this country enjoy all of the traditional civil rights and liberties enjoyed by other citizens. Homosexuals enjoy freedom of religion, association, and speech; freedom from unwarranted search and seizure; and freedom to participate fully in political decisions. They are protected against attacks on their life, person, and property by the same laws which, albeit rather imperfectly, protect everyone else; and they have the same legal recourse and remedies as anyone else. These are by no means meager blessings. Taken together, these liberties and protections constitute precisely the sort of freedom that America was founded to promote.

What, then, do many believe is lacking? What basis can there be for complaint? Contemporary claims of injustice, advanced by gay activists, focus on three distinct areas:

1. whether antisodomy laws should be retained, or if they are "unconstitutional" and therefore illegitimate;
2. whether there should be laws prohibiting "discrimination" against someone, in housing or hiring, because of his homosexual activity or orientation;

3. whether homosexual relationships should be treated the same
    as heterosexual relationships, and hence whether homosexual
    couples should be allowed to marry, to raise foster children,
    and to adopt.

Each of these issues is distinct. The first has to do with laws that
penalize behavior in which homosexuals have a tendency to engage.
The second has to do with whether the law should enforce some standard of equal treatment for homosexuals as it has done for blacks and
other minorities. The third has to do with whether homosexual relationships should entail the same privileges as heterosexual unions.

These points of contention can be ranked according to the seriousness of the challenge they pose to what remains of pre-sexual revolution laws and mores. On the one hand, to overturn antisodomy laws
is simply to remove a censure and not yet to approve of homosexual
activity or orientation. To outlaw discrimination, or the drawing of
distinctions, on the basis of homosexuality is to enforce a kind of
equality of status, and, as we shall see, it amounts to societal approval
of homosexual activity. Finally, to assign benefits to homosexual relationships is to go beyond approval, to the point of actually promoting
homosexual activity.

Note that each of these three points of contention is debated on
separate grounds. People argue against antisodomy laws by claiming
that such laws violate a putative right to privacy. In contrast, they argue
against discrimination in hiring and housing by claiming that there is
an analogy between the current plight of homosexuals and that of
blacks before the modern civil rights movement. Invoking the Equal
Protection clause of the Fourteenth Amendment, they claim that sexual
orientation should be a protected category, like race, gender, religion,
and ethnicity. With regard to the third area of controversy, there seems
to be no plausible legal argument at all in favor of extending benefits
usually enjoyed by married couples to homosexual relationships; but
clearly some people support it because they feel vaguely that the cur-

rent practice is unfair, or because they feel sorry that homosexuals seem excluded from family life.

Let us look more closely at these areas of controversy and determine how we should view them.

Antisodomy Laws

All fifty states had antisodomy laws before 1960; during the next two decades, twenty-three states repealed their laws, and eight others amended their laws to make them apply to acts between homosexuals only.[1] The traditional reason for such laws was that sodomy wrongly separated sex from procreation.[2] The early statutes therefore applied with equal force to such acts between a man and woman. But the sexual revolution of the 1960s, relying as it did on contraception, was premised upon this very separation of sex from procreation. Indeed, at the deepest level there is little difference between contraceptive intercourse and sodomy. So it is hardly surprising that, as the sexual revolution got underway, society lost its insight into why sodomy should be illegal, and states began either repealing the laws or, inconsistently, restricting them to homosexual acts only—as though what makes sodomy wrong is that it proceeds from homosexual desire, rather than, as is actually the case, what makes homosexual desire disordered is that it tends to sodomy.

The sexual revolution was very quickly read into the Constitution by the Supreme Court. But as late as 1961, traditional jurisprudence still held sway, and Justice Harlan could write, in his dissent to *Poe v. Ullman*, that "the very inclusion of the category of morality among state concerns indicates that society is not limited in its objects only to the physical well being of the community, but has traditionally concerned itself with the moral soundness of its people as well. . . . The laws regarding marriage which provide both when the sexual powers may be used and the legal and societal context in which children are born and brought up, as well as laws forbidding adultery, fornication, and homosexual practices which express the negative of the proposition, confining sexuality to lawful marriage, form a pattern so deeply pressed into the substance of our social life that any Constitutional doctrine in this area must build upon that basis."[3]

Harlan seems to go so far as to say that any regulation of sexual activity which did not promote the family would not be constitutional. However, within four years, in *Griswold v. Connecticut* (1965), the Court fabricated, out of whole cloth, a right to privacy which has since served as a kind of constitutional stamp of approval for the sexual revolution. The right to privacy was later used to overturn all laws regulating abortion, and it will very likely be used eventually to find laws against sodomy unconstitutional. It is true that the Court resisted this conclusion in the *Bowers v. Hardwick* (1986) decision, but one justice in the majority, Louis Powell, soon after said that he regretted his vote. Especially given the Court's decision in *Romer v. Evans* (1996), it seems only a matter of time before the Court reexamines the matter and overrules *Bowers*.

Putting aside, for the moment, the sexual revolution and the misguided jurisprudence which followed it, let us try to understand why antisodomy laws were first enacted and have traditionally been considered important.

We begin by observing that the state has an interest in regulating the sexual activity of its members. There are three reasons for this, all of which Justice Harlan touched upon. First, the state has an interest in promoting the family because the family is the only reliable source of good citizens—of men and women with civic virtues, goodwill towards others, peaceable habits of association, and virtues of thrift and hard work. It therefore has an interest in discouraging sexual activity that is harmful to family life.

Second, the state needs to insure that the rights of all of its citizens are protected, especially those of children, but children have a right to be raised within an intact family (or, strictly speaking, from being deprived of an intact family without grave reason). It follows that the state has an interest in regulating sexual activity so that children are conceived and raised within stable families.

Third, the state has an interest in encouraging its citizens to master their sexual desires. This is an obvious and important point, but strangely it is frequently overlooked today. Inordinate sexual desire is clearly as capable of dominating and enslaving people as are greed, power, alcohol, and drugs. Desire not infrequently drives people to neglect their responsibilities, to use power illicitly, to abuse the rights of others, to betray others, to lie, even to commit murder. Disordered sexual desire is often directly linked to depression, listlessness, and rage. Clearly, a tranquil civic order can be established only among citizens who have achieved a good degree of sexual self-control, and the state clearly has an interest in promoting this.

There are various ways in which sexual activity can be opposed to the family: it may directly harm the family, or indirectly harm it, or harm it through what it symbolizes. Adultery, for example, directly harms the family. Because it is an act of betrayal, it attacks the trust between husband and wife; since it opens up the possibility of illegitimate offspring, it attacks the bond between parent and children. A good example of an action that indirectly harms family life would be cohabitation before marriage. Various studies have shown that couples that live together before marrying are almost twice as likely to divorce.[4] If society has an interest in preventing divorce, as it clearly does, then it presumably has an interest in discouraging cohabitation, which in fact it has traditionally tried to accomplish through laws against fornication.

Every action and every law has a rationale: each carries with it a view about what sorts of things are good and bad, and how such things are to be pursued or avoided. To this extent, any action or law "makes a statement" which instructs and shapes the character of the people who view that action, or who are under that law. That this is so is clear from the advertising campaigns that often accompany new laws. For example, my home city of Worcester, Massachusetts, recently instituted a recycling program. The city's garbage trucks now carry billboards, which show the globe of the earth placed within one of the standard recycling containers, with the slogan, "Pay a little, save a lot." The implication of the billboard is that the earth's environment is more precious than the tax money the city spends on the recycling program. Of course, the law itself has this implication, even apart from the campaign. But equally so, the behavior required by the law makes a sort of statement about the value of the environment, just as wasteful disposal practices express a lack of regard for the environment. Hence, an action constitutes an indirect attack on family life if it expresses a conception of the family, or of sexuality, that is inconsistent with that required for happy family life. Laws which rule out such actions would, on the contrary, express a conception of the family, or of sexuality, that is supportive of family life.

Prostitution is a good example of an activity that is outlawed primarily because of the "statement" it makes. It is a relatively easy matter to eliminate the health dangers of prostitution, and the dangers to prostitutes from drug addiction and physical abuse at the hands of pimps, by setting up state-regulated bordellos, as is done in Nevada. But people rightly sense that this does not remove the chief evil of prostitution, which is the view, inherent in the practice of prostitution itself, that sexual intimacy can be bought and sold like a commodity and that our sex drive is an irrational urge that may reasonably be satisfied by any means available. It is because prostitution expresses this view that people do not want prostitutes in their neighborhood. It is also the reason why people typically want to see prostitution remain illegal, even if the laws against it are difficult to enforce, for such laws already achieve something simply in expressing society's condemnation of the practice. The law, even if ineffectual, goes some way towards negating the bad example of the behavior itself.

For similar reasons, the state has an interest in making sodomy illegal. Sodomy, first of all, expresses a misguided conception of sexuality. The reason for this is that sodomy is, necessarily, not a procreative act. Thus, it presupposes that genital intimacy may justifiably be regarded as something fully divorced from the possibility of procreation; yet family life depends upon the view that sex and procreation should be linked. Secondly, sodomy is an unreasonable act—it is an instance of reason being mastered by sexual desire, not sexual desire being mastered by reason. The reason for this, briefly, is that it cannot serve as a sign of love, because it lacks those features which make heterosexual intercourse a "natural sign" of love.[5]

So far I have been setting forth the grounds on which, for 180 years of American jurisprudence, and for centuries more of common law, it was believed that the state has the competence to make sodomy illegal. In contrast, the dominant view today—though, again, it has been dominant for barely thirty years—is to reject this conclusion by invoking either the so-called "harm principle" or the putative right to privacy.

The harm principle, which was articulated by John Stuart Mill in his famous essay *On Liberty*, states that the government has authority to regulate only those behaviors of its citizens which harm others in direct and specifiable ways. But the harm principle is flawed. First, it does not match our convictions about how society should be ordered. If the harm principle were applied in a thoroughgoing fashion, we would have to repeal all laws against bestiality, suicide, mutilation, drug abuse, cruelty to animals, and disrespect to corpses, since none of these actions itself involves direct and specifiable harm to others. Second, it is often the case that society can successfully discourage acts that are harmful to others only if it discourages the vices that lead to such harmful acts—and encourages the opposing virtues. The reason for this is that harmful acts are related to underlying character in the way that symptoms are related to underlying disease. Just as it is foolish not to be concerned with public health, and only to treat illnesses, so it is foolish for laws not to be concerned with character and to be aimed only at actions. Yet the harm principle rules out laws that aim at inculcating a certain sort of character.

Many argue as well that the state has no competence to enact antisodomy laws because such laws are contrary to a constitutional right to privacy. It is difficult to reply to this sort of argument since the right to privacy is so ill-defined that its content cannot easily be predicted prior to Supreme Court decisions that apply it. Part of the problem is that the right is not mentioned in the Constitution and is not supported by tradition or history. As I said earlier, the Supreme Court first asserted its existence in *Griswold v. Connecticut* (1965), which struck down long-standing state laws against the sale of contraceptives. The Court's description of that right has changed almost with every subsequent decision applying it. In *Griswold*, the Court described the right to privacy as a right possessed by a married couple. This has some plausibility, since the family is prior to the state, and we might think that it has some realm of authority that is in some way beyond state interference. But in *Eisenstadt v. Baird* (1971), the Court defined the right to privacy as something possessed by individuals, not families. This made possible the 1973 abortion decision, *Roe v. Wade*, in which the court asserted, without explanation, that the right to privacy includes the right of a woman to obtain an abortion. Now privacy no longer meant only what went on inside bedrooms; it also meant the seemingly public actions carried out by doctors in clinics.

During the 1980s, the Court expressed doubts about the right to privacy and declined to apply the right in *Bowers v. Hardwick* (1985) to overturn antisodomy laws. Then, in the *Planned Parenthood v. Casey* (1992), the Court tried to reverse this trend by reasserting the right, which it now described in these terms: "At the heart of liberty is the right to define one's own concept of existence, of meaning, of the universe, and of the mystery of human life." This seems a formula for anarchic subjectivism rather than a principle of sound jurisprudence.

Obviously, it could be used to overturn laws against sodomy, or to assert a right to die, or to overturn any sort of morals legislation. Hence, the claim that antisodomy laws violate the right to privacy is probably correct; but because privacy jurisprudence is dubious and arbitrary, without a sound constitutional basis, the claim has no force.

But suppose that the Court does not overrule *Bowers* and continues to hold that the state is competent to outlaw sodomy if it wishes. Still, we can ask the practical question of whether the state ought to do so. One could argue that antisodomy laws are unenforceable and, given current sexual mores, they will in any case be ignored. Furthermore, it is arbitrary to apply such laws to homosexuals, but not to acts of sodomy between a man and a woman. Such laws, then, merely provide radical gay activists with an easy target; it gives them a cause celebre in which they will easily gain public sympathy and thus win further support for their more extreme goals.[6]

This argument needs to be taken seriously, but I think we should reject it for two reasons. First, as we have seen, antisodomy laws make a statement about society's understanding of sexuality, and they serve to educate, even if they are not enforced. Second, such laws provide the legal underpinning for resisting the analogy between sexual orientation and race. Antisodomy laws, as well as laws against adultery and fornication, which also remain on the books in may states, are the legal expression—the only legal expression—of the judgment that sexual behavior is not irrelevant to character and can be used as a basis for decisions about hiring and housing.[7]

Discrimination in Housing and Hiring

This last point brings us to the second area of controversy, that is, whether there should be laws which prohibit discrimination in housing or hiring on the basis of sexual orientation or activity. To simplify discussion, I shall refer to such laws as "gay rights" laws.

The most important argument in favor of such laws is based upon the nature of discrimination. Although this argument is rarely stated explicitly, it underlies much gay rights activism. The essence of unjust discrimination, the argument goes, is to make distinctions among persons on the basis of accidental features not related to character. In the case of racism, for example, it is to judge people, to paraphrase Martin Luther King, according to the color of their skin, not the content of their character. But sexual orientation and activity are unrelated to character. Therefore, they cannot be used as a basis for drawing distinctions among persons, for favoring some and disfavoring others.

The flawed premise in the argument is that "sexual orientation and activity are unrelated to character." This is clearly false as regards activity: a philanderer is usually a shallow and superficial person, unable to make commitments; an adulterer has broken trust; an employer who sexually harasses his employees lacks adequate regard for the dignity of others. There are countless examples of how, in general, sexual behavior is closely connected to character. Similarly, the fact that someone engages in homosexual activity typically tells us something about his character. If he does so knowing that it is wrong, then he lacks the virtue of self-control. If, however, he does so thinking that it is right, then he at least lacks practical insight into some basic human goods, because he mistakenly takes something bad to be good. But it is also possible that he arrived at this mistaken view because he at some point allowed desire and pleasure to corrupt his conscience, and this would imply a more serious character flaw.

I am not claiming that it is always correct to draw conclusions about someone's character from his sexual activity; I am simply claiming that it is not always incorrect to do so, that in principle sexual activity is not irrelevant to character, as the argument for gay rights legislation presupposes. Note also that it may indeed be true that many people wrongly discriminate against homosexuals, in the sense that they look upon homosexual activity, but not heterosexual fornication, as a sign of bad character. But this sort of inconsistency, I think, cannot be remedied by law—certainly not through gay rights laws—but rather needs to be corrected by educating people about sexual morality and by trying to change our public culture.

Now, in contrast to activity, a homosexual orientation is not a sign of character. On its own, it is better regarded as a kind of handicap rather than a character flaw, since although a homosexual orientation is a disorder of character—in the same way that everyone's unruly desires are disorders of character—usually the condition is neither chosen nor the result of choices, and so does not reflect a person's habits of intention and will. It is sensible to take the view that decisions about hiring or housing based merely upon homosexual orientation should be illegal, even though employers and landlords should be free to take into account whether someone engages in illicit homosexual activity. A law of this sort would in fact be a good expression of the principle of "loving the sinner but hating the sin." Unfortunately there is little political support for this sensible sort of law because gay rights activists seek acceptance of homosexual activity, not merely orientation. Also, it must be conceded that what such a law would hope to achieve is already largely accomplished by current law, since typically a person's sexual orientation is simply not known to a landlord or employer unless that person also engages in the corresponding behavior.

Another argument for gay rights laws depends upon an analogy between homosexuals today and blacks before the civil rights movement. It claims that homosexuals similarly constitute a distinct and oppressed minority and that, although they do enjoy many civil liberties, they are nonetheless second-class citizens because people scorn and reject them out of prejudice. Hence, gay rights laws, modeled on civil rights statutes for blacks, should be enacted to correct this.

Yet the analogy is not sound. Homosexuals are not an oppressed minority in the way that blacks were. They have not suffered from imposed segregation, systematic economic deprivation, or denial of educational opportunities. Furthermore, they do not suffer from an inherited pattern of deprivation, since the homosexual condition is not passed from generation to generation like race or ethnicity. Rather, it has been well documented that homosexuals have, on average, incomes much higher than the national norm and that, on average, they receive several years more formal schooling than the typical American.[8] They occupy thousands of positions of prestige and influence in business, academia, the professions, and the media. It cannot plausibly be maintained that they are an oppressed minority.[9]

The concern that homosexuals are nevertheless second-class citizens would seem to be based principally on the social censure and rejection they often encounter. Now we have seen that the reasons for this censure are mixed. Undoubtedly, foolish prejudice and bigotry are frequently a cause, as is the failure of people to draw a distinction between the person and the activity. But censure is in some cases justifiable—if it is directed at homosexual activity. For example, a landlord who refused to rent to two homosexuals would be as justified in that preference as if he refused to rent to a cohabiting but unmarried heterosexual couple. The problem with gay rights legislation is that it rules out this justifiable censure along with unjust discrimination that derives from irrational prejudice.

This point leads to an important reason why we should not enact gay rights legislation: such laws directly conflict with the free exercise of religion because they outlaw actions that individuals and institutions would consider themselves obliged to do on account of their religious beliefs. For example, the owner of a small apartment building, who is an orthodox Christian and who does not wish in any way to have complicity in, or to encourage, what he considers immoral behavior, would nevertheless be forbidden to refuse rental to a homosexual couple. It is easy to imagine other cases like this, and many have already occurred. Richard Duncan demonstrates at length the necessary conflict between gay rights and free exercise of religion. Duncan points out that such legislation poses an unavoidable choice for society, between the "sexual relativism," as he calls it, implicit in such legislation, and the Judeo-Christian view of sexuality. There is no middle ground.[10]

Notice, too, that the view expressed by gay rights laws is that the reasonable and principled censure of homosexual activity is on the same level as bigotry, bias, prejudice, and malice. Such laws treat the belief that sexual activity has a bearing on character, and that sexual relations should be confined to marriage, as equivalent to racism. They therefore inevitably undermine respect for the law, since, when people are faced with a choice between, on the one hand, honoring the law and despising their religious convictions or, on the other hand, holding to their convictions and rejecting the law, they should and will choose the latter.

At the same time, gay rights laws set parental authority in opposition to public authority. Children will be taught the public morality at school and in other public forums, and according to public morality, what their parents teach as moral principle is no more than bigotry and prejudice. Of course, a rift of this sort has already opened up between the culture of many households and that of the public realm, especially with regard to abortion. But here the conflict has been muted, since public authorities have been slow to accept all of the consequences of the absurd view that the right to abortion is a fundamental civil right. But gay rights laws, precisely because they are modeled on authentic civil rights statutes, will immediately be applied, with great moral fervor, in all areas of public life. For example, programs aimed at teaching children that a homosexual lifestyle is one among many valid options were introduced in Massachusetts only a few years after the passage of a state gay rights statute. In contrast, there has been no statewide campaign to teach children to accept the premises of the pro-choice position.

Yet another bad consequence of gay rights laws is that they are harmful to the interests of homosexual persons who wish to lead chaste lives because they assign benefits principally to homosexuals who make their sexual orientation known—and the benefits will be even greater if, as seems likely, gay rights laws will eventually lead to affirmative action for gays. Furthermore, gay rights laws assign burdens to chaste homosexuals, for such people, as it were, censure the tendencies of their own sexual orientation. But, as we have seen, the law regards this sort of censure as irrational bigotry. Hence, a necessary implication of gay rights laws is that a chaste homosexual is an Uncle Tom, someone who has accepted the false ideology of the oppressor. That is to say, gay rights laws reverse what is morally the case, since they treat the corrupt condition, practicing homosexuality, as virtuous, and the heroically virtuous condition, chaste homosexuality, as corrupt.

But why is it that Americans find the claim of discrimination so compelling—when in reality it is very weak? One reason is surely that they deceive themselves that sexual behavior is independent of character, in particular with respect to their own lives, so that the basic premise of gay rights laws is plausible to them. Moreover, the true evil of discrimination, the reason we ought not to discriminate against others, is not well understood. The purpose of the principle of nondiscrimination is to foster civic friendship by encouraging people to attend to character, merit, and virtue, rather than to inessential features. But for many, "don't discriminate" has become one of a number of jingles taken from popular culture by which they live their lives, leaving them unable to distinguish just from unjust discrimination.

Moreover, people are generally reluctant to apply their religious and moral beliefs in their public lives, especially when doing so would have an unpleasant effect on others, because having had a superficial moral and religious education, they think that no objective reality underlies their beliefs. They look upon their moral convictions as at best the expression of emotion or the blindly accepted dictate of a religious authority that only other believers are bound to accept. Moreover, because Americans are generally ignorant of constitutional history, they think that the very recent and indeed revolutionary decisions of the Supreme Court are developments of previous constitutional law, when in fact they are discontinuous with it. Americans therefore look with suspicion on their intuitions about what is right and just. Finally, the argument that one should not discriminate on the basis of sexual practice has more force, clearly, if one supposes that there is a basic right to engage in sexual activity; and many people now do indeed imagine that there is something like a "right to sex."

Homosexual Marriage, Foster Parenting, and Adoption

This brings us to the third controversy, concerning homosexual marriage, foster parenting, and adoption.[11] These issues appear to many to be interrelated: if society sanctions homosexual marriage, then it would seem there is no reason why homosexuals cannot raise children. Similarly, if there is no reason not to place children in the homes of homosexual couples, there would seem to be no reason not to give legal recognition to those couples. This reasoning notwithstanding, these issues are not related; we merely imagine they are because we incorrectly apply the word "marriage" to homosexuals.

Whether children should be placed in the homes of homosexual couples[12] depends upon whether, when other options are available, it is in the best interests of a child to be raised in a household without the example of complementarity provided by a married mother and father and without the different sorts of correction and encouragement provided by male and female parents. The complementarity of male and female parents in an intact family is of fundamental importance. For each parent serves as a role model for the child, who is educated in the significance of both of these fundamental dimensions of human nature, male and female, and also in the manner in which each should relate to the other through love. Furthermore, because the complementarity of male and female is a natural complementarity, rooted in biology and nature, the male and female parents represent to the child the fact that humans are incomplete apart from society.

In a homosexual relationship, however, either the male or the female role model is missing. This is already a deficiency, so that, just as we should not place a child with a widow or widower, or with a pair of male or female friends, if other options are available, so also not with a homosexual couple. Yet there is an additional deficiency, which is that, for a homosexual couple, it is not simply that one of these dimensions, male or female, is missing: the importance of complementarity is in practice denied. A widower can admit that it would be better if the mother, the female parent, were present, but two homosexuals cannot admit, without contradicting the premise of their lifestyle, that it would be better if one of them were replaced by a member of the opposite sex. Since there is no natural complementarity between two males or two females, the homosexual couple cannot represent, in their relationship, the fact that we are by nature incomplete and fitted for completion in a social bond; rather, if anything, what a homosexual couple represents to a child is the ethic of individual autonomy, which is inevitably destructive to society.

The question of whether society should recognize homosexual couples, and regard them as marriages or as equivalent to marriage, is easy to answer. There are many sorts of friendships, and different friendships form around different sorts of activities. A marriage is a particular sort of friendship which centers around the mutual enjoyment and care of the body, together with raising children. It is the only friendship which can form between previously unrelated persons, where the joint activity has a direct basis in nature, since each spouse's enjoyment of the body of the other comes through the union of organs that are naturally fitted for each other, and the procreation of children comes as the natural and joint activity of reproduction. Because the friendship of marriage results in children, it is a burden of sorts to raise children, and society benefits greatly if it is done well; society usually distinguishes marriage from other friendships, gives it special recognition, and awards it distinctive benefits.

A homosexual couple likewise displays a certain type of friendship. But this friendship does not result in children, so there is no reason for society to reward the friends in any way. If society were to assign benefits to homosexual couples, then, consistently, it ought to assign like benefits to any pair of good friends, and furthermore, it ought to assign even greater benefits to marriages—again, in order to recognize, in a distinctive way, the good that society gains through the children who are begotten and raised in marriages, and also to compensate the parents.

Because marriage is a natural friendship, as I have described, which tends towards procreation, the bond between married partners is, in principle, as strong as that between blood relatives. This is what is traditionally expressed by saying that it is "indissoluble." True, this feature of marriage is obscured by widespread acceptance of divorce. Nonetheless, marriage must have this feature if the fabric of society is to have integrity: because a marriage bond is the basis for a family related by ties of blood, this bond must be at least as strong as blood ties. The bond of marriage, therefore, differs in kind from other friendships, in the way that ties of blood differ from other ties. Hence it is appropriate for the marriage friendship to be assigned benefits that are different in kind, and not merely in degree, from other friendships—as has in fact been the traditional practice.

Conclusion

At the beginning of this chapter I emphasized the distinctness of the three areas of controversy I have discussed. But they are also causally related. When society repeals antisodomy laws, it removes from the law the primary legal basis for drawing distinctions based on homosexual activity. Once such laws are overturned, the law, as it were, becomes blind to homosexual activity, and this then gives plausibility to the argument that some sort of inappropriate religious sentiment—which cannot be allowed to guide public policy, because of the separation of church and state—underlies resistance to the application of equal-protection reasoning to the case of practicing homosexuals. But as we have seen, once society enacts gay rights laws, it adopts the view that the judgment that homosexual activity is wrong is a kind of prejudice or bigotry. Once the law embodies this view, it is a small step to enacting affirmative action programs for homosexuals, since then it will seem that homosexuals need special protection from the sort of "religious bigotry" that gay rights legislation outlawed.

But clearly, once affirmative action programs are in place, society has moved beyond approval of homosexual activity and now has begun to reward and promote it. And once it does this, it is almost inevitable that it will reward also homosexual couples, by recognizing homosexual "marriage," granting them a status fully equal to married couples. This will be even more likely if, as seems to be the case, our contraceptive culture continues to divide, ever more sharply, sexual relations from procreation.

We must also consider what consequences, shocking as they may seem, will logically follow from the legal recognition of homosexual "marriages." The first obvious consequence is that laws against polygamy will seem to be arbitrary, since if marriage is no longer essentially for procreation, then it is difficult to see why it should exist between only two. It will not be long before various groups of people will demand to be "married," in the revised sense of that term, and we will no longer have any principled reason for denying marriage to them.

It will come to seem unfair that, among married people, only some heterosexuals can have children. This will be interpreted as kind of an unfair burden placed on homosexuals by nature, in the same way that, to the radical feminists of today, it seems an unfair burden, a curse of nature, that only women can bear children. Society will feel compelled to compensate for this perceived injustice by instituting programs designed to distribute children more evenly among heterosexual and homosexual marriages—presumably, by the active promotion of artificial insemination and surrogate motherhood.

If all this seems implausible, consider that our present society would have seemed unbelievable if described to anyone before the sexual revolution. Think of how far we have come in only thirty-five years. Moreover, many members of the gay rights movement do in fact advocate the revolutionary overthrow of traditional mores about marriage and child rearing. The world they propose in their rhetoric looks very much like the world we have arrived at by deduction.

5

Romer, DOMA, and ENDA:
Judicial and Legislative Episodes in the Culture War

Joseph Broadus

THE MOST SIGNIFICANT RECENT DEVELOPMENTS in the ongoing debate over the gay rights movement have been a Supreme Court case, *Romer v. Evans*,[1] and the passage of the Defense of Marriage Act (DOMA),[2] and the consideration of the Employment Non-Discrimination Act (ENDA).[3]

Congressional action on DOMA has been reassuring, since it demonstrates continuing support for the traditional understanding of marriage.[4] ENDA is problematic; in the 1997 session it was narrowly defeated in the Senate, avoiding a tie vote that would have permitted Vice President Al Gore to cast the deciding vote. ENDA's unmerited progress shows the growing power of the homosexual lobby and the acceptance of its curious comparison of sexual orientation and race as a category entitled to civil rights protection.[5]

These episodes reflect, on one hand, the growing conflict between the political branches, which express the values of the American people, and the courts, which impose elite preferences over popular will. On the other hand, the success of DOMA and the progress of ENDA demonstrate that the political branches are sound on social principles but growing somewhat foggy on application.

86

Romer: Autocratic Rule Restored

The Supreme Court's holding in *Romer* is deeply disturbing both because of the substance of the holding and the analysis that was applied. *Romer* is of far reaching consequences. In adopting Cass Sunstein's theory of equal protection, the court has equipped itself with a truly effective tool to constrict the rights of the people to self-governance and to expand vastly the powers of the judiciary.[6] *Romer* suggests that we may be entering an era when the courts, using Sunstein's axioms, are free to overturn any legislation which, though it passes historic constitutional standards, fails to follow the intuitions in vogue among the legal elite. Richard John Neuhaus and others are correct to ask whether this development marks "the end of democracy."[7]

Romer was a bold declaration of independence by the judiciary. As recently as *Bowers v. Hardwick* (1986),[8] the Court agreed that the history and traditions of the people were a proper limit on the exercise of judicial power. This assent appeared to go beyond the mere technical requirements of the Due Process Clause and to express a broader generic limit on judicial power.[9] In *Romer*, in a particularly offensive phrase, the Court denounced as irrational the historic religious and cultural understanding of sexual ethics. This same understanding had been identified as societal bedrock in *Bowers*. *Romer* thus serves as evidence of a changing of the guard on the Court. A majority of the Court now seems fully committed to imposing elite values on majorities. This is a revolutionary role at odds with the conservative, counter-majoritarian role of the courts.

Historically, counter-majoritarianism could be justified only because the Court acted as the people's agent, enforcing long-term political judgments against the temporary impulses and passions of majorities. The Court's role was conservative: it preserved the customs, values, and traditions of the people, a role in harmony with due process. By preserving established ways of doing things and respecting traditions and values we preserve both liberty and property.

What the Court did in *Romer* was to declare that, when it wishes to engage in social engineering, it may disregard the Due Process Clause. As Sunstein properly observed, the Due Process clause is concerned with protecting traditional practices from being overrun by short-term majorities.[10] No practice is more deeply rooted, nor should any practice be more jealously defended by the courts, than the right of the people to self-governance.

Yet the Court has decided, in general agreement with Sunstein, that the Equal Protection Clause is a general writ transferring powers of governance away from the people to the courts. While Sunstein's language is modest, its import is not. For Sunstein's proposition is that the Court, without reference to history or customs, or even in direct disregard of tradition, may without limit intrude on any other branch of government or the rights of the people.[11] The only limit to the exercise of this power to strike down a particular practice that offends its sense of justice, Sunstein instructs us, is the judicial conscience itself. A sincere reading of the Constitution should lead us to repudiate this position as an appropriate understanding of either the Fifth or Fourteenth Amendment's Equal Protection Clause.[12]

Can any knowledgeable person seriously believe that either the generation that gave us the Constitution or the generation that fought the war to preserve the Union would have bestowed such sweeping power on an isolated elite? This is a particularly distressing doctrine when one considers the origins of the Fourteenth Amendment. The country had been torn apart and plunged into war by the failure of the judiciary to respect legislative judgments about slavery. The effect of the holding in *Dred Scott* was to cripple Congress in dealing with slavery in the new territories.[13] A judicial act intended to end a political controversy led to war. It is unthinkable that the generation that had witnessed that bit of judicial arrogance and suffered its consequences would have written a provision granting the courts the sweeping powers Sunstein claims for them.

But, then, original intent, however interpreted, plays no role in postmodern jurisprudence. The role of the courts is no longer to insure loyalty to past practice or broadly shared democratic ideals. Their new role, it seems, is to provide a mechanism whereby the enlightened few may triumph over the majority.

DOMA: *The Defense of Marriage*

After the ruling in *Baehr v. Lewin*, it became apparent that Hawaii might soon recognize same-sex marriage.[14] The state court had ruled that the state's equal rights amendment required that the government show a compelling reason why same-sex couples should be denied marriage licenses. Other states and the federal courts had determined that neither due process nor equal protection required the government to recognize same-sex marriages.[15] Judges in Hawaii, however, chose to conclude that adoption of the state equal rights amendment forced the court to ignore centuries of custom and social and moral practice. For the court, marriage was little more than an act of recording and the conferral of enumerated benefits.

The discovery that they had commanded the courts to establish same-sex marriage probably came as a surprise to the 74 percent of the voters in Hawaii who were opposed to same-sex marriage, but the courts were not interested in what the voters intended when the voters enacted the ERA.[16] Instead, the courts were concerned with their own rather vague notions of privacy.

The case sent shock waves across the nation. Soon other states were passing legislation to block recognition of Hawaiian same-sex marriages.[17] This sparked an immediate controversy. Under the Full Faith and Credit Clause of the Constitution, states are obligated to recognize the acts and records of their sister states.[18] Historically, however, states have written their own rules on marriage and certain aspects of family law and have refused to recognize conflicting rules from other jurisdictions. States have been able, for example, to set age limits on marriage or decide which cousins may wed and to refuse to recognize marriages from other jurisdictions that violate these rules. It is a murky area of law and requires determining the interest of the forum state—the one where the controversy is being disputed—and of the other states.

Fortunately, the Full Faith and Credit Clause provides Congress with the authority to establish rules for deciding conflicts.[19] DOMA is intended to provide interpretive rules for federal purposes and to use full faith and credit authority to provide decisional rules for controversies over same-sex marriage. It employs a device common in conflict cases: it permits the forum state to apply its rule but permits other states to reject Hawaii's extraordinary innovation.

Harvard's Lawrence Tribe wrote Senator Edward Kennedy to suggest that DOMA spelled the death of the republic. Citing *Romer,* he suggested DOMA might violate the Fifth Amendment by being little more than an irrational act of prejudice based on sexual orientation. Tribe, however, declined to answer the *Romer* question and instead expounded his theory of the proper role of Congress in establishing procedures for full faith and credit. He asserted that DOMA exceeds congressional authority and violates the rights of the states to have their measures enforced. He claimed DOMA awarded to some states the power to void the acts of others. This exceeds the power to determine mere procedures.

The argument ignores, however, well-established principles in the area of conflict of laws. Those principles recognize as appropriate procedural rules regarding how a jurisdiction's law will be applied in a dispute. Across a range of issues states have been permitted, under their own local rules, to decide cases they see as significant to their public policy interests. Hence, Tribe's concern appears beneath the surface to be substantive, not procedural.

Congress acted on a theory similar to that of the states. Marriage is a central institution with historic limits and is entitled to protection. Tribe's views on marriage and state protection, which he has set forth in his textbook on constitutional law, are very different. He believes the state has little interest in protecting marriage by prohibiting extramarital sexual acts. In Tribe's view, the Constitution protects sex acts of every variety, with the exception of acts that involve violence and (curiously) incest.[20] Tribe's views reflect the preferences for unrestricted sexual activity typical of establishment liberals. Sexual activity, for Tribe, is central to the process of self-definition and requires the widest range of personal experience an expression. This is the position rejected by the Court in *Bowers* but implicitly accepted in *Romer*.

Tribe was not alone in seeing a danger to DOMA presented by *Romer*. Professor Hadley Arkes argued that *Romer*, which had snaked its way through the courts on limited issues of voting rights, had blossomed into a general statement about sexual orientation. It would be argued that the state was generally prohibited from regulating or considering sexual orientation in a negative way.[21] At the heart of Tribe's objections is his conviction that marriage, for constitutional purposes, is largely meaningless and that few state actions can be justified in its defense

ENDA: Not Simple Justice

In the 1995 Congress, ENDA (the Employment Non-Discrimination Act) was narrowly defeated in the U.S. Senate by a vote of 50 to 49. In 1997, the bill (S. 869, by Senator Jeffords) was reintroduced in the Senate with thirty-four sponsors. It had the support of President Clinton.[22]

ENDA would prohibit workplace discrimination on the basis of sexual orientation, which it defines to include homosexuality, bisexuality, and heterosexuality.[23] It would accord the same protection on the basis of sexual orientation as is accorded other classes: race, religion, gender, national origin, age, and disability.[24]

In introducing the bill, Jeffords stated that "people who work hard and perform well should not be kept from leading productive and responsible lives because of an irrational, non-work-related prejudice. Unfortunately, many responsible and productive members of our society face discrimination in their workplaces based on nothing more than their sexual orientation."[25] Jeffords insisted that ENDA provided equal rights but not special rights on the basis on sexual orientation. As an assurance of this, he cited provisions prohibiting preferential treatment based on sexual orientation. He also noted that the bill would not require benefits for same-sex partners and that employers would not be compelled to justify employment practices that have disparate statistical impact based on sexual orientation.[26] Jeffords said that in response to privacy concerns expressed in the previous session, the EEOC was prohibited from collecting data or compelling employers to collect data on employee sexual orientation. Further, the EEOC was prohibited from entering consent decrees providing for quotas or preferential treatment as a remedy for sexual orientation violations.

Jeffords's remarks, however, misrepresent both the need for ENDA and the consequences of its enactment. He implied that the proper model for understanding sexual orientation is discrimination based on race. He suggested not only that sexual orientation discrimination threatens the productivity of particular workers but also that the global competitive position of the United States and its major corporations is threatened by sexual orientation discrimination. Yet he introduced no evidence to support these claims, no evidence that people were being irrationally prevented from living useful lives because of sexual orientation discrimination in the workplace. His claim that a new and improved ENDA had eliminated many of the problems present in the old bill was at best misleading. An analysis of the legislation reveals that the changes were largely cosmetic and that in some cases the results of the changes were both counterintuitive and counterproductive.

This bill is unlike any prior civil rights legislation in critical ways. In the past, civil rights legislation has been enacted to open economic opportunities to groups that had previously been disadvantaged. Frequently great disparities in income existed between the proposed protected class and the average population. African-Americans and women as groups, for instance, earned substantially less than majority whites and males. The handicapped were frequently denied education, employment, and an opportunity for a good life. Certain religious believers found substantial barriers to economic opportunity.

Great disparities exist in income on the basis of sexual orientation. But they do not establish the presence of discrimination in the workplace—quite the opposite, in fact. The economic statistics for homosexuals are impressive. Homosexuals are more likely than the average American to have a college degree, a graduate degree, or a doctorate; more likely to hold a job in a profession; more likely to earn one hundred thousand dollars a year than other Americans. On almost any measure of economic success, homosexuals compare favorably with straight Americans. And their success is not just financial: they are more likely to work in prestigious jobs in the academy and the media, where they have great influence shaping public taste, values, and perceptions.[27]

ENDA will not lift the burden of discrimination from an oppressed group. There *is* no oppressed group—and only episodic or anecdotal claims of discrimination. Jeffords and other supporters of ENDA come close to admitting this when they dismiss concerns that ENDA will result in a litigation explosion. Supporters of ENDA are quick to explain that state and local sexual orientation laws result in few, if any, cases (for example, since 1991, there have been only twenty cases in the District of Columbia and nineteen in Vermont). The overwhelming majority of the cases that have been filed have been dismissed without a finding of discrimination.[28]

In introducing ENDA, Jeffords cited statistics to claim that most

Americans oppose discrimination against homosexuals and therefore support legislation like ENDA to protect homosexuals. Actually, most Americans—84 percent—do oppose discrimination against homosexuals, but the same *Newsweek* poll showed that fully 66 percent oppose new legislation. Forty percent believe government has already done too much, and 26 percent believe government has done enough.[29]

Yet hidden inside the Pandora's box marked ENDA are the seeds of quotas and special privileges that will blossom into the full flower of red tape, litigation, and special favors which can be expected to stifle American business large and small. Presently classes or groups are only protected by civil rights law to the extent it can be said information about class membership is irrelevant to the workplace.[30] ENDA forgets that character is frequently revealed by sexual behavior; and that certain sexual conduct is very relevant to certain jobs.[31] Federal courts have held that sexual orientation is or may be relevant to several areas of employment, including those related to child care and education. ENDA would effectively reverse these cases. It endangers state laws and regulations that protect children from those with known histories of child sexual abuse.[32] ENDA carelessly includes in its protection a known class of youth sexual abusers and is loosely enough written to accommodate others.

This reveals that laws such as ENDA are not about workplace discrimination but about putting a government seal of approval on conduct and silencing critics by branding them bigots.[33] Hadley Arkes asserts that the bills will result in a form of "Christian removal" from the work place. A person's traditional ethical views on sexual behavior will be used as grounds to separate him or her from employment. Arkes explains how that process is already underway. He notes that law schools bar discrimination on the basis of sexual orientation by firms that recruit on campus, and firms have responded by relieving of recruiting duties partners who adhere to religions with strict views on sexual behavior. Arkes insists that it is a short step from that exclusion to not hiring persons with traditional mores in the first place.[34]

The Family Research Council published "The Other Side of Tolerance: The Victims of Homosexual Activism," which recounts the real discrimination in the marketplace today. The true victims are people like Ron Greer, a firefighter, and eighteen-year veteran of the Madison, Wisconsin, fire department. He is also a pastor who was suspended without pay for circulating to coworkers the pamphlet "The Truth About Homosexuality." Greer, like dissidents in communist regimes, has been ordered to reeducation or, as it is called in Wisconsin, "diversity training." Or take the case of California Superior Court judge John Farrell who was accused of unethical conduct and faced with removal from the bench for bigotry. Why? Because he had agreed to volunteer to chaperone hikes for the Boy Scouts which prohibits homosexuals from serving as scoutmasters. Or from Texas there is the story of Betty Sabatino who worked for Texas Commerce Bank, that is until she dared politely to ask her employer why the company nondiscrimination policy was being extended to cover sexual orientation. Betty, in the language of the diversity training session she was in, had been promised a "safe zone" where she was free to question. The bank explained her dismissal tersely: "Management loss of confidence with employee."

These episodes should chill anyone seriously concerned with the First Amendment as a shield from governmental abuse. In the past, under both labor law and First Amendment law, a worker has remained a citizen free during free times at work to privately speak his mind to his coworkers. Think of the possibilities. Could newspapers reporting the wrong side of an issue on sexual orientation discrimination be banned from the workplace? Could a homosexual employee at a newspaper unhappy with the coverage file a discrimination complaint because reporters in meeting their obligation to report both sides had manufactured "hate speech"?

ENDA's proponents claim that the bill provides substantial safeguards through exemptions for religion. But ENDA in fact represents an attack on the religious exemption contained in Title VII-style legislation. ENDA language is so slyly worded that it may in fact cover no one. The religious exemption in ENDA is contained in Section 9 (a) and (b) which provide in relevant part:

(a) IN GENERAL—Except as provided in subsection (b), this Act shall not apply to a religious organization.

(b) UNRELATED BUSINESS TAXABLE INCOME—This Act shall apply to employment or an employment opportunity for an employment position of a covered entity that is a religious organization, if the duties of the position pertain solely to activities of the organization that generate unrelated business taxable income subject to taxation under section 511(a) of the Internal Revenue Code of 1986.[35]

Section 9 (a) only appears to provide a broad religious exemption. First, present Title VII law does not distinguish between the taxable and nontaxable aspects of a religious organization. ENDA, therefore, attempts to achieve by stealth a change in basic policy. Further, by linking the general exemption to tax status ENDA may abolish the exempt status, with the exception of religious schools, which are expressly excluded. But even religious schools are placed in jeopardy by the tax requirement.

The problem is the *Bob Jones University* case, in which the Supreme Court held that religious schools and institutions could be subjected to taxation, without express congressional authorization, for conduct exempted from antidiscrimination laws. The Court held that, while the conduct was not reached by the regulatory language of the antidiscrimination policy, because of the exemption it nonetheless violated the spirit of the public policy and therefore was not entitled to tax exemption.

Applied to ENDA, this line of analysis would say religious institutions are generally exempt under paragraph (a) because their discrimination is permitted. Then under paragraph (b) the institutions would be declared taxable because they violate the spirit of the policy while remaining within the exemption—at which point the exemption disappears because every exemption granted under paragraph (a) must survive the test of paragraph (b). The religious exemption provision is an enormous hoax under which everyone is exempted, until they exercise the exemption, at which point they are covered. Because ENDA does not define unrelated business income, it seems all income which is taxable is deemed unrelated. This provision transforms any activity into an unrelated business activity if it "discriminates." It effectively prohibits courts from balancing religious interests against statutory interests when conflicts emerge, and declares there are no legitimate interests that conflict with the statute.

ENDA destroys the traditional respect and accommodation for religious faith and practice found in civil rights laws. Instead it adopts a narrow and hostile view that seeks to use the law to transform or extinguish disfavored religious practices. America does not need ENDA. It needs the First Amendment. It needs freedom of religion and speech.

6

Homosexuality and the Military

Melissa Wells-Petry

PRESIDENT CLINTON'S 1993 INITIATIVE to lift the ban on homosexuals in military service seems ancient history now. Nevertheless, while this initiative had short-term political consequences for the president, both positive and negative, the initiative's philosophical implications have had an enduring impact on the armed forces. Apart from any particular result for the cause of homosexual "rights," the commander in chief's advocacy of a cause organized around the principles of pansexualism was bound to have a subtle, but nonetheless profound and persistent, impact on the philosophy of soldiering.

There is no doubt that the debate on military personnel policies and force structure—a debate presently encompassing not only homosexuality in the armed forces but also the related issue of women in combat—is extremely important in its own right. While the nation mostly focuses on its military when war is either imminent or actually underway, history counsels that often it is a nation's policies in interwar years that prove most decisive.[1]

An examination of President Clinton's adoption of the philosophy of pansexualism, however, does more than illuminate various implications for military service. It also provides a valuable case study, first, of how homosexualist rhetoric plays out in public discourse and, second, how homosexualism—that is, the philosophical principles that are centered on homosexuality and inhere in the cause of homosexual rights—effects fundamental shifts in an institution's paradigm. Homosexualism is for practical purposes interchangeable with pansexualism, which is, in turn, a gloss on radical individualism as described by, among others, Judge Robert Bork.[2] While the military is the immediate context for examining the institutional consequences of adopting pansexualism, it is imperative to keep in mind that this same phenomenon is presently changing other social institutions as well—most notably, the institutions of marriage, the family, and the church.

First a word about language. I have already used the term "homosexualism" to indicate the philosophical underpinnings or principles of homosexuality. If ideas have consequences, and certainly they do, perforce behavior has consequences and, clearly, one consequence of behavior is that it engenders ideas. The term homosexualism is used here to denote the ideas—in other words, the organizing principles—which spring from the personal and political conduct of homosexuality. A more accurate and more ideologically revealing way to describe homosexualism is as pansexualism. I use the term pansexualism to indicate the belief that sex has no public or institutional consequences, that all consensual sex is an affirmative moral good, and that no consensual sex must be regulated by the state or restrained by the culture. Homosexualism is a kind of pansexualism because it is impossible, logically as well as politically, to support social, cultural, or legal limits on one form of sexual behavior without admitting that public morality demands such limits in general.

Thus, homosexualism, consonant with its philosophy of pansexualism, views government limits on sexual behavior as paternalistic at best and evil at worst. Pansexualism, therefore, is a form of sexual capitalism, in which all forms of sexual behavior must be allowed to flourish without any social intervention. Limits on sexual behavior, if

there are any, arise solely from the market—that is, the participants
in sexual activity. Patently, pansexualism is a proxy for an even broader,
radical individualism. Therefore, for purposes of this discussion of the
philosophical implications of the commander in chief's initiative to
create a legal right for homosexuals to serve in the military, these three
"isms" will be used interchangeably: homosexualism, pansexualism, and
radical individualism.

Homosexualism and the Military

It is illuminating to highlight some of the concrete ways that homosexualism changes an institution's philosophical underpinnings and,
therefore, inexorably changes the institution. What is interesting from
the military example is how philosophical shifts create practical change,
with or without—in other words, apart from—corresponding changes
in institutional policies. The military, for example, was changed simply by the commander in chief's adoption of pansexualism. In short,
for fundamental institutional change to occur, an institution need not
go so far as to accept homosexuality as a matter of official policy; nor
is it required that the institution align itself fully and explicitly with
the policy goals of homosexualists. All it takes to cause fundamental
institutional change is for there to exist some level of institutional
adoption of the principles of pansexualism. Change—philosophical
change, followed by incremental practical change—is effected the
moment there is any institutional adoption of the principles of radical individualism, because radical individualism rejects authority.

As a practical matter, this undermining of institutional authority
cannot be confined to matters of private sexual relations. Once, at
some level or in some sphere, pansexualism becomes a de facto institutional norm, the practical result is that an armed force—or a church,
or a marriage—increasingly lacks the institutional authority to direct
the lives of its members. Once subjected to the principles of pansexualism, the institution of marriage no longer has the capacity to im-

pose institutional responsibilities or delimit institutional benefits, and it certainly lacks authority to establish and enforce norms of sexual activity.

In short, radical individual autonomy is inconsistent with—indeed, antagonistic to—institutional authority. This fact is key to understanding the philosophical implications of the president's initiative to open the armed forces to homosexuals. There is no doubt that the commander in chief, *as an institutional authority*, was modeling a particular understanding of military service. And, plainly, it was his institutional authority that rendered his advocacy of pansexualism highly effective in causing philosophical change in fundamental aspects of the military. The adoption of the principles of pansexualism brought about three fundamental changes in military culture: the primacy of the individual's needs and wants, the loss of a special military calling, and the toleration of sexual license as a moral imperative.

The Primacy of the Individual

First, pansexualism dictates that the individual's wants and needs are more important than the military mission. Almost the entire debate on homosexuals in the military has focused on the homosexual individual's wants and needs—first, *sexual* needs and, then, *political* needs. When the commander in chief took up the fight on behalf of the homosexual rights movement, the principle that emerged—and was expounded and fought for politically—was that, regardless of the context, the individual's wants and needs come first. Indeed, they take precedence per se.

Quite explicitly in support of the commander in chief's initiative to put homosexuals in the military, for example, arguments were advanced that, to the extent homosexualism changes the military, ipso facto it needs to be changed. Similar arguments are heard in regard to the institutions of marriage and the family; that is, to the extent homosexualism changes the social function or value of these institutions, it is appropriate, and indeed necessary, to change those institutions. Hence, the truly radical aspect of Clinton's initiative was not that he wanted to put homosexuals in the military, but that—like all pansexualists—he advocated a fundamental shift in the balance of power from the institution to the individual. Since the pansexualist notion of individual autonomy admits no limits (other than the requirement of consent in actions involving others), in the end there is no principled way to justify military authority.

This fundamental shift in the balance of power from the institution to the individual—a shift that inheres in pansexualism as an organizing principle—brings about a fundamental change in society's understanding of the very nature of military service. Historically, military service was summed up by the idea that soldiers *subordinated* (a word rarely used these days) their needs and wants to the good of the service, and if they did not, the military was justified in bringing down on them the full weight of military discipline. In the pansexualist world, however, soldiers have the right to decide for themselves what constitutes the good of the service, and the military is not justified in punishing soldiers even when they break explicit rules. For example, under the present policy on homosexuals in the military—called "don't ask, don't tell," but more aptly described as "don't get caught"—even if a commander quite innocently stumbles upon evidence that a soldier is violating the law by engaging in homosexual conduct, *it is the commander, not the lawbreaker, whose conduct is at issue.*

No Longer a Special Calling

The second change generated by the institutional adoption of the principles of pansexualism is the notion that soldiering is not a special calling and the military is not a separate, specialized society. In this view, the military is not an institution; it is an employer. Defending one's country, perhaps with one's life, is not a duty; it is a job.

This second change is the flip side of the pansexualist notion that individual wants and needs take precedence over military authority because the good of the individual is the highest social good. In other words, the first point, discussed above, demonstrates that pansexualism advances a *positive* view of radical individualism. In the reduction of military service to a commercial endeavor, pansexualism holds that individual wants and needs take precedence over military authority because the military mission lacks seriousness. In other words, pansexualism also advances a *negative* view of the function and value of institutions in society.

When an institutional authority adopts pansexualism, the upshot is the poignant message that there exists no reason—no justification—for that institution's culture to differ from the larger society, whether the institution is the military, marriage, family, or the church.

Therefore, to adhere to the pansexualist principle that the individual is sovereign, the military, like all institutions, must be dethroned. Not only must the individual be exalted, but the institution must be debased. For pansexualism to thrive, the armed forces must be viewed as an employer, not an institution, and defending one's country must be viewed as a job rather than a duty. This reductionism was pervasive in the debate surrounding the commander in chief's initiative to lift the historical ban on homosexuals in the military and remains prominent not only in current debates on military personnel policies but in the ongoing push to redefine other social institutions, such as marriage. One way to articulate the present controversy regarding homosexualism and marriage is to ask whether marriage is a special calling and a specialized society, that is, a society of one man and one woman called together in sexual fidelity for life. Or is marriage a "job," a contract in which individuals are free to negotiate all manner of terms, without regard to any extraindividual authority?

The pansexualist demand to reduce the function of institutions, and thereby to reduce institutions' authority over individuals, presents particular problems for the military. It is impossible to reconcile this reductionist view with the fact that military service requires special sacrifice—and may require the ultimate sacrifice. I doubt it is possible to find many who think it is their "job" to die for their country—nor does there seem much to commend such a view. Indeed, as a soldier, I would say, on a number of grounds, it is deeply distressing, not to mention destructive, to have military personnel held up to the nation essentially as mercenaries.

The notion that military service is just a job is demonstrably false, and treating it as nothing more than a job exacerbates the institutional damage. There can be no doubt that everyone participating in the debate on homosexuals in the military knows that what is at issue is combat readiness, national defense, and the survival of soldiers. The commander in chief, in his choice to support pansexualism in the armed forces, treated these matters as trivial.

What inhered in the push to put homosexuals in the military was the conclusion—the pansexualist principle—that military service was not special enough to justify institutional limits on individual behavior. It was not special enough to have institutional standards that exceeded the lowest common denominator of individual behavior. It was not special enough to resolve policy controversies by erring on the side of caution, that is, against the individual and in favor of the institution.

This conclusion was not confined, and is not confinable, to homosexuality. Logically, as demonstrated by subsequent events, this conclusion is equally applicable to all sexual conduct. Again, this is the primary point: The debate on homosexuality in the military is not about homosexuality. It is about sex and the meaning and result of disqualifying social limits on sex. In other words, the philosophical fallout from the commander in chief's policy initiative supporting homosexuality in the armed forces was the clear message, not delimited by homosexuality or even pansexuality, that no institutional mission or goal is big enough, important enough, or valuable enough to make the individual accountable to the institution. In plain terms, pansexualism concludes that no matter what the institution is trying to accomplish—and after all, we have to ask ourselves, if not the military, what? if not the military, where?—the institution cannot tell you what to do. That is a fundamental change in our attitude toward, and our general understanding of, military service. And it is the type of shift that pansexualism brings to every institution that, implicitly or explicitly, adopts its principles.

Tolerating Sexual License as a Moral Imperative

Finally, and this sums up the first two points, pansexualism generates the wide-ranging notion that tolerating sexual license is a moral imperative.

As a young major in the Judge Advocate General Corps, I was in the audience of military officers at the National Defense University in Washington, D.C., when, in 1993, the commander in chief explained his reason for supporting homosexuality in the armed forces. He said he would permit it because supporting homosexuality was "the right thing to do." Likewise, from the commander in chief and others, it often was heard that it is "wrong"—that is, morally wrong—to regulate homosexuality in the armed forces. Recently, senior political leaders declared that it is not "right"—that is, it is not moral—to punish an officer in the United States military for adultery.

What else, by word and deed, would this teach us, except that tolerating sexual license is a moral imperative? All freely chosen sex is an affirmative moral good. No sex should be limited by the law or restrained by the culture. Sex, and sexual license, is more important than, and always outweighs, any negative social consequence it may cause. Sex is more important than military readiness. Sex is more important than life. (Indeed, Justice O'Connor, in noting that women have "organized" their lifestyles around the availability of abortion, has opined that abortion on demand cannot be limited because that might chill sexual activity—thus deeming the moral imperative of sexual license a constitutional imperative as well.[3]) This is the fundamental working out of pansexualist principles, first, in social institutions and, then, in society at large.

In conclusion, these are the three broad implications that inhere in pansexualism, the philosophy that all consensual sex is an affirmative moral good and no sex should be restricted by law or restrained by culture: First, individual needs and wants always outweigh the institution's goal, mission, function, ideal or value. Second, no social goal, aspiration, ideal, function or mission is weighty enough to justify institutional limits on individual autonomy. Finally, in and of and for itself, tolerating sexual license is a moral imperative.

These principles must be fully contemplated before it is possible even to begin to discern the full implication of the increasing coalescence of American government around the principles of pansexualism. To our nation's detriment, the armed forces provide a presently subtle, but predictably incremental, case study of the mechanism by which pansexualism changes an institution's philosophical underpinnings and, thereby, changes the institution.

7

Homosexuality and Adoption

Mary Beth Style

SINCE THE FIRST ADOPTION LAWS were enacted in the United States in the mid-nineteenth century, the explicit focus of public policy in adoption has been the best interest of the child. There has always been a certain tension in child welfare and adoption, as the nature of the proceedings often involves competing interests of the various parties. However, because the child is the most vulnerable party and will be affected the most by adoption decisions, it has long been agreed, at least in theory, that the child's needs should be paramount. Therefore, adoption law and advocates continue to view the best interest of the child as the guiding principle.

The current discussion about whether homosexuals should have a right to adopt threatens to challenge the very nature of adoption because it shifts the focus from the needs of the child to a discussion of the rights of adults. Unfortunately, this shift in focus is not unprecedented, and each time adoption policy has changed in this way, the results have been disastrous. I will discuss two examples—the rights of unmarried putative fathers and the current fad in child welfare services for "family preservation"—in order to illustrate the danger for children of following a similar line of reasoning advanced in favor of the adoption by homosexuals of children to whom they are unrelated. The parallels will become clear as I address each issue.

Putative Fathers' Rights

A "putative father" is a man who is presumed by reputation to be the biological father of a child. He has not been judged to be a legal father by virtue of marriage to the child's mother, by a court in a paternity action, by a blood test, by his paternal actions toward the child through physical or emotional support, or even by his admission of paternity. Until 1973, fathers who did not legitimate children by marriage to the children's mother had virtually no parental rights. In that year, in *Stanley v. Illinois*, the Supreme Court ruled that an unmarried man could have legal custody of his children.[1] Since then states and courts have given broad rights to all fathers, often at the expense of the rights of all other parties, including the child's mother and the child himself. The public policy which has emerged since *Stanley* goes far beyond what the Court required, and it is important to review this decision in light of the discussion of adoption by homosexuals.

The *Stanley* case involved a man who had a long-term relationship with his children and their mother and had for many years lived with them. The mother died, and the father was initially denied custody because under the law in Illinois, as in most other states, there was an *irrebuttable* presumption that unmarried fathers are unfit, and no opportunity was given them for a hearing to seek custody. The Supreme Court rightly, by virtually all accounts, gave custody to the unmarried father because he had a long-standing parental relationship with his children. The Court acknowledged in *Stanley* that it may be "that most unmarried fathers are unsuitable and neglectful parents. But all unmarried fathers are not in this category; some are wholly suited to have custody of their children." And so the Court ruled that under the Due Process Clause putative fathers must be given the opportunity for a hearing.

Had this decision been interpreted from the traditional child-welfare standpoint of protecting the best interest of the child while assuring that the rights of others are not violated, there would have been a change in the adoption process, but there would not have been the wholesale disruption of adoption that has occurred since *Stanley*. But instead of merely changing the law to allow unmarried fathers their day in court, the states overreacted and changed adoption laws to create a *rebuttable* presumption that unmarried fathers are fit—that is, they would be considered fit unless proved by the state to be unfit. In adoption cases involving a newborn, there is no evidence one way or another about the fitness of a particular individual to be a parent to this particular child. In many cases courts have ruled that prior abuse of other children cannot be used to show unfitness to parent the child in question. The result has been that states are now burdened with the task of tracking down every biological father, including sperm donors, and providing a hearing, rather than merely assuring that all fathers who wish to assert their rights have the opportunity to do so. The rights and needs of children and the other parties to the adoption have often been set aside as the state attempts to provide a day in court for an individual who may not want it.

The state has a legitimate interest in assuring that children are born with legal mothers and fathers. Therefore, it is clearly justifiable to have a rebuttable presumption that unmarried fathers are unfit, as law professor Lynn Wardle and others have argued, because they have not legitimated their children to assure that the children have their basic physical and legal needs met.[2] The fact that the presumption is rebuttable allows the father who has taken responsibility for the child, even though he has not married the child's mother, to show that he is a fit parent and deserves all the rights and responsibilities afforded married fathers. This approach leaves room for a discussion of the best interest of the child, since, as one is proving his fitness to be a parent, the unmarried father will necessarily show how it is in the best interest of the child to be raised by him. Stanley would have retained custody under this law. Subsequent Supreme Court decisions have required that unmarried fathers show, in order to claim parental rights, that they have attempted to establish a meaningful relationship with the child. The Court stated clearly in *Lehr v. Robertson* that "the mere existence of a biological link" was not enough to provide constitutional protection. The father must grasp the "opportunity" to develop a relationship with his child and assume parental responsibility. The *Lehr* Court also stated "that the most effective protection of the putative father's opportunity to develop a relationship with his child is provided by the laws that authorize formal marriage and govern its consequences."[3]

However, if one looks at adoption practice and policy in many states today, it is almost as if no clarifying decisions had followed *Stanley*, which is treated in many states today as a precedent that gives blanket rights to unmarried fathers. Often, when a group is given new rights, it pits them against other groups, and when a new right emerges it tends to overshadow rights that already exist. This appears to be what has happened with the issue of putative fathers' rights. In fact, in many states, courts will not even consider the child's rights and needs unless an unmarried father is proven unfit.

As a result of this shift in focus from needs of children to the rights of unmarried fathers, adoption policy and practice are in great turmoil today. Many states require adoption agencies, biological mothers, prospective adoptive parents, and the courts to jump through many hoops in order to track down unknown fathers. The process is lengthy and expensive, leaving children in legal limbo for many months. Often, after multiple attempts, a father who has shown no interest in the child still cannot be found. In other cases, after many months of searching, a father who has provided no support or shown any interest comes forward at the last minute to object to an adoption. Many judges will grant his petition for custody based solely on his biological connection to the child. In some cases such as the 1995 *Baby Richard* case, even though the state of Illinois had specific procedures and timelines that unmarried fathers had to follow to assert rights, a father who failed to act within the parameters of the law was granted custody of the child without any consideration of the child's best interest. The Illinois Supreme Court, apparently misunderstanding *Stanley* and believing that paternal rights are paramount, claimed that the biological father's rights were the most important. The sad result was that a child was removed from an adoptive family after four years and placed with the biological father who subsequently abandoned the child and his mother. Had the court considered the best interest of the child, it would have examined the father's previous behavior as well as the devastating effect of a child's losing the only family he has ever known. Instead, the court's decision that the father's rights come first led this child to a second serious loss.

This case is not unique. Judges often state in opinions and public comments that the father's rights must always be protected, with the best interest of the child secondary in considerations. Therefore, unless it can be proven that the child will suffer imminent danger, the biological father will always get custody, regardless of his relationship with the child and in the face of the child's other significant relationships. Only the claims of a biological mother can trump those of a biological father. Again, this ignores the best interest of the child when a mother has determined that she is not prepared to raise him or believes, as most women choosing adoption do, that the child will be better off raised by a married couple so that he can have both a mother and a father.

There have been recent cases where a judge has declared a biological mother unfit precisely because she considered adoption for the child, believing adoption to be in her child's best interest. In one of these cases, known to the author, custody was granted to a biological father who had encouraged abortion and adoption during the pregnancy and who had numerous complaints leveled against him by former employers, acquaintances, and legal authorities. The judge refused to hear any testimony that was not directly related to the father's parenting. Since the child was a newborn, no information on the father's ability to raise him was available.

It is not only the courts that have created this situation, but the child welfare field and society in general, which have shifted their focus from the child to the rights of the adults. No one would like to see the rights of adults trampled, but most would agree that when the rights of various parties are in conflict, the state should make an extra effort to protect the rights of the most vulnerable. One of the reasons that society is so ambivalent about these cases is its reluctance to have the state intrude on private life. This is a legitimate concern, and public policy must be clear that the state may only become involved in family life when there is a clear state interest such as the protection of children. If, in fact, the rationale for the state's involvement in custody cases is the protection of children, then it is clear that the state's primary concern in all proceedings must be the best interest of the child. Therefore, in considering only the rights of adults the state is not fulfilling its responsibility to protect children.

Family Preservation

This is even clearer in the issue of "family preservation," a term designed to win support from all quarters. It is certainly good public policy to preserve families. Nevertheless, as with most slogans, there is more behind it than meets the eye. "Family preservation" was a concept developed to justify increased federal funding for services to families who have abused or neglected their children. The rationale is that families abuse or neglect because of a lack of economic and social supports. If the government provides these services, children can be removed from foster care and returned home safely. This is a laudable goal in the abstract, but unfortunately it is not based in reality. There are many reasons that parents abuse and neglect their children, including serious character defects which cannot be corrected by buying a family groceries, providing babysitting or housekeeping services, or even counseling. But the driving philosophy is that the parents are victims who need help and that to deny them their children is a violation of their rights. It is often heard from drug treatment programs that the promise of a return of children to a drug-addicted parent is necessary to provide the addict an incentive to clean up. It is not considered whether it is in the best interest of a child to return to a parent who has repeatedly abused the child, after perhaps years of separation in which the child has finally begun to feel secure in another household. Again, adult rights supersede the best interest of the child because public policy defines the family by biology and treats children as the parents' property. Public relations has been very important in getting society and the courts to accept this policy, which is clearly harmful. I have heard more than one judge state quite innocently, upon being informed of the dangers of returning a child to an abusive parent, "I thought it was a settled matter that children are always better off with their biological parents."

If the child welfare and foster care system would return to its original mission and make the protection of the best interest of children its primary concern, services would still be given to challenged parents so that children could remain with them when it was appropriate. But there would be a recognition that some parents will never have the capacity, motivation, or resources to provide the consistent loving care and safe environment that a child needs. In these cases what is best for the child is to place him in a family that can provide for his needs adequately. This brings us to the issue at hand: homosexuals adopting children.

Homosexuals and Adoption

The issue of homosexuals adopting children is not an adoption issue but a homosexual rights issue. This puts it into the category of the previous two issues, where adults wish to claim rights over children without considering the child's best interest. In the last ten years, the topic has become more prominent, not coincidentally during a period when the gay rights movement has begun to assert itself in many different arenas. The movement of homosexuals to adopt comes not merely from an interest in parenting, although that is the motivation of many. For the homosexual rights movement the right to adopt is a symbol—a goal which must be achieved in order to achieve broader victory. Whether the reason for promoting homosexual adoption is personal or political, the chief concern still must be what is in the best interest of a particular child. Clearly, adoption as a political statement does not take into account a child's needs at all. And an individual parent, whether heterosexual or homosexual, who is seeking to adopt principally to meet narcissistic needs is also not concerned about the best interest of the child.

The purpose of adoption is to provide a child with a permanent, legal family, when the family he was born into cannot or will not fulfill its responsibilities to him. As such, society attempts to replace as far as possible the family the child would have had by birth under the best of circumstances. The world is not perfect and children sometimes get less than desirable families. But when you have the opportunity to plan for a child's family, as you do with adoption, you might as well do it right. And since the state has taken on the role of creating families, it has a special obligation to look after the best interest of the child—the only legitimate reason for the state to be involved in the first place.

The adoption law in virtually all states makes it clear that children may be adopted—by a married couple or a single individual—only after a finding that it is in their best interest. Historically, state statutes have not allowed two unmarried adults to adopt a child—whether they are an unmarried heterosexual couple, a homosexual couple, or two sisters who are aunts to the children.[4] The reason is that adoption gives family membership to a child but does not create the whole family. The child, in other words, is not what binds everyone together. It is the parental dyad, that is, the most important relationship for the functioning and stability of a healthy family. When there are problems between the parents, the children suffer. The state, therefore, has a legitimate interest in insisting that the parents have a legal commitment to each other before they can make a permanent legal commitment to a child. While marriage may not always be reliable as a lasting relationship, it at least provides some indication that the couple intends a permanent legal relationship.

Now some will claim that this provision discriminates against gays because gays are not allowed to marry. Nevertheless, this argument overlooks that a child needs more than a legally committed family. It is widely agreed that children do best in a loving family with a mother and a father. Some will maintain that children raised by single parents or homosexuals do just fine, and undeniably many do, but as a rule children still do better with a mother and a father.

Lynn Wardle, in his article "The Potential Impact of Homosexual Parenting on Children,"[5] reviewed the literature on the impact of homosexual parenting on children. What he found, which unfortunately is all too common in social science research, is that the studies have generally been done from a particular advocacy perspective. In studies of homosexual parenting, the overriding hypothesis has been that children are not harmed by homosexual parents. As Wardle and numerous others have pointed out, all of the studies have methodological problems: Because of the nature of the issue and the small percentage of parents who are homosexuals, the sample sizes are small. There is also the problem of identifying homosexual parents, so it is impossible to do random sampling. Virtually all the studies depend on volunteers generally identified from clinical samples of individuals in therapy or through some homosexual support group, which generally indicates an involvement in the political agenda of the homosexual rights movement. The studies' authors invariably conclude that children of homosexuals are not at greater risk for various problems. But even those who make these claims have pointed out some particular problems that the children experience but downplayed them by suggesting that all children will face challenges and that what is important is a nurturing family to help children meet those challenges.

In addition, the comparison groups for homosexual parents are virtually always single parents, not married parent families. It is revealing that the authors choose not to make the comparison with the ideal (married parent families), presumably suspecting that the homosexual group would come up short. No one is suggesting that any family can be perfect and that every family headed by a married man and woman will be superior to a single-parent family regardless of sexual orientation. But as a general rule, the married model provides more protection for children and an environment more conducive to healthy development.

I cannot say that homosexuals cannot or will not make loving parents who provide for many of the needs of their children. I believe they can and do. But providing a nurturing environment is not enough. A homosexual parent cannot provide the parental experience of a parent of the opposite sex, and this is as critical to the child as anything else. When discussing a child's needs, it is not just a discussion of what a particular parent can provide—it is just as important to consider what a parent cannot provide and, in this case, it is half of a child's needed parenting experience.

This is where the research is a little clearer. In recent years, with the discussion of welfare reform and the growing concerns of illegitimacy and fatherless children, many authors have reexamined studies on delinquency, school performance, and mental health, controlling for the presence of a father in a child's life, and they have found that the lack of a father is the most important factor in predicting maladaptive behavior in children, particularly boys. The same analysis has not been done on mother absence. Possibly no one has thought to do the comparison because mother absence is not as prevalent as father absence. Yet most of us know intuitively that the loss of a mother is devastating to children. Society has always fostered policies to keep mothers and children together while it has allowed for some separation of fathers from children. It is undisputed that mothers and fathers behave differently with their children in play, in terms of demands, discipline, and social interaction. Both parents contribute to intellectual, emotional, moral, psychological, and social development of children in different ways, enabling a child to be more secure in his identity. Therefore, if we know that mothers and fathers bring different but equally important parenting styles and attributes to children, doesn't it follow that the state, whenever it is entrusted to represent the best interest of a child, should do all that is possible to provide both of those experiences to the child?

This is the only legitimate question in adoption and foster care. But unfortunately the debate is not being held on this level but has been framed as an issue, not of children, but of adults and their demand for "rights." It is important to remember, when discussing whether homosexuals should have rights to adopt, that *no one* in our society has a right to adopt, since adoption is about a child's need for a secure, permanent family. If there were a right to adopt, a logical conclusion would be the state has a responsibility to guarantee adoption to anyone who wants to be a parent—an impossible task.

The gay rights movement's public relations campaign has already begun to redefine "best interest of child" by asserting that it is best for children to be adopted by homosexuals. Proponents of nontraditional parenting models understand that to promote their agenda they cannot compare their parenting model to the married mother-father model. On one talk show I was asked if it is my position that it was better for a profoundly retarded child to be raised in an institution or be adopted by a loving lesbian couple. On another program I was asked whether it wouldn't be better for a child to be adopted by a single person than an abusive married couple. The answer to both of these questions is to ask if these are ever the state's only two options? If so, then of course, keeping with the philosophy of the best interest of the child, the lesbian couple and the single person are the most appropriate persons to adopt these particular children.

Some in the gay community, to their credit, have come forward to be resources to families affected by AIDS, stepping in to care for children when mothers become ill or die. In many of these cases, the homosexual individual may be the only support the family has and play a critical role for the children. It is arguable in some of these cases that it is in the best interest of the child to be adopted by this adult, who has been a stabilizing source of support during a very traumatic time. There are other cases where a homosexual has had a significant custodial relationship to a child, and it is in the best interest of the child to protect that relationship legally and permanently through adoption. These relationships may include situations where children were left by their parents in the care of a homosexual and then subsequently abandoned. They may also include some situations where a child was being raised by a homosexual biological parent and his partner until the biological parent's death. If the child has no other significant relationship with an adult, it may be appropriate for the parent's partner to adopt the child. This case would be similar to the *Stanley* case, where the court would protect an existing critical bond for a child. This is the scenario which appears to result most often in a favorable court opinion for a homosexual adoption. Unfortunately, these individual cases, which are fact-specific, are being promoted as if they are general precedents. They should not be treated as such.

The parallels to *Stanley* are great, and for the sake of children we should not allow the same mistake to occur. These cases should be about an individual child's best interest, not about creating a new right of adoption by gays, but the Lambda Legal Defense Fund does not seem to agree. Lambda has been quoted in news reports as saying that, while two states have statutes prohibiting gays from adopting, twenty-one states expressly allow gays to adopt. This information came as a surprise to those of us in the adoption field who closely follow legislation because statutes generally do not state who can and cannot adopt by personal characteristics, except with a few exceptions like convicted felons. On closer examination of Lambda's data it was found that there had been cases in twenty-one states that Lambda was able to identify which resulted in an acknowledged homosexual adopting. They concluded from this information that twenty-one states allow homosexuals to adopt. Theoretically, all but the two states which specifically prohibit homosexuals from adopting would allow homosexuals to adopt, but only when it was judged to be in the best interest of the child.

Changes in Adoption Policy

This commitment to the best interest of the child by all in the child welfare field has assured that most adoptions were accomplished by married couples. This has been changing, and nontraditional parents have been more successful in adopting in the past two decades. Several factors are responsible for this change.

The first was the increase in the focus on placing children with special needs. A child with special needs is a child who is physically, emotionally, or mentally disabled, older than infancy, or a member of a racial or ethnic minority or sibling group. These children are also defined as "hard to place" because there is not the same large pool of prospective adoptive parents that is available for healthy infants. Because there are not always married couples lined up waiting to adopt these children, agencies have expanded their pool to nontraditional families. There has been some debate in the field about this practice, as it can be argued that a child with a special need or challenge needs a stable family with a mother and a father even more than a child who is healthy. Most have agreed that if an agency truly could not find a married couple family and the only alternative for a particular child was nonpermanent foster care or institutional care, it is better to have one parent than no parent. The question that still remains, and that responsible agencies need to continue to answer in the affirmative before making such placements, is whether the agency truly has done everything possible to find a family able to serve the best interest of the child, which by definition is a married couple?

With the acceptance of single-parent adoptions for children with special needs came the argument that if it was acceptable for children with special needs, it ought to be acceptable for healthy infants. Proponents of single-parent adoptions argued that there was an increase in single parents in society and many were doing a superb job. Therefore, not to allow singles the opportunity to adopt is discriminatory and judgmental on the part of the adoption field. This is perhaps the most effective charge to make against the social work community in order to get it to change its practices. Social workers as a group view themselves as the champions of the oppressed and believe it is their mission to rid the world of prejudice.

During this period there were also many changes occurring in adoption practice. Many criticize the home study process which was designed to screen prospective adoptive parents as being too intrusive. Increasingly the field began to talk about being inclusive of adoptive parents rather than exclusive and focused the home study process on preparing adoptive parents for the experience of adoptive parenting. In fact some adoption reformers, such as a governor's task force in Ohio, recommended removing the prohibition against convicted felons adopting, and one of the most contentious custody battles in Cleveland in recent years involved a potential adoptive parent who had been convicted of killing his first wife against a family of a race different from that of the child. The social work community sided with the convicted murderer because his race was the same as the child's. Accordingly, so-called adoption reformers have advocated focusing on issues such as attitudes of adoptive parents toward birth parents and willingness of adoptive parents to share their children with birth parents, attitudes about discipline (usually including prohibitions against corporal punishment), feelings about infertility, and the like.   .

What is not included in the recommended updated home studies is investigation into an individual's sexual and social relationships. It is still acceptable to ask these questions of married couples, because there is recognition that a couple's relationship will affect the children. Nevertheless, since a single person is not in a permanent relationship at the time of adoption, the question is often viewed as irrelevant or intrusive. Most homosexuals who successfully adopt probably withhold information about their sexual orientation and relationships, and since often no in-depth investigation is done in this area, the court is often unaware of the facts. It can be argued that the instability of nonmarital relationships will have more of an impact on children than a marital relationship with some difficulties. Certainly, a child who is exposed to various sexual partners of a promiscuous parent, regardless of sexual orientation, is put at considerable risk. Even a parent who is discreet about his sex life but nevertheless allows his partners to form emotional attachments with his child can cause harm to the child, who must endure loss whenever a relationship ends.

As is apparent, the shift from the child's best interest to a focus on an adult's right to adopt a child without any interference has lowered the standards in practice, so that a careful investigation into critical relationships to which the child will be exposed is not being done as a matter of routine by social reformers who have decided that a parent's sexual relationships and orientation are irrelevant to the parenting role.

In addition to the segment of the adoption field that believes single people, heterosexual or homosexual, should receive the same consideration as married couples, there are other groups that wish to end adoption as we know it by changing the structure of adoptive families. Some want to end adoption because they believe that all organized social institutions are oppressive, that marriage was invented by men to oppress women, and that adoption is by association problematic because it has traditionally been used to assure that children have married parents. If one argues that women are capable of raising children alone, then an institution like adoption is contrary to one's goals.

Other reformers who want to end adoption are motivated by a belief that adoption causes unresolvable grief, and hence a pathology. Among these advocates are individuals with a personal connection to adoption who believe all their problems can be traced to the adoption experience. Others include so-called "adoption therapists" who view all problems by individuals involved in an adoption to be connected in some manner to unresolved issues of the adoption. Parallels to therapists involved in recovered memory therapy are striking, as all clients, regardless of their presenting problem all end up with the same diagnosis and the suggested treatment is to undo the adoption by reconnecting the adopted person with the biological parents. These reformers have gone one step further and recommended preventing adoption from occurring in the beginning and have suggested a new form of parenting sometimes called open adoption, sometimes called cooperative adoption, and sometimes just referred to as a form of guardianship. In this new adoption, adoptive parents would take on full parenting responsibility for a child, but the biological parent would have a continuing relationship with the child, with varying rights and privileges depending on how the individuals involved agree to define the relationships.

The argument is that the structure of the family does not matter. What is important is that the child is in a loving, nurturing environment. The argument continues that it cannot hurt a child to have more than one set of parents to love him and in fact will be beneficial. Notice the parallels between the arguments for open adoption and the ones made in the 1970s for open marriage—structure does not matter; how can it hurt to have more than one spouse; each family will define its own relationships with rights, responsibilities. The idea of open marriage did not succeed except among a fringe group, probably because it affected adults adversely, and adults would not stand for it. Unfortunately, the proposal of open adoption has not been as slow to fade and at this point is increasing in popularity. Yet it ignores the needs of children, who do need structure and a sense of stability and security that one set of parents brings. A child needs to know that his mother and his father will be there always for him and not worry about whether other parents will have a right to disrupt his life in the future.

The recent case in Hawaii involving same-sex marriage featured four expert witnesses advocating same-sex marriage. One witness was Dr. David Brodzinsky, a professor of psychology from Rutgers and a self-proclaimed adoption therapist. Dr. Brodzinsky first gained notoriety in the adoption field from his studies of school-age children's understanding of adoption. He concluded, in essence, that children did not begin to comprehend adoption until around the ages of seven and eight, and while some struggled with understanding the concept of two sets of parents and some even were preoccupied with concerns about losing their adoptive parents if biological parents reclaimed them, most children resolved the issues successfully without trauma by adolescence. These findings reflected the experience of most in the adoption field.

Dr. Brodzinsky has been called in numerous cases and before legislatures to give expert testimony. His statements in those instances have often gone beyond the scope of his research and have instead been based on personal opinion he claims he has formed from his clinical practice. Dr. Brodzinsky is an advocate of open adoption, claiming that all adopted persons will seek out their origins. This is contrary to what he reported in his own research, that the majority of adopted persons integrate the knowledge of their adoption without any problem and have a good sense of self.

It is important to be wary of generalizations about a particular population coming out of a clinical sample, which is not representative of an entire population group but only of the segment of that group that is having difficulty and (therefore) seeking assistance. It is possible that Dr. Brodzinsky only sees patients who are seeking contact with their biological parents. The ones he does not see are the adopted persons who are content with their lives and are not seeking therapy or their biological parents. Yet he concludes that all adopted persons feel the same way as his patients.

In his testimony in Hawaii, Dr. Brodzinsky stated that he has counseled numerous gay parents, who were doing a fine job of parenting, but did not claim to have done any objective research on this population. It is not clear how many of his patients fall into this category, why they sought counseling, or how Brodzinsky himself defines successful parenting, though he claims that what is important to a child is nurturing, not the structure of the family.

Yet the recognition of a child's need for one mother and one father, even in divorce and cases of remarriage, has led to stepparent adoption laws being worded carefully. In adoption, it is necessary to terminate the rights of the biological parents before an adoption can occur. In a stepparent adoption an exception is made so that it is only necessary to terminate the rights of the noncustodial parent for the spouse of the custodial parent to adopt the child. Reformers may ask why the noncustodial parent's rights must be terminated in order to have the stepparent adopt the child. Isn't it better for the child to have two legal fathers or mothers to love and support him? To have two mothers or two fathers is confusing for the child and for the state. The more the roles, responsibilities, and privileges are spread around to numerous people, the more watered down the role of parent becomes and the more confusing to all involved.

The law in most states is very clear that the child can only have one mother and one father at a time. This is a further prohibition on homosexual couples adopting a child. While it is possible for one of the parties to adopt as a single person, it is not possible for the other partner to adopt because the two are not married and the child would have either two mothers or two fathers. Some cases have challenged these laws successfully and judges have allowed gay couples to adopt under traditional stepparent laws. Other judges have rejected this approach, choosing instead to follow the intentions of the legislatures that passed the laws.

Conclusion

Public policy in adoption that has traditionally made the best interest of children the paramount concern has been very successful. The institution of adoption boasts a failure rate of less than 2 percent for all adoptions and a disruption rate of about 12 percent for adoptions of children with special needs who have a history of multiple placements and abuse. In a society with a divorce rate around 50 percent, this success is tremendous. When a shift away from the best interest of the child has occurred, such as in the case when the rights of putative fathers or abusive parents are given preference over the needs of children, the results for children have been devastating, with children suffering severe trauma and loss and instability which will affect their ability to form stable relationships in the future.

Creating a right to adopt by homosexuals would be another shift from the focus on the child. The research is clear that while many homosexuals are good parents, providing a nurturing environment, homosexuals cannot give the child the experience of having parents of both genders. It is also indisputable that children who have the benefit of both a mother and a father do better than children raised by single parents. Therefore, while homosexuals may do a laudable job as parents, just as many single heterosexual parents do, their children are missing out on a very important parenting experience.

It is the role of the state in adoption to assure that a child is adopted by a family in the best interest of the child—not a "good enough" family, but the best possible one the state can find. Therefore, if the slate is clean and the child has no significant emotional attachments to any potential parents, the state should always opt for an available married mother and a father. There may be individual situations where, because of a child's specific needs, no married couple is available for adoption for a particular child and the state may need to look to a nontraditional parent. However, in those cases it should be the responsibility of the state to prove that efforts have been made to find a married couple to adopt the child. It is not good enough for the state to show that it is not detrimental to the child to be adopted by a nontraditional parent, but the state must show that it is in the child's best interest to be adopted by this particular parent.

There are other situations where a homosexual may have had custody or a significant relationship with a child who is in need of a permanent family. In these cases it may be in the child's best interest to be adopted by the homosexual parent rather than disrupting the child's life and forcing him into a new family situation. In these cases, judges should have the discretion to grant an adoption which is proven to be in the best interest of the child, again not just not detrimental to the child.

These exceptional cases make it clear that the law ought to be flexible enough to allow for some homosexual adoptions when it is clearly in the child's best interest. However, as a rule, adoption by homosexuals should not be allowed. This probably can only be enforced against agency adoption since most of the exceptions will result from a parent leaving a child in the custody of a homosexual for such a length of time as to create a substantial bond between the child and the homosexual. Often the original placement was not for the purpose of adoption but for temporary care. Therefore the law would have to specifically state that no agency or individual may place a child with a homosexual for the purpose of adoption. This prohibition should be expanded to include foster care, since that is the point of entry for many adoptive parents. If homosexuals are allowed to foster, it will follow that they will develop significant relationships with children who may eventually be available for adoption. It can be argued in most of these cases that since the child has formed a significant bond with the individual it is in the child's best interest to be adopted by that individual. A prohibition against placing a child with a homosexual for the purpose of foster care would prevent this dilemma down the road.

This proposal will be judged as a harsh treatment of homosexuals. But as I have stated repeatedly, this is not about homosexual rights; it is about children. It is irrefutable that children do better with a mother and a father, and a policy which promotes that end is defensible. It is interesting to note that the Scandinavian countries, which have historically given much freedom to sexual expression by adults and which recognize a legal relationship between homosexual partners, prohibit homosexuals from adopting or fostering children. Public policy should not, in general, discriminate against any individuals because of sexual orientation. But nondiscrimination does not mean establishing new rights to meet the narcissistic needs of individuals. Providing someone with a child so that the individual can experience the joys and challenges of parenting is narcissistic when that parenting relationship will deny the child the equally necessary parenting relationship with someone of the opposite sex.

8

Translating Science into Policy: A Sound Approach to AIDS and HIV

Shepherd Smith

ERHAPS NO DISEASE IN HISTORY has become so politicized, and certainly none other has so challenged the process of translating fundamental tenets of science and medicine into sound policy, as AIDS/HIV. More than a decade after the first cases of the then mysterious syndrome were reported by the Centers for Disease Control and Prevention (CDC), physicians and public health authorities are still embroiled in debate over how best to confront HIV and AIDS. Policy continues to evolve, if ever so slowly, as illustrated by the following news item.

Buried on page A26 of the December 7, 1990, edition of the *New York Times* was a five-paragraph report entitled "Doctors Back Mandatory AIDS Reporting." It began: "In a significant policy change, the American Medical Association's governing body voted on Wednesday to support routinely reporting to public health authorities the names of people who test positive for the AIDS virus." The AMA also voted to declare AIDS a sexually transmitted disease—a fact that had been obvious for nearly a decade. Yet by the late 1990s only a few more than half the states had implemented infectious disease reporting practices for HIV, and none of these were the most heavily affected states.

Never before in medical history have we made it the responsibility of the individual exposed to a contagious or infectious disease to end such an epidemic. With AIDS/HIV, the medical and public health communities during the first fifteen years of the epidemic largely removed themselves from the intervention through aggressive diagnosis and reporting consistent with their approach to similar diseases. Instead, they have relied on those infected—most of whom have no idea they have been exposed to HIV—to voluntarily come forward to be tested. Ordinarily, when a person visits a physician he or she gives informed consent to be treated to the best ability of the physician. It is the physician's responsibility to order whatever tests he deems appropriate in order to properly evaluate the health of the patient and prescribe effective treatment. This is how medicine has been practiced in the United States and still is today—except in the case of HIV. Special, and often extraordinary, consent must be obtained before any HIV antibody test can be ordered. Some states are removing this burdensome, nontraditional practice.

We find ourselves in a continuum of changing policy. To understand where we are in respect to policy and where we are headed, we must look at how and why policy has developed. In doing this we shall consider the role and responsibility of the medical and public health community, AIDS activists, various governmental agencies, and the general public. All have already played roles to varying degrees, and all will in the future, especially as the dynamics of the epidemic change.

Discovery

On June 5, 1981, the CDC publicized the first cases of HIV in its *Morbidity and Mortality Weekly Report*. Michael Gottlieb, a doctor in Los Angeles, had reported five similar cases of pneumocystis carinii pneumonia (PCP) appearing in otherwise relatively healthy young homosexual men.

Another syndrome associated with early cases was Kaposi's sarcoma (KS). So prevalent, in fact, was KS that the first CDC working group on HIV was called the Kaposi's Sarcoma and Opportunistic Infections (KSOI) Task Force. It was critically important for these syndromes to be identified so the causative agent could be found and the risks the disease posed better understood. As the number of cases increased—sixty-seven in the first month after the initial June report—it became evident that other communities would be affected by this new disease. Clearly, intravenous (IV) drug users were also at risk. Women seemed virtually exempt, with only one report in 1981 of an infected woman—an IV drug user. This early pattern of discovery would ultimately shape—and haunt—HIV policy development.

Early Science

Shortly after the initial discovery, the CDC developed an excellent case definition for AIDS, which facilitated the discovery within three years of the cause of the syndrome and its methods of transmission. AIDS was caused by a virus known as human immunodeficiency virus, HIV. The discovery was made by Robert Gallo of the National Cancer Institute of the National Institutes of Health, the same scientist who had previously discovered the only other known human retroviruses, HTLV-I and HTLV-II. The methods of transmission were established to be sexual (heterosexual and homosexual), parenteral (blood and blood product transfusions and sharing drug paraphernalia), and perinatal (mother to infant).

Traditionally, the discovery of the etiology of a syndrome is followed by the death of the syndrome. Medical uncertainty is replaced with knowledge of disease pathogenesis. Dorland's medical dictionary defines a syndrome as an aggregate of signs and symptoms without an etiology. In 1983, AIDS remained accurately defined as a medical syndrome just as Chronic Fatigue Syndrome still is today. The same dictionary defines a disease as a disorder of bodily function with a defined etiology. In 1984, AIDS was no longer a mysterious syndrome, nor technically a syndrome at all, but rather a disease—HIV.

It remains nearly unprecedented in medicine to continue to focus on an arbitrarily defined syndrome in the presence of full knowledge of a disease process. How did this happen? Why weren't fundamental tenets of medicine and public health practiced or utilized throughout much of the early stages of this epidemic? The reasons are complex and varied, but it is less important to analyze why this occurred than to acknowledge that it did occur and to understand its impact on present and future policy.

Since 1984, the clinical spectrum and natural history of HIV infection has been further defined. Early studies suggested only a minority of patients with "pre-AIDS" or HIV infection would develop AIDS. Unfortunately, time now shows us conclusively this is a progressive disease which will claim, absent a cure a number approaching 100 percent of those infected. HIV is fully understood to cause a clinical spectrum of disease, of which AIDS—as initially defined by the occurrence of opportunistic infections, or as redefined in January of 1993 to also include a depleted T-4 lymphocyte count under 200—represents only the terminal phase.

In spite of this knowledge, society and many within the medical community continue to define today's HIV problem in terms of AIDS. Because the time from infection to symptomatic AIDS ranges from five to ten years or more, our continued focus on end-stage disease causes us to respond to events of the past rather than create policy based on the reality of the present. Such a strategy is doomed to failure. Unfortunately, the pattern of dependence on AIDS data rather than HIV data is difficult to change. Certainly policy development has been dictated nearly entirely by AIDS infections rather than HIV infections.

The report of the Presidential Commission on the Human Immunodeficiency Virus Epidemic, issued in June 1988, begins with an executive summary. The first point of that summary states: "The term 'AIDS' is obsolete. 'HIV infection' more correctly defines the problem.

The medical, public health, political, and community leadership must focus on the full course of HIV infection rather than concentrating on later stages of the disease (ARC and AIDS). Continual focus on AIDS rather than the entire spectrum of HIV disease has left our nation unable to deal adequately with the epidemic. Federal and state data collection efforts must now be focused on early HIV reports, while still collecting data on symptomatic disease."

While most today would agree that this is a reasonable position, it was considered radical in 1988. When the report was issued the media focused almost exclusively on its antidiscrimination section, virtually ignoring this critical opening statement. Just two months later Congress created a new commission, taking a step backward by naming it the National Commission on AIDS. And that commission lived up to its name by ignoring the advice of the first commission—whose recommendations it was charged to implement—and focusing its attention almost entirely on AIDS.

The Centers for Disease Control, responsible for reporting all diseases in the United States, responded to the June 1988 report by changing their monthly report title to *HIV/AIDS Surveillance* from simply *AIDS Surveillance*. Nevertheless, it was not until 1994 that any HIV data were listed. And in July 1995, a *Lancet* commentary stated that "in view of the central role of HIV in disease pathogenesis we should strongly consider abandoning the term 'AIDS' in favor of 'advanced HIV disease,' and make greater use of HIV staging systems that describe the full spectrum from symptomless infection to severe disease." Sadly, the commentary did not acknowledge that the United States military had already developed just such a comprehensive staging system in 1985—a decade earlier.

Again, AIDS is an anachronism. The consequence of our obsession of focusing on it rather than HIV disease is devastating. Our opportunity to develop sound policy from the dramatic scientific advances made to date is rapidly disappearing. Despite our best intentions, our strongest resolution, our sincerest commitment, our response to this epidemic will be inappropriate unless we ultimately change our focus from end-stage disease to the full spectrum of disease caused by HIV infection.

Laying the Foundation

The starting point for understanding the full extent of the HIV problem—offering optimal medical care and developing effective policy—is early diagnosis. In understanding diseases and providing care it has always been an imperative to focus on the entire disease process and intervene as early as possible. Not to diagnose is not to practice the fundamental responsibility of medicine and public health.

Today's real epidemic—the HIV epidemic—remains unrecognized, undefined, underground, driven there not by fear but by a lack of proper response from the medical and public health authorities. There presently is little solid foundation for understanding the size of the epidemic, its rate of growth, or its direction. There is opinion, some scientific studies, but no comprehensive knowledge. This after spending billions of dollars on what has been described as America's number one health issue.

To confront HIV effectively, limit its spread, and care for those infected, we must establish policy which facilitates and enhances opportunities to practice sound medicine and allows for the enrichment of the public's health. This is accomplished by treating HIV as we have other serious diseases, not pretending it is something it is not, or ignoring the medically, socially, and politically devastating consequences of the illness. To do this we must answer to some of the most pressing issues this epidemic has raised, from discrimination to access to health care, to a medical and scientific solution.

Policy Objectives

The building blocks for policy development are knowledge, need, and leadership. One cannot provide an informed response without adequate knowledge, nor should one establish guidelines without a need to do so. Clearly the need for sound policy existed from the outset of this epidemic. The level of knowledge required can still be debated, but few would dispute that the element most lacking of the three has been leadership.

Policy should be established which facilitates the accumulation of knowledge, provides optimal support to those most affected, and promotes the public's health and confidence. Anything that hinders knowledge should be scrutinized carefully, and ways found to provide sound policy while protecting access to scientific understanding. The following points should be considered when seeking to formulate HIV policy.

1. Define The Problem.

Is it HIV or is it AIDS? If it is HIV, then we must evaluate the extent of the problem in as many ways as possible; we must neither underestimate the problem nor blow it out of proportion. Ultimately we must inspire the confidence of the public to sustain the level of commitment this disease will require. The CDC's estimate of one million Americans infected—virtually the same number each year from 1986 to 1997—does little to bolster public confidence. Until we accurately define the size and scope of the HIV epidemic, we will be unable to commit the resources needed to defeat this modern-day plague.

2. Articulate the Benefits Of Early Diagnosis.

Fundamentally, it is knowledge of infection that is the beginning point of good science, good medicine, and good public health. Strategies that mask knowledge must be examined carefully. Universal precautions, for example, may dictate treating everyone as if they are infected, but do nothing to inform us of who actually is, negating our ability to offer optimal medical care and limit the spread of the disease. Knowledge of infection, it goes without saying, is for the personal benefit of the patient, and not for public disclosure. Time has now shown that the medical community's ability to respect the confidentiality of HIV-positive persons is consistent with its handling of personal knowledge of all other diseases. Rarely, if ever, is confidentiality breached in the medical setting. Nearly always it is the infected individual sharing his HIV status with a friend, relative, or co-worker that causes HIV status to become more widely known.

3. Use HIV Data to Limit The Spread Of the Disease.

One case makes an anecdote; many cases define trends, rates of progression, direction of spread, possible changes in transmissibility, and other critical factors. It was not until the early 1990s that studies were begun which would better define HIV progression in women. Because we were reluctant to compile fundamental information on HIV-positive patients, including women, we had to begin belatedly collecting critical data which had been available for the better part of a decade. Communities of color were never appropriately warned, for instance, of the extent of their coming HIV problem, even though early HIV data indicated they would be hit hard. Basic science, critical to resolving any medical disorder, became little more than an afterthought because of AIDS activists' initial obsession with end-stage disease research.

4. Balance Policy Between Those Infected and Those Uninfected.

At the same time, we must consider replacing the "rights" debate with a "needs" and "responsibility" debate. The needs of all involved should be balanced in a way which allows for patients to receive optimal medical care, permits the medical community to provide it, allows the public health service to protect the uninfected, and encourages the public to support it. For example, when fear of disclosure and the right to privacy dictated policy development in the early years, we saw enacted laws such as one in California which would have sent a physician to jail for a year and levied a fine of ten thousand dollars if he or she shared HIV-patient data with a fellow physician specialist—for the purpose of helping the patient—without first obtaining the written informed consent of the patient. Certainly laws like this, and there are still some on the books in other states, are unbalanced and prevent the needs of at least one of the parties, the medical community, from being met. Rights given any party should be paid for by being responsible to others.

5. Always Act to Enhance the Condition of Individuals Infected by HIV.

Persistent focus on AIDS rather than HIV facilitates discrimination among patients with HIV infection. Health care benefits provided to some because of fulfillment of an arbitrary case definition, while denied others equally "diseased" as a consequence of HIV, is discriminatory. Our continual overfocus on symptomatic AIDS also works against both those asymptomatic with HIV disease and those uninfected. It leaves at risk for infection those exposed to the undiagnosed asymptomatics, and provides little care for those newly infected.

6. Make All Policy Take Into Account the Diversity of Communities Affected by HIV.

When case definition, for example, is based on gender specific syndromes of adults, it immediately is weighted against the opposite gender and the young. When knowledge of infection is discouraged in one community because of excessive fear of disclosure, it also prohibits knowledge in other communities that do not harbor these same fears. When policy prevents the medical community from providing optimal medical care because physicians are ignorant of HIV status, then the needs of many communities are not met. Likewise, education must be structured in a way which acknowledges the diversity of communities. Messages must be targeted, and policy must respect the ethnic, cultural, religious, and socioeconomic backgrounds of all affected by this disease. Cost consideration of treatments must also be considered as more and more underserved communities become impacted.

7. Continually Monitor Policy

The process of scientific discovery creates an environment for change. Policy that cannot be altered or is too inflexible to accommodate a new understanding is flawed from its inception. By the same token, science must acknowledge that new information will continue to enhance both our knowledge and response to this epidemic. Vaccine therapy, for example, may show that the earlier we intervene in the disease the more effectively we can prolong life, and if not with a therapeutic vaccine then with some other combination of antivirals or treatment modality. Likewise, vaccine development may need additional support should research on antivirals bog down as the epidemic continues to expand. Policy that cannot be readily changed, or restricts the medical community's ability to identify those who can benefit most, is policy in need of review today.

These seven policy objectives are broad, yet inclusive. They do not, however, address the critical need for leadership. The medical and scientific communities can no longer abrogate responsibility regarding policy development to others concerned about this issue. We must return to the fundamental tenets of science, medicine, and public health in order to translate our knowledge into sound policy. We must demand that leadership.

Early Policy Development

The first debate surrounding AIDS policy centered on the blood supply, the second on gay bathhouses. Both illustrate the immense pressures brought to bear on the medical and public health establishments and how early decisions set a precedent for future policy development. Few aspects of this epidemic have been discussed without controversy, yet without a focus on fundamental medical practices the fires of controversy have been fanned more fiercely.

The conflict between individual rights and public health came to the forefront nearly immediately. Those involved in the blood and bathhouse industries adamantly resisted acknowledging that HIV is a blood-borne, as well as a sexually transmitted, disease. Bathhouses, where multiple anonymous sexual encounters occurred nightly, were clearly a place where HIV was transmitted. Although this was recognized almost immediately after the first hundred AIDS cases had been reported, it was not until three years later (October 1984) that San Francisco took the necessary steps to close them. Amazingly, other cities hardest hit, like New York and Los Angeles, would not take such action for quite some time. And in the mid-1990s gay bathhouses began reopening in major U.S. cities (and with them came new HIV infections among young gay men).

Why was there even debate on this issue? Because competing interests intervened to prohibit the establishment of traditional public health strategies to limit the spread of this deadly epidemic. The first roadblock thrown up was the issue of individuals' freedom of choice and with it their right to privacy. Shouldn't people have the right to choose whom they associate with, even sexually? In the case of bathhouses, the issues of freedom of assembly and speech quickly entered the argument. For many, public health should not infringe on the private rights of the individual. Those arguing for leaving bathhouses open never said they wanted to do this simply to allow uncontrolled libidos to reign or to make money from hypersexual activity. They couched their arguments cleverly in weightier issues related to fundamental freedoms and public health. Bathhouses, it was said, were excellent places for AIDS education to take place. Certainly this type of free speech shouldn't be restricted. So effective, in fact, were the proponents of bathhouses in San Francisco that the public health department vacillated for years on whether to close them.

Many in New York argued that closing bathhouses would cause the epidemic to go underground. The public health department delayed closing New York's bathhouses a year longer than in San Francisco. Randy Shilts in *And the Band Played On* notes that anonymous anal sex in public parks and other hidden places by the frequenters of bathhouses turned loose on the streets never occurred as bathhouse proponents had argued it would. The epidemic was not driven underground by this loss of protection of alleged privacy; it was already underground. And it will remain underground until we acknowledge the failure of "volunteerism" in this epidemic.

While arguments raged over the advisability of keeping bathhouses open, the CDC was warning the blood industry that HIV could be blood-borne, first requesting in July of 1982 that blood banks not accept blood from the then-defined "high-risk groups"—gay men and IV drug users. Another powerful group, the blood industry, now argued with the CDC much as the bathhouse owners had. Self-interest and civil rights arguments soon clouded rational discussion of what was sound public health policy, setting a precedent which would linger for a decade or more.

Incredibly, so strong was the denial of reality that in 1984 both the American Red Cross and a majority of blood centers denied that HIV could be transfused through blood products—even after a *New England Journal of Medicine* article by the CDC documented transfused HIV cases. In March 1984 the New York Blood Center still refused to screen blood by testing for core antibody-positive hepatitis B, a recommendation of CDC to the Public Health Service made in August 1982. When in March 1985 the first HIV blood test was developed, attention was directed not at its usefulness as a diagnostic tool but first at whether blood donors should be notified of a positive test, whether their records could be retained, and whether positive donors' previous donations should be traced. To many today this seems almost incredible, especially since the National Blood Registry has had no breaches of confidentiality in its entire history.

In September 1995, the Institute of Medicine issued a report on early blood transfusion infections and concluded "that a failure of leadership may have delayed effective action during the period from 1982 to 1984." The document, "HIV and the Blood Supply: An Analysis of Crisis Decisionmaking," notes that both the FDA and the blood-banking industry not only played down the risk of HIV transfusions but rejected suggestions to screen donors for risk behaviors or test for surrogate viral indicators. This could and should have been done in January of 1983, the report concludes.

But the aspect of diagnosis versus screening was very controversial in 1984 and 1985. The gay community had a near paranoiac fear of identity disclosure, witchhunts, and discrimination because of their lifestyle. Identifying the virus that causes AIDS possibly meant identifying (in some never-defined public fashion) the individual carrying the virus. Randy Shilts, in *And the Band Played On*, describes events leading up to the licensing of the first antibody tests:

> Just forty-eight hours before [Secretary of Health and Human Services] Heckler announced the Abbott licensure, the National Gay Task Force and Lambda Legal Defense and Education Fund filed a petition in federal court to stay the licensing of the antibody test, pending verification of the test's accuracy and a guarantee that the test labeling would not mark the start of massive HTLV-III (HIV) screening of gay men. . . .
>
> The pressure was on. Within hours of the suit's filing, Lambda lawyers and NGTF leaders met with FDA Commissioner Frank Young, who quickly acceded to the gay demand for government-required labeling of the test. Under the agreement, each

test was labeled with the warning, "It is inappropriate to use this test as a screen for AIDS or as a screen for members of groups at increased risk for AIDS in the general population." With the test clearly defined for use in blood banks or laboratories, gays hoped to avert its use as a blood test for homosexuality.

The process of translating science into policy quickly became something altogether different from past medical and scientific experience. The logical scientific outcome for utilization of an extremely accurate diagnostic tool would ordinarily have been to use it for legitimate medical diagnostic purposes. This test could and should have been used to intervene early in the disease, to allow for optimal medical care, to learn about HIV progression, to give individuals the opportunity to avoid infecting others, and to better understand the full scope of the epidemic, its size, rate of growth, and direction.

Instead, the first thing a clinician, physician, or scientist read was, "It is not appropriate to use this test as a screen for AIDS." Inappropriate to diagnose! Incredibly, having that knowledge might result in a fine or prison sentence. In effect, when it came to HIV disease in 1985, it was inappropriate to practice fundamental medicine. Even worse, the practicing physician could face criminal prosecution if he or she did. Bumper stickers passed out at the First International AIDS Conference held in Atlanta in April 1985 proclaimed "No Test Is Best." And when testing was mentioned in a positive vein it was cached in the sophistry of the day, "Test blood, not people."

In this environment it quickly became impossible to translate the fundamental tenets of medicine and science into rational policy. The medical and scientific communities had abrogated their responsibility, and the government enjoyed the support of neither the medical profession nor the general public. The dearth of leadership created a nonscientific AIDS policy.

Nowhere was this lack of medical and public health leadership more evident than in the discussion over how to develop a staging system for the full course of HIV disease. Only the United States military moved quickly to define the entire spectrum of disease by developing a comprehensive staging system from point of infection to death. A young military doctor (a major at the time), Robert R. Redfield Jr., used all available information on the disease to define the various stages of progression of HIV.

His system was put in place in 1985 and required three fundamental criteria in addition to some outward symptoms. Central to the military system were HIV seropositivity, monitoring of T-4 lymphocyte counts, and determining the innate strength of each individual's immune system through delayed hypersensitivity skin (DHS) testing. Because HIV is asymptomatic (has no outward symptoms) during the majority of the time one is infected, the Walter Reed Staging System, as it became known, focused on the need to stage individuals during the critical times when no symptoms were apparent.

A year later, the U.S. Public Health Service met in Atlanta at the CDC to formulate an official U.S. government HIV staging system. Many of the fifteen experts assembled argued that getting people to come back to have their skin test results read was impractical. Having T-4 counts monitored was costly and may not actually be predictive of disease progression, a majority said, so that critical component was also not included. And as for requiring serologic diagnosis of a mostly asymptomatic disease (that would require HIV testing), it was argued such a practice could somehow drive the epidemic underground. The result was a 13 to 2 vote to base the staging system of a mostly symptomless disease solely on symptoms. The two dissenting votes came from members of the U.S. military.

Years later, as the tuberculosis (TB) epidemic expanded on the back of an expanding HIV epidemic, the CDC argued strenuously for more TB testing of HIV positive patients—never arguing people might not comply with having to come back to have their skin test read. In 1993, T-4 lymphocyte counts became a prime marker in the CDC's revised

AIDS case definition. And by 1995, the CDC was strongly encouraging anyone at risk to be tested for HIV, particularly all pregnant women.

Ten years after a comprehensive staging system had been developed by the U.S. military, the U.S. Public Health Service had yet to develop one that had broad appeal, or even limited use, in the scientific and medical community. By this time T-4 counts had shown themselves predictive of disease progression, and delayed hypersensitivity skin testing had proved to be an independent predictor of disease progression. Because, in the beginning, the fundamental tenets of medicine and public health were not embraced, because the irrational fears of AIDS activists were allowed to determine policy, and because few had the courage to speak out for what was right, a deadly disease began to spread to more segments of our population.

Perhaps the best—and saddest—illustration was the spread of the disease to both the heterosexual population and African-American communities. Active duty military data showed higher rates of HIV infections among black women than among white men in 1985-1987, yet it was not until 1994 that Congress held its first hearings on AIDS in the African-American community. Civilian military applicant HIV data showed a heterosexual epidemic coming, yet in the mid-1990s debate continued as to whether or not AIDS would strike American heterosexuals, even though worldwide HIV was predominantly a heterosexual epidemic.

Present Policy Defined

In a word, present policy is based on the syndrome we identified at the beginning of the 1980s—symptomatic AIDS—not on the disease we know today—HIV. Until America and the world change their focus to HIV, it will be impossible to translate science into sound policy. The obstacles to policy formation must be addressed forthrightly and corrected.

For example, it was believed that offering complete protections against privacy breaches and discrimination would encourage people to come forward to be tested. Yet even after the passage of extensive legislation toward these ends we have not seen more voluntary testing or diagnosis. A 1990 AIDS behavior study from San Francisco of fourteen thousand individuals showed only 62 percent of gay men and 53 percent of IV-drug users had been voluntarily tested. A June 1991 GAO report showed only 39 percent of those getting tested returning for their results, with possibly fewer who go in for testing actually staying to be tested. By the mid-1990s, this dismal record had not improved; it was estimated only one-third to one-half of the one million infected Americans knew their HIV status in 1995. Is there something that is keeping or driving this epidemic underground?

The answer is the scientific and medical communities themselves, by not accepting responsibility to implement basic tenets of public health and medicine. When has it ever been the primary responsibility, either in diagnosis or disease control, for the infected individual to discover infection or limit its spread (especially individuals who often participate in irresponsible or illegal behaviors that put them at risk in the first place)? How does putting this burden on the backs of those who need help alter the course of this epidemic? Since most people who are infected have no idea they carry the virus—or even that they have been exposed to it—they should not have the burden or responsibility of discovering it. The medical and public health communities should undertake this important task.

In respect to partner notification, for example, many AIDS activists have proposed self-referral (where the infected individual informs past sexual or IV partners of exposure to HIV) over allowing the public health community to perform this function. Some in the medical community agree. Yet when one examines the issue more carefully, it becomes apparent that self-referral immediately breaches the long fought for confidentiality of the infected individual and is equally suspect in compliance.

Likewise, universal precautions mask knowledge of infection by detrimentally hiding from the medical community those who are HIV positive. Treating everyone as if they are HIV positive does nothing medically for those who are not—nor anything for those who are. In a similar fashion, condoms are less an answer and more of an impediment to allowing people to make fully informed decisions about sexual relations. Many of those who depend on condoms rather than knowledge of their partners' HIV status will ultimately suffer the same fate.

With respect to patients and healthcare workers who are HIV positive, again knowledge of HIV infection should dictate policy. The medical community has an obligation to provide optimal medical care; likewise, patients should not be subjected to possible accidental infection by infected healthcare workers during risk-prone invasive surgery without their consent. Knowledge of infection in the healthcare setting, particularly, must become an example of how HIV should be treated. This is a serious disease with grave consequences. Masking its presence through well-intentioned programs ultimately proves harmful to both the infected individual and society. Ignorance can no longer shape present policy.

A Model Policy

Where should we look for examples of the type of medical leadership now translated into sound AIDS/HIV policy? Is it to the most affected and infected state, New York? There we saw the New York State medical society and the state public health department locked in battle over whether HIV is a sexually transmitted disease, with the public health department ultimately prevailing in court so that HIV is not a legally recognized STD in New York. There we saw over eleven thousand individuals diagnosed for HIV in 1989 and not one reported to the public health department for standard follow-up. There we saw all AIDS "leadership" arguing against knowledge. There we saw in 1995 the state AIDS institute arguing that infants should not be routinely tested, because they believe the privacy rights of an HIV infected mother come ahead of the right to life of her child. There we see an ever-growing HIV epidemic. Recent changes in New York, brought about largely through the efforts of a courageous member of the New York State Assembly, Nettie Mayersohn, give us hope.

The one community which has implemented solid antidiscrimination measures, which has identified its extent of HIV infection, has offered comprehensive care, and provided traditional public health intervention strategies such as confidential and voluntary partner notification to interrupt the chain of transmission is the United States military. More than ten thousand personnel on active duty have been found to be HIV positive. All have received optimal medical care.

Critics of the military's HIV response say it was easy because they had the authority to do these things. It could be argued that all communities have had the responsibility and authority, but few have had the will or the leadership. In fact, the establishment of sound policy in the military was not an easy process. For example, a July 1985 *Life* magazine article asked what HIV testing of civilian military applicants might do to the all-volunteer recruiting program. Would young men and women no longer volunteer if they knew they would first be tested for HIV? Those with responsibility for bringing in new recruits with over a hundred million dollar budget were nervous, if not hostile, at the time to HIV screening. But medical leadership was offered which allowed sound policy to arise.

The basis of that policy initially required identifying the extent of the problem through aggressive screening programs, protecting from irrational discrimination those found to be positive (this was challenging in a community which legally prohibited homosexuality and drug usage), and offering optimal medical care based on knowledge. Fundamental public health elements of this program included spousal and partner notification, routine HIV diagnosis in all medical settings, projecting future needs and cost based on complete knowledge of numbers infected and disease characteristics. The underlying premise was, and has continued to be, that knowledge of infection dictates the military's response. Rates of new HIV infections fell four-fold by the mid 1990s among active duty personnel, while it grew among their civilian counterparts.

Beneficiaries of the military's response were both those found to be infected and those who did not acquire HIV who might have otherwise had they not been associated with the armed forces. For example, military physicians and clinicians quickly became aware of the need to treat pneumosistis carini pneumonia, PCP. They began treating it with Bactrim or Septra in 1986 (and servicewide by 1987) as a standard of care for later stage patients, having ruled out aerosolized pentamidine as too expensive, less effective, and burdensome.

In 1989 the AIDS community made prophylaxing PCP with aerosolized pentamidine a major issue. In 1991 the National Institutes of Health issued a report stating Bactrim and Septra were superior to aerosolized pentamidine because they were less expensive, more effective, and easier to administer. Regrettably, this example is only one of many where the lack of knowledge of HIV infection and the lack of medical leadership to implement sound policy has proven detrimental to so many.

The Rewards of Sound Policy

Policy derived from science has clearly been shown to be superior to policy derived from unreasonable fears. Policy based on knowledge is unquestionably far superior to policy based on ignorance. And policy structured to implement fundamental tenets of science and medicine will prove effective in limiting the spread of this epidemic while offering optimal medical care to those already infected.

Such policy facilitates benefits beyond science and medicine. Questions regarding personal religious belief, race, lifestyle, educational messages, discrimination, and other issues even more sensitive are quickly resolved or replaced by the medical solution. The burden of responsibility for obtaining knowledge of infection is shifted to those who should be responsible—the medical and public health community—allowing the public to gain the needed confidence to appropriately address and support this issue. And such policy creates an environment in which honest debate can occur, accurate information can be exchanged, and many more people helped.

The knowledge model of test-linked education has proven effective over the widely used practice of AIDS education alone, which is not linked to individual knowledge of infection. By using the medical model in respect to appropriate messages, we can differentiate between optimal versus suboptimal ones. And the distinction between prevention and risk reduction can be more easily articulated and understood.

The medical model also allows educational policies to be based on fact rather than theory. The biggest predictor of an STD, including HIV, for example, is the number of sexual partners one has. Having more than one lifetime partner increases risk, and having intimate contact with an HIV infected individual indicates great risk. Hence, knowledge of infection and fundamental medical and public health tenets point directly to optimal educational and policy development messages.

We must remember that diagnosis can be done in medical settings without violating privacy rights. The Denver Public Health Department has routinely tested for HIV (with a provision to opt out if one chooses) in its public health clinics for over fifteen years without a single breach in confidentiality; the CDC has collected data on over a half-a-million people with AIDS and HIV since the inception of the epidemic, all reported by name to state public health departments without a single breach in confidentiality. We do not have to test everyone (which AIDS activists refer to as mandatory testing), but we do need to target testing as we have with blood donors and make it a routine practice in a diversity of medical settings.

Finally, sound policy will dictate the critical allocation of financial and human resources. This can be done only, however, if the medical and scientific communities offer the needed leadership both in articulating fundamental tenets of medicine and public health and identifying individuals to carry these messages to all affected. Without this leadership the knowledge gained to date and the need to implement it will not occur quickly enough to prevent an even greater tragedy.

III

The Culture War

9

Homosexuality and the
Entertainment Media

Michael Medved

N O ONE CAN FORGET one of the truly remarkable events in the panorama of western civilization: Ellen DeGeneres declaring her lesbian orientation before a huge television audience on her weekly sitcom produced by the Disney company on ABC-TV. Now, Ellen's coming out was, in the view of most mainstream observers, perhaps the greatest advance for humankind since the discovery of the wheel. The amount of attention and the volume of the hosannas that greeted this event were astonishing. It was on the cover of news magazines, and there were news specials on television—it was surely the best publicized show ever on television.

Now was this in truth a magnificent advance for civilization, for decency, and for fairness, or was it, as some other Americans believe, a confirmation of the anti-family and anti-marriage agenda of the entertainment industry? And does that alleged antifamily agenda relate in any way to the very strong representation of homosexual individuals in positions of creative influence in that industry?

That question was, of course, very much on the minds of the twelve thousand delegates to the 1997 Southern Baptist Convention annual meeting in Dallas who voted overwhelmingly for a boycott of

153

all things Disney. I will address whether that was good strategy, but for the moment we can ask how many Southern Baptists would honor a boycott, for instance, of ABC-TV, which is owned by the Disney company, if ABC were covering the Super Bowl one year?

In any event, the boycott that was announced by America's largest Protestant denomination (there are 15.7 million members of the Southern Baptist Convention) was a very serious challenge to the entertainment industry and was directly related to the treatment of homosexuality in the mass media. The people at the convention spoke very specifically of the "Ellen declaration," Ellen's emergence from the closet, as being the final straw that provoked the boycott. They were also objecting to the family benefits policy towards homosexual partners that the Disney company had instituted.

I am going to ask three fundamental questions concerning the mass media—particularly movies and television—and the media treatment of homosexuals and homosexuality.

First, is the over-representation of homosexuals in positions of influence in the media either primarily or prominently responsible for negative messages concerning the family that many observers perceive? Second, is monetary gain the prime motivation for mass media treatment of homosexuality? Is that motivation simply the profit motive—which, of course, usually explains and is used to explain almost everything in Hollywood. Third, is there a consistent set of messages regarding homosexuality being sent in television series and motion pictures and in other mass media, and are those messages being accepted and having an influence on the larger American public? Let me take each of those questions in turn.

The Influence of Gays in the Entertainment Industry

Let's turn to the first question, whether there is some sort of association between the very prominent role of gay people in the entertainment industry and the very derisive attitude towards the family and towards marriage that many people perceive throughout the world of television and the movies. A reader familiar with the mainstream press might assume that he would know my answer to the question because of a fascinating book by Michelangelo Signorile, a columnist for *Outweek* and author of a recent book entitled *Outing Yourself*.[1] An earlier book of his in which I am discussed at some length is called *Queer in America*.[2] I was delighted when my friend David Horowitz called to my attention that the final chapter in *Queer in America* is called "Queer in Hollywood, from McCarthy to Medved." Now, truly, during the era of the blacklist there *were* some lives ruined in Hollywood, and people suffered—it was a huge upheaval. Still, I am enormously "flattered" in this dubious context to be considered influential enough to be compared to Senator McCarthy.

In his imputing to me some of these powers of darkness and destruction, Signorile writes the following: "For Medved to side with the Christian right without qualifying their criticisms is not only disingenuous, it is dangerous. But more disturbing than Medved's failure to distinguish these nuances is his warped belief that gays in the industry actually create what he perceived to be Hollywood's negative and 'permissive' atmosphere. According to Medved, Hollywood's obsession with violent and deviant behavior must be the work of 'Hollywood's powerful homosexual community.'"

Now, when I read this, I was a little nonplussed, because in my book *Hollywood Versus America*,[3] which he misquotes, I have a chapter entitled "The Myth of a Gay Conspiracy." In that chapter I write: "The willingness of the networks to accept major losses on gay-themed programming raises the sensitive but unavoidable issue of the impact of Hollywood's powerful homosexual community." "Some of the popular culture's most outspoken critics," I continue, "contend that the over-representation of homosexuals in every corner of the creative community leads directly to the entertainment industry's anti-family bias and its obsession with violent and deviant behavior." Then *in the sentences immediately following* I write:

These charges offer a one-dimensional and misleading explanation of a complex phenomenon and should be rejected by all fair-
minded people. Those who look for evidence of some huge gay
conspiracy at the heart of Hollywood will be frustrated in that
search for the simple reason that no such conspiracy exists. Some
militant gay rights organizations may indeed pursue a radical
agenda in their efforts to influence the messages of the popular
culture. But homosexual performers and film-makers are far from
unanimous in advancing that agenda in their work. The gay men
and lesbian women who play prominent roles in the entertainment industry are as diverse and dissimilar as their straight colleagues. They are involved on every side of every significant issue
that currently divides the popular culture.[4]

That is my position. Anyone who assumes that one's position in the
entertainment industry is determined by the all-powerful influence of
your sexual orientation is someone who ignores history and ignores
the present. That simply is not the case.

In recent biographies of Danny Kaye it has become fairly clear that
the great entertainer actor, singer, and comedian was bisexual. He had
certain involvements and died of AIDS, apparently from a blood transfusion. The fact that Danny Kaye was bisexual in no way detracts from
my eagerness for my children to enjoy his wonderful movies, which
remain truly classic family entertainment. Similarly, Howard Ashman,
who also died of AIDS and who was an uncloseted homosexual, was
one of the guiding creative forces behind what I consider to be one of
the finest children's movies of recent years, *Beauty and the Beast*. He
wrote the lyrics for, and was one of the producers of, the film.

The truth is—and we have to confront it—that it is unjust to
blame Hollywood's disgusting work on gay people. Overwhelmingly,
the people who do that disgusting work are rampagingly heterosexual—and they are out of the closet. Oliver Stone has been accused
of many things, but no one has ever accused him of being gay, and he
most assuredly is not. Paul Verhoeven—the creator of such ornaments

to our civilization as *Basic Instinct*—which I reviewed under the title "Basically It Stinks"—is most assuredly heterosexual and feels called upon to prove his orientation frequently. The notion that somehow it is the presence of gay people in the industry that is the cause of all this dismal work is simply ignorant and, moreover, dangerous. The problem in Hollywood is not the gay presence. Hollywood's treatment of homosexuality is not governed by the sexual orientation of those inside the industry but by social pressure from people largely *outside* the industry.

Some of that pressure was brought to bear on me in April 1992, when I was covering the Academy Awards. That year the ceremony was saturated with the ubiquitous red AIDS ribbon, which everyone was compelled to wear. When I say "compelled to wear" I am not exaggerating. I was out in front of the music center where the Academy Awards were held and was about to go on the air to broadcast the arrival of the various stars, when one of the producers came up to me and said "all right, you're about to go on air." They touched up the makeup, and he said, "Oh, here is your AIDS ribbon," and they put the AIDS ribbon on my lapel. I immediately took the AIDS ribbon off and said, "No, it's not my AIDS ribbon, it's *your* AIDS ribbon." The producer responded, "No, you're going on our air, you're representing our network, you will wear the AIDS ribbon." I replied, "I will not wear the AIDS ribbon," to which he responded, "Are you a bigot, are you a hater, do you want all gay people to die"? I said, "I emphatically do not. However, my grandmother recently passed away of Alzheimer's disease and I am extremely conscious of the fact that there are many more victims of Alzheimer's. If there were a ribbon I could wear for Alzheimer's I would wear that, but I resist the idea of being forced to wear this one." Then he said, "You will be the only person within a square mile of this spot who is not wearing an AIDS ribbon tonight and we will not have it." I said, "I am willing to take that risk." I was thrilled later that night when one other person appeared without an AIDS ribbon, Clint Eastwood. In any event I then heard a hysterical

lecture along the lines of "Well, you'll never work in this town again."
And that in fact was the last year I covered the Oscars live—but I did
go on the air, despite threats and imprecations, without my AIDS ribbon.

At that same ceremony, there were a great many and very angry
gay demonstrators. Why were they protesting the Oscars? Because
1992 was the year *Silence of the Lambs* won several awards, and in *Silence of the Lambs* the mass-murderer—the one who skins his victims
(not the one who eats his victims)—is a rather effeminate character
who is by implication gay. The activists were protesting what they
saw as the movie's homophobia. One of their targets was Jonathan
Demme, who won best director that year for directing *Silence of the
Lambs*. The protestors had signs and chanted slogans condemning
Jonathan Demme for his insensitivity, for his hatred of gay people. The
result of all that condemnation was a movie called *Philadelphia*, which
completely restored Jonathan Demme to the good graces of the gay
community.

Now why did Demme make *Philadelphia*? Did he believe that the
truly minuscule gay community in this country could end his career?
No—he had just won the Academy Award. But he became convinced
that it was necessary to make a sincere gesture of contrition, a sincere
demonstration that he was not a bigot, because no one in Hollywood
wants to be accused of homophobic bigotry. A complex combination
of expectation and criticism and demonstrations, not sexual orientation, led a heterosexual filmmaker, with the support of heterosexual
studio executives, to make *Philadelphia* to advance fundamental claims
and purposes of the gay rights movement.

A Response to the Market?

That brings us to the second question I want to ask. Can you explain
the current plethora of gay material in the media as simply a response
to the market? *Philadelphia* is a good place to begin, because *Phila-*

delphia was deemed a very difficult project to sell, but the film became a substantial box office hit. I believe part of the reason it became such a hit was that there were many Americans who felt that going to *Philadelphia* was some sort of good deed, as if by going to see the movie and paying your money to see it, you would help to deal with this AIDS crisis, which we all feel as a painful and lamentable situation in the United States.

But *Philadelphia* has not been alone. Many recent films on gay themes have been substantial box office hits. You can explain the success of *Philadelphia* because it was a good movie. There is an absolutely wretched movie called *To Wong Foo, Thanks for Everything Julie Newmar*, which is really one of the worst films I have seen in recent years—and that covers a lot of territory. It is a film about a bunch of transvestites (played by John Leguizamo, Wesley Snipes, and Patrick Swayze) who get stranded in a homophobic small town in Kansas and then later convert the small town to the charms of platform shoes and Judy Garland. The film is dreadful, and it became a huge box office hit. Even more strikingly, a film called *The Birdcage*, starring Robin Williams, based upon the old French film and musical *La Cage Aux Folles*, became a very major box office hit.

People in Hollywood can argue that what they are doing is not in any way catering to a specific group or a certain agenda but simply responding intelligently, as the market system says they should. There is a market for this material, they say, so they distribute it. But consider that the films I have mentioned are rare exceptions among the gay-themed material which has been released, most of which is emphatically rejected by the public, and in which the public seems to have absolutely no interest at all.

For instance, there are other films like, *Love, Valor, Compassion*, a film I reviewed, which is about eight gay males who meet over three summer weekends and disport themselves in a sylvan lake, comparing lesions and talking in witty but rather depressing terms of their problems and difficulties and their AIDS medication regimens. The film, an adaptation of a Tony Award-winning play, received superb reviews everywhere except in the *New York Post*, where I reviewed it. I found it a dreary, pretentious, almost unwatchable piece of work. When the film opened, people had to be subpoenaed to see it. It had no discernible box office impact.

That same was true of the motion picture *Priest*. It was a film about a right-wing Catholic priest in Great Britain who leads a double life, secretly dressing in black leather and going to gay bars on Friday nights and picking up young boys—and it has some very graphic sex scenes in it. The film was released with much fanfare because it is a profoundly anti-Catholic film, not just because of the portrayal of the one gay priest, but because of the entire portrayal of the Church and its teachings. I spoke to theater owners under contract to show the film, and there were showings in different parts of the country where literally the only person watching *Priest* would be the projectionist, who had a union contract and had to unspool this film even though nobody was there. The film was not a huge box office hit.

Nor was *It's My Party,* a film starring Eric Roberts about a farewell party for an AIDS patient. Nor was *Jeffrey,* which features a whole subplot about a homosexual priest who tries to molest a handsome young gay male in the confessional. *Jeffrey* was released with much fanfare and, again, very positive reviews. Have you ever heard of this film? There was *Go Fish*, a grainy film in black and white.

In *My Best Friend's Wedding* there is a homosexual character who plays the boss and close friend of Julia Roberts. One reviewer described the person who played this character, Rupert Everett, as terrific—listen to this—as the "voice of sweet homosexual reason in the midst of this heterosexual hubbub." That sort of part, the voice of sweet homosexual reason, the nice-guy neighbor in the flat next door, has appeared in countless movies and it appears in countless television shows. I checked with the Gay and Lesbian Alliance Against Defamation, which keeps what they call a scoreboard of gay characters in television. Prior to Ellen's emergence from the closest, in April 1997, their scoreboard reflected that there were twenty-nine identified gay characters on network television, twenty-two of them on prime-time, virtually all supporting characters. They are not there for financial reasons or for ratings, I can assure you. If Rupert Everett's character had not been a gay male, *My Best Friend's Wedding* would not have done a dime less business at the box office. No one is tuning in to *Roseanne* or to *Friends* in order to see the supporting gay character or the occasional appearance of a gay character. After all, there is absolutely no evidence, there is no marketing study, there is certainly no statistical analysis of America that suggests that this kind of characterization is necessary to appeal to a large audience.

Consider how many religious characters are on television—Catholic, Protestant or Jewish. There have been a few shows in recent years about clergy—such as Dan Aykroyd's *Soul Man*, in which he plays a comical clergyman—but still, are there anywhere near twenty-nine *religious* supporting characters? Of course not. Now does anyone believe this is a representation of reality? Does anyone believe there are more gay people in America than religious people? This is a profoundly religious country where, in every survey done, fifty percent of us go to church or synagogue at least once a month. Over 40 percent of us go once a week. That is *never* reflected on television.

Any one who argues that the inclusion of homosexual characters in movies and television is a reflection of reality or the box office is simply not paying attention. Because, frankly, if you want to make money—if that is your prime motivation—there are easier ways to make money than by handling gay themes, which are not popular with advertisers. Even with *Ellen,* before the "coming out" episode, the show lost hundreds of thousands of dollars in advertising from Chrysler, J.C. Penney, Wrigley, and other corporations that normally sponsored her show but did not want to be associated with that episode. One network even announced that when *thirtysomething* had one scene where they briefly showed two gay males expressing affection to one another one night in bed they lost *more than a million dollars* in advertising revenue on that show. This is not a safe and easy way to make money. The idea that gay characterization and the gay themes in American media is only a response to box office demands is wrong.

Why Gay Portrayals in the Media?

And that brings me to the final question. If it is not the gay orientation of people in Hollywood, and if it is not simply a desire to make money, why do we all of a sudden have this tremendous upsurge in gay themes and gay characterization—nearly all quite positive? Are there, in fact, some messages and values that are being consistently communicated by mass media in this country, and is that communication proving effective with the public at large?

Now, in answering this question I am going to do something which very few straight people do: I am going to take the gay press seriously. For a variety of reasons, most straight people do not read the gay press. Nevertheless, in the same way you have absolutely no idea of what the Palestinian Liberation Organization really is about if you only read its statements in English language press (that is, if you never read its statements in Arabic newspapers), you have absolutely no idea about the agenda of the radical elements in the gay community if you only read statements given out to the straight press. The PLO talks only about peace, brotherhood, understanding, and acceptance when they speak to English language press, the *New York Times* or the *Washington Post*, but then in Arabic papers talks about blood and horror and pushing people into the sea. Likewise, if you simply read the straight press and hear from the gay organizations there, all you hear about is acceptance and tolerance and love and kindness and brotherhood and human rights. There is a very different agenda that emerges if you look at some of the material in gay publications. For instance, going back a good deal, in January of 1983 Dennis Altman wrote in *NY*

Native, a New York homosexual newspaper, "We are essentially a radical movement and in as far as we are successful we do indeed break down the hegemony of certain traditional values about sex and relationships. Often this perception is argued in terms of the need to defend our own minorities, whether they be man-boy lovers, transvestites, or sadomasochists—a point with which I would agree."

Most significant to me is an absolutely remarkable article that appeared in another gay publication, a magazine called *Christopher Street*. It also appeared many years ago, and the reason I am bringing it up now, even though the article appeared in December of 1984, is that it reflects exactly what has happened in the American media. It is a step-by-step approach that has been realized with admirable precision. The article is called, "Waging Peace: A Gay Battle Plan to Persuade Straight America." The authors are two officials of the National Gay Task Force, Marshall K. Kirk and Erastes Pill. In one section of the article they list six principles for the persuasion of straights. We can actually break this down into three primary focuses: one, to desensitize and normalize; two, to emphasize gay victim status; and three, to demonize defenders of the family:

> As already stated, we think the first order of business is the desensitization of the American public concerning gays and gay rights. To desensitize the public is to help it view homosexuality with indifference instead of with keen emotion. Almost any behavior begins to look normal if you are exposed to enough of it. The way to benumb raw sensitivities about homosexuality, is to have a lot of people talk a great deal about the subject in a neutral or supportive way. Constant talk builds the impression that public opinion is at least divided on the subject and that a sizeable segment accepts or even practices homosexuality. Even rancorous debates between opponents and defenders serve the purpose of desensitization so long as "respectable" gays are front and center to make their own pitch. The main thing is to talk about gayness until the issue becomes thoroughly tiresome.

I would say "mission accomplished." They continue, with remarkable prescience and accuracy:

> Where we talk is important. The visual media, film and television, are plainly the most powerful image-makers in Western civilization. The average American household watches over seven hours of television daily. Those hours open up a gateway into the private world of straights, through which a Trojan horse might be passed. As far as desensitization is concerned, the medium is the message of normalcy. So far, gay Hollywood has provided our best covert weapon in the battle to desensitize the mainstream. Bit by bit, over the past ten years, gay characters and gay themes have been introduced into TV programs and films. On the whole the movement has been encouraging.

Here they begin to talk about the opposition: "We can undermine the moral authority of homophobic churches by portraying them as antiquated backwaters badly out of step with times and with the latest findings of psychology. Against the mighty pull of institutional religion one must set the mightier draw of science and public opinion. Such an unholy alliance has worked well against churches before on such topics as divorce and abortion. With enough open talk about the prevalence and the acceptability of homosexuality, that alliance can again work here."

This brings us to point two: "Portray gays as victims, not as aggressive challengers. In any campaign to win over the public, the gays must be cast as victims in need of protection, so that straights will be inclined by reflex to assume the role of protector. If gays are portrayed instead as a strong prideful tribe promoting a rigidly nonconformist and deviant lifestyle, they are more likely to be seen as a public menace that justifies resistance and oppression. For that reason, we must forgo our temptation to strut our gay pride publicly whenever it conflicts with the gay victim image." They continue: "An additional theme of the campaign should be more aggressive and upbeat, to offset the increasing bad press that these times have brought to homosexual men and women. The campaign should paint gays as superior pillars of society."

And then they come to the final point:

> At a latter stage of the media campaign for gay rights it will be time to get tough with remaining opponents. To be blunt, they must be vilified. ["Hollywood from McCarthy to Medved"] Our goal here is twofold. First, we seek to replace the mainstream pride about its homophobia with shame and guilt. Second, the public must be shown images of ranting homophobes whose secondary traits and beliefs disgust middle America. These images might include: the Klu Klux Klan demanding that gays be burnt alive or castrated; bigoted southern ministers drooling with hysterical hatred to a degree that looks both comical and deranged; menacing punks, thugs, and convicts speaking cooly about the "fags" they have killed or would like to kill; a tour of Nazi camps where homosexuals were tortured and gassed. We have already indicated some of the images which might be damaging to the homophobic vendetta. These images should be combined with those of their gay victims by a method propagandists call "the bracket technique." For example, for a few seconds an unctuous, beady-eyed southern preacher is seen pounding the pulpit in rage about these sick abominable creatures, and, while his tirade continues over the sound track, the picture switches to pathetic photos of badly beaten persons or to photos of gays who look decent, harmless, or likeable. Then we cut back to the poisonous face of the preacher, and so forth. The contrast speaks for itself. The effect is devastating.

I submit that the effect *has* been devastating. Hearing the agenda outlined so brilliantly in this article, can anyone doubt that part of the problem, in what some people have called the culture war, is that one side is prepared and organized and determined, and the other side is just gradually beginning to wake up?

Responding to Entertainment Media Trends

In this context, I happen to believe that the decision by the Southern Baptist Convention to boycott Disney was a profound mistake, and an unforgivable mistake, frankly, because the Baptists are not boycotting certain objectionable material, but everything Disney. It should have been obvious how this would be portrayed by the very sophisticated people who favor gay rights. The Baptists have been portrayed as drooling, intolerant southern preachers of hate who are against Mickey Mouse, against *Beauty and the Beast*, against *Hercules*. Disney owns ESPN—are people going to give up games on ESPN? Disney owns the major part of A&E—are people going to stop watching *Biography*? Are people going to give up watching "Good Morning America" on ABC? As Talleyrand said about Napoleon's assassination of the Duc D'Enghien in 1804, "It is worse than a crime, it is a blunder!" Such a boycott cannot work and will achieve nothing except to make opponents of gay rights look silly. It is a mistake that encourages the idea that we in the pro-family community are fanatics. Instead, we should call on all people of conscience to boycott, for instance, all R-rated movies or, what would be most effective, to watch less television and to see fewer movies in general.

The average American spends thirteen uninterrupted years of life watching television. Twenty-four-hour days, seven-day weeks, fifty-two-week years. It is too much.[5] *That* is the problem, and it is the wrong response to pick on Disney, which is disgusting and despicable, but is no more disgusting and despicable than Twentieth Century Fox, or Paramount, or Warner Brothers, or Sony. At least the Disney Company produces *some* family entertainment. What is the last wonderful family film you have seen from Fox? The boycotters are sending a message that somehow watching an R-rated Fox bloodbath is acceptable, but watching a G-rated Disney delight is not. We are asking people to consider a movie's label—whether it is a Disney film or not—rather than its substance. It is the wrong strategy at emphatically the wrong time.

What we need is to respond with the same kind of coordinated and self-conscious approach that people in the gay rights movement have used. They have emphasized desensitization and normalization, victimization of gay people, and the demonization of their opponents. What we must do is to renormalize family life. The important message here, and it is crucially important, is one that Bill Bennett has talked about: we will get nowhere if this conflict is framed as people who are promoting homosexuality versus people who are opposed to homosexuality, because then it is very difficult for those who oppose gay rights to make the case that we are anything other than hostile. We must not define ourselves as antigay, but as pro-marriage—an essential distinction. Homosexuality is a threat to the family, to marriage, to the unique sanctity of one male and one female bound together in monogamous, eternal, and sanctified heterosexual union. That is an important standard to maintain.

But let us be clear, the main threats to the family in America do not come from the gay community. They come from infidelity, they come from divorce, they come from all of the temptations that heterosexuals fear and feel in a hedonistic culture. Our response should not be targeted specifically at homosexuals or homosexual issues. It should be targeted on the need to uplift and sanctify and defend the family and the institution of marriage.

In the second area—victimization—we have to show the victimization of the institution of the family. We have to show the way parents who are trying to defend the innocence of their children are being assaulted everywhere, not only in the media but in the schools, by an increasingly hostile government, by advocacy groups who will tolerate every sort of freedom of speech except the freedom of speech which says that the institution of heterosexual monogamous marriage is uniquely valuable and uniquely important, and uniquely worth fighting for. We have to show how the family has been victimized, how it has been a victim of intolerance.[6] We should answer this approach of emphasizing gay victims by showing these ordinary Americans—and there are literally millions of them—who have been victimized and harmed and reviled for their attempts to defend their own children and their own families and the institution of marriage.

The third area in their strategy, demonization, is one we should leave alone. We do not need to demonize any one. Our approach should include love, not demonization; compassion and accentuating the positive, not assaulting the people with whom we disagree. That is a temptation that people of conscience and people of faith in particular must resist.

Can we win this argument? We can, but more than that, we must. For the sake of our faith, for the sake of our families, for the sake of our civilization. Most of all, for the sake of our children and their grandchildren and their future.

IO

Opposing Homosexual Advocacy

Robert H. Knight

AMERICA IS IN THE MIDST of an enormous cultural struggle over homosexuality. This is evident every time you pick up the newspaper or turn on the television. On one day, Ellen comes out as a lesbian; on another day, the Southern Baptists announce a boycott of the Walt Disney Company.

Through highly publicized lawsuits, left-wing groups like the ACLU play a key role in promoting homosexuality to the American public. The ACLU has harassed the Boy Scouts and defended smut peddlers and Internet pornography—even when it is accessible to children in public libraries. Recently, they announced that they had filed a suit defending "campaign lies" as a form of free speech.

Their agenda seems obvious enough. The ACLU's ultimate goal, as Joseph Sobran has noted, is to make all manner of perversion, from pornography to sexual dysfunction, public, while making religion private. C. S. Lewis pointed out that the goal of liberals in general is to make religion entirely private, while shrinking the private sphere and enlarging the public sphere. This leaves little room for disagreement with certain premises, such as that homosexuality is normal, wholesome, and deserving of public support.

As "gay rights" laws advance, the freedom to disagree with homo-sexual activism recedes. The cultural struggle we face is no longer about whether Judeo-Christian morality will prevail as the dominant value system. It is now about whether biblical Judaism and Christianity will be permitted at all.

The Boy Scouts have spent millions of dollars to defend themselves from lawsuits by homosexuals, atheists, and feminists, all of whom seem curiously reluctant to start their own youth organizations. Perhaps they realize that any group with their value systems would have difficulty filling those pup tents with recruits. So they try, instead, to subvert an institution that succeeds largely because of the very traditions that the activists wish to destroy.

The press, our window on the world, is almost uniformly on the side of sexual excess. Whenever traditions are under attack, they say silly things like "activists seek to create new tradition," or "gay couples seek to redefine tradition." But they really want to smash tradition.

Homosexual activists have commandeered virtually all mainstream media, including television, print and the entertainment industry. They also have a commanding presence in academia and an increasing role in corporations. Only one side of this contentious issue is being aired. As a result, a number of outright lies and distortions have become commonly held public opinions:

- that homosexuals are "born that way" and cannot change;
- that "gay teens" commit a third of all teen suicides, mostly due to homophobia;
- that church doctrine concerning homosexuality is mixed; the Bible itself is said to be unclear;
- that homosexuals are disproportionately victims of "hate crimes";
- that opposition groups hate homosexuals and are therefore bigots;
- that homosexual behavior is not very different from that of heterosexuals.

These claims fall apart upon examination, but they take on lives of their own through their amplification in the media. Dissenting views are routinely suppressed.

Some had hoped that the gay rights movement, which began making headway in the 1970s, was just a fad. We know now that it is much more serious than that. The homosexual rights movement is the spear point in the cultural war to destroy traditional religion. Its goal requires nothing less than the public marginalization of Christianity and, in some cases, the criminalization of conduct based on Christian principles.

In the U.S. Supreme Court case *Romer v. Evans*, which struck down Colorado's Amendment Two, Justice Anthony Kennedy himself discarded 3,500 years of moral law by equating opposition to homosexuality with mere bigotry ("animus," he called it).[1] If the law is changed to reflect his view, then much power can be brought to bear against those who cling to the idea of natural sexual morality. It is already happening, as more and more Christians are denied tenure at universities or admission to medical and law schools because of their "outmoded" attitudes toward life and morality. Employees in corporations and in government are being subjected to diversity training that directly challenges their most deeply held religious beliefs.

Over the last few years, homosexual activists have achieved stunning victories:

- forcing a national debate on the meaning of marriage;
- overturning the sodomy laws, usually through liberal court decisions, in more than half the states;
- reconfiguring the psychoanalytic profession's understanding of human sexuality;
- securing gay rights laws in eleven states and more than one hundred cities and counties;
- introducing millions of schoolchildren to homosexuality through sex and AIDS education;
- capturing many unions and professional associations, includ-

ing the two-million member National Education Association;
- holding highly publicized celebrations, such as the Gay Olympics, Gay Days at Disneyland and Disney World, and Gay Pride festivals in major cities;
- undermining military morale by promoting homosexuality in the armed forces and an abandonment of sexual restraint.

People often ask, how could a tiny group of people—most of whom are not activists—wield so much power? The short answer is that the activists are single-minded in purpose, well organized, well funded, and have the support of all major values-transmitting institutions. Moreover, they have been at this for several decades, while most Americans were worrying about other things, like the Cold War, global warming, and getting to the little league game on time.

Homosexual activists drafted a platform of demands in 1972 and updated them for the 1993 "March on Washington." They have achieved in part, if not entirely, many of their goals. Nevertheless, they have yet to lower the age of consent, establish "same-sex marriage" (they demanded multiple-partner marriage in 1972), pass a federal civil rights law, force the legalization of prostitution, secure access to the Boy Scouts, among other goals. But they have achieved much in a short time.

Today it is clear that the battle has reached beyond the faculty lounge and literary set and is now exploding in nearly every walk of life. To illustrate how the fight is shaping up, let me use a boxing match scenario: in this corner, weighing in at less than 2 percent of the population, and followed by an entourage of Oprah Winfrey, Garth Brooks, Laura Dern, Michael Eisner, Barry Diller, David Geffen and other Hollywood personalities, along with Abigail Van Buren, Ann Landers and most of the working press, and the president of the United States, is the Gay Rights Movement. Collectively, the movement is constituted of:

- the ACLU and its Gay and Lesbian Rights Project;
- the National Gay and Lesbian Task Force;
- the Lambda Legal Defense and Education Fund;
- the National Education Association and other education groups;
- People for the American Way;
- the Gay, Lesbian and Straight Teachers Association;
- the American Psychological Association and the American Psychiatric Association;
- Hollywood Supports;
- the Gay and Lesbian Alliance Against Defamation;
- the National Gay and Lesbian Journalists Association;
- liberal church denominations such as the United Church of Christ and much of the Episcopal Church;
- Act-Up, Queer Nation, the Lesbian Avengers, and other shock-tactic groups;
- hundreds of AIDS services organizations that double as cheerleaders for homosexuality, including the Whitman-Walker Clinic in Washington, D.C., which offers lesbian parenting workshops and helped sponsor this year's D.C. gay pride festival;
- major corporations such as AT&T, Walt Disney Company, Subaru, American Express, Kodak, Apple Computer, Ben & Jerry's, Miller Beer, Budweiser, Coors, Pacific Bell, U.S. West, Bank of America, Wells Fargo, Levi-Strauss and others;
- corporate diversity trainers such as Brian McNaught, who made a video, *On Being Gay*, that has been shown to many Fortune 500 employees;
- almost the entire entertainment industry;
- liberal judges;
- most women's magazines;
- MTV;

- last but by no means least, the working press, which transmits a litany of distortion about this issue daily to hundreds of millions of people.

In the other corner, weighing in at 98 percent of the population, is the traditional values opposition—the Traditionalists. The trads, as Maggie Gallagher calls them, seem indomitable on paper, but upon closer look they more resemble the Pillsbury Doughboy. They have numbers but are taking a lot of shots. Luckily, that flab protects them in a way. The sheer inertia of the mushy middle slows down the process, but it also inhibits an effective resistance. The traditionalist forces are:

- Catholic doctrine, when not mangled by liberal bishops;
- Family Research Council;
- Focus on the Family;
- American Family Association;
- Concerned Women for America;
- the Christian Life Commission of the Southern Baptist Convention;
- Coral Ridge Ministries;
- Traditional Values Coalition;
- Eagle Forum;
- Colorado for Family Values;
- the grassroots folks at Christian Coalition;
- Accuracy in Media;
- Accuracy in Academia;
- Americans for Truth About Homosexuality;
- *Lambda Report*;
- Media Research Center;
- Stop Promoting Homosexuality America;
- various state-based organizations;
- the National Coalition to Protect Marriage;
- Free Congress Foundation;

- conservative and Christian talk radio;
- a handful of brave academics and psychoanalysts;
- a handful of brave Christian pastors;
- a handful of Orthodox Jews;
- God's Word.

Given the power of this last element, one would think this fight would end in the first round. In fact, if you look at the span of human history, the trads may eventually prevail. Sodom is not exactly known, as we Americans like to say, as a big winner. Rome and Greece also met their demise amid decadence.

But right now, the gay rights movement is making impressive gains because traditionalists have not mobilized their forces, fashioned a plan, or constructed a simple, effective message. Homosexual activists, on the other hand, have pounded out a compelling three-part message: we are born this way; we cannot change; therefore, we deserve civil rights status. In *After the Ball: How America Will Conquer Its Fear and Hatred of Gays in the 90s*,[2] Hunter Madsen and Marshall Kirk counsel homosexual activists to:

- talk about the issue incessantly so Americans become jaded;
- focus on abstractions, such as civil rights;
- keep attention off behavior; hide the more unsavory aspects at all cost;
- demonize opponents through linkage to hate groups and words such as "bigot" and "hatred";
- marginalize the church by creating dissent within it;
- steadily employ a series of laws to reduce the ability of traditionalists to fight back;
- paint homosexuals as victims—the "born that way" message works best.

A compliant media have repeated this message, publicizing politically-charged genetic studies while suppressing almost any dissent from scientists.³ Using this cover, activists have appropriated the moral capital and the rhetoric from the black civil rights movement and seek to elevate homosexual behavior to minority status.

Corporations are buying into homosexual activism at a rapid rate. Many include "sexual orientation" as a minority category in workplace protection rules. Some, including IBM, Kodak, Bank of America, Intel, and Disney, have even elevated homosexuality to virtual marital status by offering domestic partner benefits. Major corporations advertise in homosexual publications. Miller beer, Budweiser, and Coors routinely run ads in *Out*, *The Advocate*, *The Washington Blade* and other publications. One Miller beer ad even carries the rainbow flag, the symbol of the gay rights movement, and proclaims "pride" in homosexuality. A Budweiser ad in *The Advocate* shows a bottle being pulled from a six-pack, with the slogan: "Another one coming out."⁴ Left unspoken is the rest of the phrase "of the closet," which means revealing one's homosexuality. At the bottom of the page, Bud advises the reader to "Be yourself and make it a Bud Light." This constitutes open endorsement of homosexuality.

Bank of America says it was prodded into providing domestic partner benefits by San Francisco's passage of a law mandating such benefits at all companies that do business with the city. That law, which took effect June 1, 1997, is being challenged by the Air Transport Association, which represents more than twenty airlines; by the American Center for Law and Justice, which is representing an electrical contractor; and by the Alliance Defense Fund, a conservative Christian legal group.

In Hawaii, the state was sued on July 11, 1997, by Bank of Hawaii, Hawaiian Electric Industries, and three other major employers over a law requiring companies to offer "reciprocal partners" benefits that took effect in July 1997 as part of a legislative deal to pass a constitutional amendment protecting one-man, one-woman marriage.

The Walt Disney Company is being boycotted not only by the American Family Association but by the Southern Baptist Convention, which represents sixteen million people, the Assemblies of God, Concerned Women for America—the largest women's group in the nation—and by some Catholic groups. Does everybody know Disney's sins? To mention a few: The 1995 film *Powder* was directed by a convicted child molester, Victor Salva. Disney has produced NC-17-rated *Kids* (1995), the anti-Catholic *Priest* (1995), the pornographic *Color of Night* (1994), the ultra-violent *Pulp Fiction* (1994), and many other objectionable films. Disney tacitly allows "gay day" at its theme parks, facilitates homosexual relationships by offering partner benefits to homosexual employees, places ads in gay publications, and employs rock groups such as Danzig, which feature openly Satanist and anti-Christian themes. Disney has used extremely suggestive imagery in many of its feature films aimed at children. In *Dick Tracy*, *Who Framed Roger Rabbit*, *Little Mermaid*, *Pocahontas*, and *Aladdin*, the kids are treated to double entendres and a good deal of cleavage by frisky females, live or animated. *The Hunchback of Notre Dame* includes an erotic, leering dance in the city square by the film's heroine, the gypsy Esmerelda. Disney-owned Hyperion Press turns out such classics as *Growing Up Gay* and transvestite Ru Paul's autobiography, *Lettin' It All Hang Out*.

American Airlines, which donates to homosexual activist groups such as the Human Rights Campaign and People for the American Way, sponsors all-night gay "circuit" parties such as Cherry Jubilee in Washington, D.C., offers discount fares to homosexuals' partners, and advertises in the gay press. The airline has been targeted by several large pro-family groups, which took out a full-page ad in June 1997 to publicize an open letter to then American chairman Robert Crandall. Sponsored by Family Research Council, Focus on the Family, American Family Association, the Christian Life Commission of the Southern Baptists, Concerned Women for America, and Coral Ridge Ministries, which represent more than twenty million constituents, the ad was turned down by *USA Today*, *Dallas Morning News*, and Disney-owned *Fort Worth Star-Telegram*. It ran instead in *The*

Washington Times and several Dallas-area papers including the *Allen American*, *Lewisville Leader*, *Plano Star-Courier*, *Coppel Gazette*, *McKinney Messenger*, and *Mesquite News*. The effort garnered some radio coverage but did not reach a national audience.

Some more dispatches from the front:

- Political battles loom over the pro-homosexual federal Employment Non-Discrimination Act and state efforts to protect marriage. As of July 1997, twenty-five states had enacted laws barring recognition of same-sex unions as "marriage."
- Family Research Council released *The Other Side of Tolerance*, a thirty-two-page compilation of cases in which people have been harassed, persecuted, or fired for opposing some aspect of the homosexual agenda.
- People for the American Way released a 112-page report, "Hostile Climate: A State by State Report on Anti-Gay Activity." In the foreword, actor Alec Baldwin summarizes the aims of the gay rights movement: "[T]o make anti-gay prejudice and bigotry as appalling to Americans as racism; to make discrimination against gay men, lesbians and bisexuals just as illegal as discrimination against African-Americans and other minorities; and, finally, to make diversity *something we celebrate as a people, not just tolerate*." (italics added)

Looking over the landscape, one sees the fight heating up on all levels. Unless traditionalists and Christians step up their efforts, they will soon find themselves out of jobs, and some will even land in jail. It is that serious. The gay rights movement is the greatest threat today to religious freedom, free speech, and freedom of association. It will be stopped only when the truth emerges about the threat it poses to civil liberties and how "tolerance" has become a one-way street.

The greatest threat to the gay rights movement is the ex-gay movement, with its message of compassion, hope, and healing.[5] These groups directly confront the lie being told by gay activists that homosexuals are so different from the rest of us that they are exempt from natural law or so warped by sin that they are unqualified for salvation and spiritual renewal. Groups like Exodus International, Homosexuals Anonymous, Regeneration, and Parents and Friends of Ex-Gays are providing hope to an estimated six thousand people at any given time. Thousands have left homosexuality behind and entered a life far richer in possibilities for happiness. Their stories, rarely told in the media, need to be heard. Lives—and souls—are at stake. As always, hope lies in the truth, delivered in love.

11

*The Homosexual Movement in
Churches, Schools, and Libraries*

David M. Wagner

I N THIS CHAPTER, I will examine the activities of the homosexual
movement in certain key institutions of our society: churches,
schools, and libraries. In looking at highlights in each of these
areas, I will be speaking of the "homosexual movement," meaning the
organized and energized movement that seeks to attain complete social and legal acceptance of same-sex acts, especially by delegitimizing
and marginalizing traditional sexual ethics and those who hold them.
This movement is not coterminous with homosexual persons as such,
many of whom reject the shrill identity politics practiced by what I
refer to as "the movement." With that caveat, I will look at certain
instances of the movement's influence in these three important areas.

Churches

Homosexual individuals who are Christians, and who experience this
dual identity as a dilemma, can find a wealth of self-confident churches
and denominationally-linked groups that will neutralize the dilemma,
or seem to do so, by offering them a gay-affirmative version of Christianity. There is the nationwide homosexual denomination known as

the Metropolitan Community Churches, founded in 1968 by the Reverend Troy Perry, a Pentecostal.[1]

In addition, nearly every denomination has a homosexual organization claiming to be part of it. One of the best-known is Dignity, which calls itself a gay Catholic organization. It has been repudiated by the leadership of the Catholic Church, but manages to hold meetings and services in Catholic churches in some dioceses. A list at the Queer Resource Directory website includes, besides Dignity, several similar organizations in other churches: AWAB, or Association of Welcoming and Affirming Baptists; Axios, an organization of gay Eastern Orthodox; Integrity, for gay Episcopalians; PLGC, Presbyterians for Lesbian and Gay Concerns. One entire denomination finds its own name on this list: the United Church of Christ. Other organizations on this list with neutral names are the Evangelical Anglican Church in America, the Interfaith Working Group, and the aforementioned Metropolitan Community Church.[2]

For the homosexual movement in the United States, the two religions that have historically played the largest role in American culture, Christianity and Judaism, present a problem. Both the Old and New Testaments contain what the movement calls "clobber texts," meaning texts that condemn homosexual activity in rather clear terms. Furthermore, both the Jewish and Christian traditions affirm the traditional, heterosexual, procreation-oriented, and—if you will—"patriarchal" family as an ethical norm. These "clobber texts," and the traditions of thinking and living that they have fostered, must be discredited. As a columnist in *OutNOW!* put it some time ago, "the chief opposition to gay equality is religious. We may conduct much of our liberation efforts in the political sphere or even the 'cultural' sphere, but always undergirding those and slowing our progress is the moral/religious sphere. If we could hasten the pace of change there, our overall progress would accelerate—in fact, it would be assured."[3]

When movement theologians try to cope with the "clobber texts," they have a rich tradition of scriptural subversion to draw on. The notion that the Bible records merely the time-bound perceptions of its human authors is, of course, very old, though that does not prevent every generation of religion reporters and liberal clergy from thinking that their professors discovered it. Any technique used to find that the Bible does not really frown on adultery, fornication, or greed can be used to find that it does not frown on same-sex activity.

One of the classic methods of this genre is to acknowledge that the Bible contains authoritative lists of prohibitions but then declare that it blesses any activity that it does not specifically prohibit. In this way, the illusion of a benediction for homosexuality can sometimes be achieved by pointing out that no explicit condemnation of it is attributed to Jesus in the Gospels. For example, Barbara Brooten, in her book *Love Between Women: Early Christian Responses to Female Homoeroticism*, writes: "We know of no saying attributed to Jesus, either within the New Testament or within any of the many ancient gospels not included in the canon, in which he comments on sexual love between men or between women. Such love was apparently not a major concern to him. In spite of this, the early church set itself on a path that in the late twentieth century has resulted in opposition to lesbian, gay and bisexual civil rights and ecclesial recognition as a hallmark of most forms of Christianity."[4] Still, for most people, the aforementioned "clobber texts" are just too plain to allow the conclusion that negative judgments on homosexual conduct only crept into Christianity in the twentieth century. Even John Boswell (of whom more in a moment) only wanted to push the origins of such judgments as far as the twelfth.

The "clobber texts" still have to be dealt with, and there are four other claims by which people attempting to be "gay Christians" endeavor to deal with them. First, they claim the Bible reflects only the views of its human authors, who were guided only by their feelings about God, which were not as enlightened as ours. One example of this would be the words of Melanie Morrison, a founder of Christian Lesbians Out Together (CLOUT): "I know in my heart that the canon is not closed—I know this because the Bible does not reconcile me with the earth and the Bible does not reconcile me with my sexual self."[5]

Second is the claim that the Bible is generally reliable, but Leviticus and the Pauline Epistles reflect interpolations by "homophobes." An example of this would be a letter by a liberal rabbi to his homosexual brother, made public on a movement website: "I know what the Torah says about homosexuality in this week's portion: it's called 'abomination punishable by death.' But I don't believe a loving God could have written such a thing. It could only have come from well-meaning but ignorant people who could not see that homosexuality was part of God's diverse plan for humanity."[6] The rabbi is obviously an extremely nice person, but for humanity in general, there is a huge and dangerous pride lurking behind making one's own instinctive, pre-Scriptural notions of goodness the standard against which God will be measured.

Third is the claim that the text of Romans accurately reflects what Paul wrote but we need not accept it as normative. For an example of this, there is the remark of homosexual Episcopalian minister Robert Williams: "So what: Paul was wrong about any number of other things too. Why should you take him any more seriously than you take Jerry Falwell, Anita Bryant, or Cardinal O'Connor?"[7] Adding to this argument, as a reason for rejecting what Paul said about homosexual activity, is the theory that he himself was a repressed homosexual.

These three claims illustrate how the attempt to create a gay-affirmative version of Christianity almost always involves knocking out the support struts on which Christianity rests. If Scripture can be disregarded when it condemns homosexuality, it can be disregarded on any other issue as well. Under this approach, if we continue to believe, say, in the Incarnation, it can only be because we somehow "feel" the Incarnation to be true, just as we "feel" that Paul's words on homosexuality are wrong. The source of the believer's belief becomes the believer himself, or "God" conceived as somehow inside the believer, rather than an independently existing God Who seeks and is sought by the believer. Thus, the gay Christian movement can be seen as part and parcel of liberal religion in general.

There is still another claim, one that preserves the outward form of respect for the authority of Scripture as written: The text of Romans accurately reflects what Paul wrote, and we should follow what Paul wrote, but what he actually meant was something very different from what everyone has thought it was for two thousand years. This is the approach of the late Professor John Boswell, the Yale medievalist who, despite being widely dismissed by his colleagues as an activist-scholar, is treated by the movement as having forever settled, in their favor, the question of what St. Paul meant. Of course, reinterpretation of Scripture to neutralize troublesome texts did not start with Boswell. For instance, the "hospitality theory" of the Sodom and Gomorrah episode in Genesis—the theory that the sin of Sodom was not same-sex lust but a lack of hospitality—was advanced by Anglican theologian Derrick S. Bailey in his 1955 book *Homosexuality and the Western Christian Tradition.*[8]

I should mention here, as a Yale medievalist myself, that I took several courses from Professor Boswell, both as an undergraduate and graduate student. I learned a great deal from him about medieval law and about the close reading of primary texts. Unfortunately, there is such a thing as reading a text so closely that the words start to swim, especially when—as Boswell often did—you are dealing with languages so obscure that you have effectively no peers who can review your work and especially when you have a personal axe to grind, as Boswell did.

He was an engaging lecturer and seminar leader, and he dealt courteously with dissenting views, provided they were reasoned and based on the historical sources. He professed Catholicism with evident sincerity. I once heard him lecture at a forum on Christianity and academia, an event that had no connection to the homosexual movement one way or the other. On that occasion, and also in his introductory medieval history course, he attacked the myth that the people in the Middle Ages were more superstitious than people to-day. Unlike most of those who have contributed to gay theology, he was free from "chronological snobbery"—the idea that currently popular ideas, just because they are recent and modern, are better than old ideas. But of course, this reverence for the past had a twist to it, as he believed that acceptance of homosexuality was an ancient and early medieval idea, not a modern one. As he defined the landscape, he was a reactionary.

The gravamen of Boswell's work is that opposition to homosexual acts is not part of the authentic deposit of Christianity but was the result of theological and political trends that characterized the passage from the "early" to the "high" Middle Ages. Even though he is not the first scholar ever to be able to read the Biblical languages and situate the texts in their historic setting, he trusts you will assume he is the first one without bias. That he had a different bias from most of his predecessors can easily be granted, but not that he had *no* bias.

At the risk of oversimplifying Boswell's work, I summarize it as follows. He argues, largely from linguistic evidence, that every scriptural text that appears by its plain terms to condemn homosexual conduct in fact condemns other types of conduct, such as ritual impurity, rape, or prostitution. Boswell's academic credentials and his undisputed zeal for delving into obscure primary sources have caused many to accept his views simply on his own authority. However, his Yale colleague Ramsay MacMullen, a specialist in Roman history, has criticized the theory that Roman civilization accepted homosexuality[9] and sharply questioned Boswell's reading of certain Roman primary sources.[10] Boswell's credibility as a philologist of ancient languages rests more on the absence of others with such expertise within the community of historians than on validation by those who do have such expertise. His belief that moderns should not snobbishly dismiss the views of past generations did not prevent him from maintaining that the words of Moses and Paul had to await the late twentieth century to be correctly interpreted.

Though Boswell's works have scriptural status in homosexual religious circles, they have their problematic side even from the gay point
of view. For instance, if Boswell is right in holding that the ancient
world did not categorize sexual relations as hetero- or homo- as we
do today, then the fact that Jesus did not condemn homosexual conduct by name ceases to have any probative value. Furthermore, his
project of rehabilitating Paul from the gay point of view runs afoul of
the work of other pro-homosexual scholars who wish to demonize Paul
and find new depths of oppressiveness in his writings.

There is an interesting example of this tension in the March-April
1997 issue of *More Light Update*, a publication of Presbyterians for
Lesbian and Gay Concerns, in the form of a review by the Reverend
Thomas D. Hanks, a Scripture professor and gay activist based in
Buenos Aires, of Barbara Brooten's *Love Between Women*. Brooten
summarizes her conclusion: "I have argued that Paul's condemnation
of homoeroticism, particularly female homoeroticism, reflects and helps
to maintain a gender asymmetry based on female subordination. I
hope that churches today, being apprised of the history that I have
presented, will no longer teach Rom. 1:26ff as authoritative."[11] Hanks,
the reviewer, is of the Boswell school and would rather rehabilitate
Paul as a gay advocate than throw him over. As Hanks explains:

> (1) fundamentalists may rush to use Brooten in their exegetical
> battle to brandish the Bible as a homophobic club full of handy
> clobber texts, but politically she is firmly and militantly on the
> side of full rights for lesbigays;
>   (2) those who suggest alternative interpretations for the tra-
> ditional clobber texts, while seeking to maintain some concept
> of Biblical authority (following John Boswell, William Country-
> man, Daniel Helminiak, Robin Scroggs, etc.), will be happy nei-
> ther with Brooten's exegesis nor her more radical questioning of
> Biblical authority, but will find plenty of exegetical insights and
> ideological ammunition—and be glad for the political alliance;
>   (3) fundamentalists and progressive revisionists may agree

with one another in upholding some concept of Biblical authority, but find themselves radically disagreeing about the interpretation of the relevant texts and on opposite sides of the political
battle and cultural wars.[12]

For Hanks, cultural warfare is primary, and while he wants to give
Brooten the full credit due her for her loyalty to the homosexual cause,
he repeatedly falls back on wishing she agreed with him in reading
Paul along Boswellian lines: "We should add the obvious, that in an
age before safer sex, condoms and precise understanding of the way
venereal diseases are transmitted, Leviticus (and possibly Paul) referred
to UNPROTECTED male anal intercourse. So if Paul follows
Leviticus, any implied prohibition of male homoerotic acts would refer only to unprotected male anal intercourse. Even this may not
qualify as a valid ethical absolute (but neither Paul nor any other Biblical author ever pretends to give us 'ethics' or 'morals' [Greek philosophical categories alien to the Bible])."[13]
So, on Hank's reading, Paul certainly transcended his time. Even
though Hanks promises to revise his "soundbites"—his term—in light
of Brooten's work, he is nonetheless irritated at her for breaking party
line. He summarizes the differences between his views and Brooten's:
"The question remains whether all that Paul writes should be flattened
to simply reflect these limitations, or whether he does not soaringly
transcend these cultural limitations at many points and thus faithfully
extend the radical Jesus tradition deeply into the gentile world."[14]
Hanks and Brooten agree that Jesus proclaimed the sexual revolution;
they disagree only on whether Paul was a mere product of his times
who undermined that revolution or a subtle propagandist for it.
It must be stressed that, while the academics of the homosexual
Christian movement acknowledge the existence of what they call "fun-
damentalists" and will even acknowledge that there are "fundamen-
talist scholars," they are nonetheless quite serene in their conviction
that they are within the fold of Biblical orthodoxy rightly interpreted.

Commenting on how we got to this point, pastor and ex-gay coun-sellor Joe Dallas, in his book *A Strong Delusion*, admonishes his fel-low conservative pastors. In the first rush of reaction to the nascent homosexual movement in the 1970s, some conservative pastors, ill prepared to respond, said things that confirmed the hateful stereotypes about them that appear in gay propaganda. But even more impor-tant, Dallas points out, conservative churches are often either igno-rant or in denial about the presence of people in their own congregations struggling with homosexuality: "When the subject is mentioned from the pulpit, it's usually framed as a problem 'out there in society' (which it is), yet few pastors add, 'Perhaps someone here is wrestling with this sin, as well. Resist it—God will be with you as you do. And so will we.' As one who has known countless women and men who have renounced homosexual practices and who resist, sometimes daily, temptations to return to them, I can attest to the world of difference one remark like that from a pastor can make."[15]

Schools

Looking into the movement in schools, we find that it is building a network of sympathetic teachers and forming clubs in public high schools. These clubs aim primarily at delegitimizing resistance to ho-mosexuality.

The pitch is based on two themes: rejection of hate and safety. The antihate theme seems to be more for students, the safety theme more for parents and teachers. The literature of the high school area of the movement seems to be of two minds about the legitimacy of oppos-ing views. It contains disavowals of any intent to change anyone's views on the morality of same-sex relations. On the other hand, by characterizing all opposition as "homophobia" and as a social disease to be expurgated rather than recognizing moral conservatism as a body of thinking to be argued with, it pretty obviously seeks to close stu-dents' minds to the possibility that there might be reasons for withholding approval from same-sex relations. The homosexual movement in the schools does not feature the approval-or-else approach that we find elsewhere in the movement. Rather, it presents a soft and friendly face, a face of welcome and "inclusion."

The apparent cutting edge of the movement's influence in schools is an organization called the Gay, Lesbian and Straight Teachers Network, or GLSTN, and a wave of high school clubs commonly called Gay/Straight Alliances, or GSAs, which are officially sponsored by the schools at which they take place.

The patronage of former governor William Weld during his term of office permitted the movement to become further entrenched in the public schools in Massachusetts than in most other states. The Bay State has an official Safe Schools Program for Gay and Lesbian Students, which publishes a handbook on establishing GSAs in the schools.[16] This student guide comes with a warm letter of endorsement from the state commissioner of education, and its title page bears the logo of the Massachusetts Department of Education.

The student guide makes a number of assumptions, the most basic of which is that there is such a thing as a "gay youth," as distinct from youths who are confused about sexual matters amid the bizarre welter of conflicting signals that society is sending them at their own time of maximum uncertainty and vulnerability. For the reasons given by noted psychologists, I believe this is a very shaky assumption. Of course, it is nowhere defended in the student guide, for to defend an assumption is to admit that reasonable persons can disagree. In theological debate, as we have seen, the movement cannot altogether avoid this admission, but it is unwilling to let it into its high school materials. It has learned that people selling revolutionary concepts cannot, like their nineteenth century predecessors, do so by orating in Hyde Park or leafleting the factories. When the sale is a hard one to make, you make it by presuming it is already made and that the only problem remaining is installation.

In the student guide, the curtain rises on a set that strains the imagination, especially in liberal Massachusetts. First, there is the aforementioned block of "gay youth." Then we are asked to believe that in the state of New Lights and Route 128, of Thoreau, Holmes, and Weld, the state with 50 percent of the openly gay representatives in the 104th Congress, these "gay youth" face daily peril to their lives or, when their lives can be considered secure, to their ability to learn.

"Safety," therefore, is a key selling concept for GSAs. State Commissioner of Education Robert V. Antonucci in his "Dear Student" cover letter describes the intended audience of the student guide as "students who want to improve your school by making it safer for gay and lesbian students." The student guide describes the program's "vision of inclusion" as "a school that is safe for all students, that uproots all forms of discrimination and oppression."[17] As a response to those who question spending school time and resources on homosexual issues, the student guide, suggests arguing that "since public schools have an obligation to educate all students and provide them with a safe learning environment, making schools safe for gay and lesbian students is part of their role."[18]

The "safety" theme has barely been introduced before we are starting to talk about "uprooting" some baleful foe. Already it sounds very much as if the safety we are talking about is not safety from terminal disease—the safety parents are perhaps most apt to think about first in connection with homosexual issues—but safety from some undefined yet terrifying threat posed by the very existence of the opposition. In a word, it sounds like the safety being envisioned is somewhat selective. It does not sound as though a Massachusetts school with a flourishing GSA will be a very "safe" environment for anyone who comes within the ambit of the term "homophobe." And since that term was coined by ideological cadres for ideological purposes, its ambit can be as wide as those purposes require them to be.[19]

There are several passages in the student guide that disavow any intent to promote homosexuality or to repress dissent concerning it.

For instance, "superintendents and principals have stressed the need to distinguish between 'supporting gay and lesbian students' and 'promoting homosexuality.'"[20] Many of the suggestions offered in the student guide show that, for purposes of GSAs, the emphasis is on outreach, and identity politics is on the shelf. However, there is room to doubt whether this distinction is scrupulously preserved in GSA activities.

Slogans for meeting ads include "You don't have to be straight to go" and "Homophobic? So am I. Come deal with it at the Gay/ Straight Alliance meeting." Two sets of students will not be affected by these slogans: those who have already absorbed the mainstream conservative message that homosexual persons must be respected as persons even though their sexual acts are morally wrong (as are those of many straights), and those who simply enjoy name-calling and put-downs and thus meet not only the gay movement's definition of a bigot but more objective ones as well. But within the universe of students not already sympathetic to the movement, there is probably a substantial set who have only a sense that there is something wrong with same-sex activity but are uncertain as to why. They also have an equally correct sense that bigoted behavior is wrong, and about this they are more certain than about their views on the morality of same-sex activity. Weighing a doubt against a certainty, they attend the meeting and take the first step along a road that will end in approval of same-sex activity and condemnation of opposition to it.

The student guide frequently stresses the strong official support that GSAs enjoy in Massachusetts; this theme is especially noticeable in passages that deal with overcoming official resistance. For instance, when dealing with refractory school officials, student-activists should "offer them a copy of the Governor's Commission on Gay and Lesbian Youth Education Report" and "encourage them to speak with other administrators who work at schools that have formed GSAs."[21] You do not need an advanced degree in management to see what's going on here. The school official is a relatively low person in the education bureaucracy, and the program "representative" and "other administrators" are relatively high ones. This thoughtful offer to inform superiors of a failure to get with the program is probably very effective in inspiring school officials to "overcome" their "homophobia."

Though we have looked at GSAs in Massachusetts, it would be premature to conclude that they will be flourishing in every state in the short run. Utah banned them last year. Interestingly, the rationale used by GSA opponents there was the same used by proponents in Massachusetts: safety. One state representative who supported the anti-GSA bill had a brother who died of AIDS, and he characterized the bill as aimed at preventing the "recruiting" of young people into a "lifestyle that can kill them." Newspaper accounts suggest the issue was rather an emotional one for him.[22]

Libraries

In the brief space I have to deal with libraries, I would identify the contours of homosexuality issues as basically two issue-clusters: availability of either gay-affirmative or gay-critical books, and availability of free gay newspapers.[23] In both cases the issue is not so much availability *tout court* but whether and in what way they should be restricted where children are concerned.

The leader of the movement to implement an age-appropriateness standard in these areas is Fairfax County's Karen Jo Gounaud, whose organization is called "Family-Friendly Libraries." Mrs. Gounaud does not seek to remove gay-affirmative children's books such as *Daddy's Roommate* but rather to place alongside them books such as *Alfie's Home*, said to be a true story about overcoming homosexual temptation. Sensitive to the charge of being a censor, her strategy on books is to add rather than subtract. This puts library officials into a quandary, with a minority that concedes Mrs. Gounaud has made a valid diversity argument, and a majority that relegates gay-critical or hetero-affirmative materials to the category of KKK leaflets.

The issue is different with regard to news racks containing free copies of homosexual-oriented newspapers. Mrs. Gounaud suggests a gay-neutral test for deciding whether such publications should be distributed in public libraries: whether they advocate conduct that violates the jurisdiction's criminal code.[24] The ongoing relevance of sodomy statutes, even if not enforced in flagrante, so to speak, becomes evident here.

When it's a question only of adult access, Mrs. Gounaud becomes as much of an access advocate as anyone in the American Library Association. Her reasoning: "Ignorance doesn't help anyone. Parents with traditional values need to know what's out there, and they're by and large not going to get it by visiting gay bookstores."[25]

Mrs. Gounaud identifies the ALA as her principal organized opponent, because, she says, persons of left-leaning values have come into leadership positions in that organization. This hypothesis seems to be borne out by a glance at a report on the organization's 1996 conference, which included a panel on "Watching the Right: What Librarians Need to Know." At this session, Chip Berlet of Political Research Associates urged attendees not to characterize all "bad people"—his words, apparently—as "extremists," because if they do, then "no one will take responsibility for racism, sexism, homophobia." Berlet characterized the present era as the "longest right-wing backlash in history." The next panel was about local coalition-building, and the eager beaver who was writing up the conference prefaced this section with the words "For those who can't wait for the pendulum to swing left..." There followed a fair amount of thundering about "fundamentalism" and "religious-right politics." There is, therefore, evidence that the ALA is consciously involved in ideologically-charged cultural politics, in addition to its laudable professional programs and services.

Conclusion

At a minimum, one can conclude that the movement is and has been very active in churches, schools, and libraries I have pointed out in the main body of this chapter the ways in which it seems to be that the movement distorts theology and threatens the freedom of the tradition minded in schools and communities. Having said that, I want to finish as I began—with a caveat.

As Joe Dallas points out more than once in *A Strong Delusion*, the conservative churches have occasionally been guilty of genuinely bigoted tirades against homosexuals and of ignoring the spiritual agonies of their own congregants who are subject to homosexual temptation. We may need to remind ourselves from time to time that sexual sin—or *porneia*, I will add in deference to the late Professor Boswell—is universal, to one extent or another, and equally bad in its homo- or hetero- varieties. In my lay understanding of Christian morality, there is no basis for considering a heterosexual adulterer less sinful than a homosexual. Perhaps it could even be said that we do not have any special rules about homosexuality at all. There is just one rule for sexual morality—marriage, as traditionally defined, or continence.[26] Homosexual acts are merely one species of departure from that rule.

Concerning the literature of the Gay-Straight Alliances, it is worth remarking that the vast majority of the injustices that GSA proponents seek to redress could be eliminated if our society could only rediscover *manners*. Calling a classmate a "fag" or a "fairy" is simply rude. I call on those who engage in such conduct to stop or else go live in a zoo; and I challenge those who would use such conduct as leverage for a revolutionary social agenda to come clean about that agenda, and especially about what liberty they envision, if any, for those who cherish a vision of human sexuality different from their own.

IV

RELIGION

12

John Boswell and Historical
Scholarship on Homosexuality

Robert Louis Wilken

JOHN BOSWELL, late professor of history at Yale University (he died of AIDS in December 1994), is the author of two books on homosexual practice in Christian history. The first is a general study of Christian attitudes toward homosexual behavior in the Scriptures, in the early Church, and in the Middle Ages. The second is a more specialized study of what Boswell calls "same-sex unions," an ancient practice within Eastern Christian churches of blessing friendship between two males or two females.

When John Boswell's first book, *Christianity, Social Tolerance, and Homosexuality*[1] appeared in 1980, it received lavish praise. The reviewer for the *New York Times* said that "John Boswell restores one's faith in scholarship as the union of erudition, analysis and moral vision. I would not hesitate to call his book revolutionary, for it tells of things heretofore unimagined and sets a standard of excellence that one would have thought impossible in the treatment of an issue so large, uncharted and vexed. . . . the book's argument is of such richness—its empirical base so broad, its reasoning so fierce—that it succeeds in making one think the unthinkable. It forces us to re-examine even the most fixed notions about our moral and cultural heritage."[2]

A year or so later, and over the course of the next several years, when scholars in the field began to publish reviews in learned journals, Boswell's accomplishment took on quite a different appearance. D. F. Wright, a Scottish scholar who has published widely on sexuality in the early church stated that "the conclusion must be that for all its interest and stimulus Boswell's book provides in the end of the day not one firm piece of evidence that the teaching mind of the early Church countenanced homosexual activity."[3]

But the damage had been done. The initial celebration of the book in the popular press had fixed a certain view of the book in the minds of many intellectuals and columnists sympathetic to the argument, and this view persists. The considered judgment of the scholarly community has been ignored, and *Christianity, Social Tolerance, and Homosexuality* has become for the chattering classes and many others the definitive work on the topic.

When Boswell's second book, *Same-Sex Unions in Premodern Europe*,[4] appeared in 1994 the scholarly community was more attentive and within a few weeks the book had been dismissed. Scholars from all over the world weighed in with devastating criticism—Robert Taft, a student of Eastern Christian Liturgy at the Oriental Institute in Rome, and Brent Shaw, a medievalist from Canada, to mention only two. Speaking from quite different perspectives, each showed that Boswell's claim that the medieval Church had blessed gay marriages was bogus. *Same-Sex Unions in Pre-Modern Europe* is a premier example of advocacy scholarship, pseudohistorical learning yoked to a cause, tendentious scholarship at the service of social reform, a tract in the culture wars.

Of the two books, the first has been the more influential, in part because of its reception but also because in it Boswell advances an argument, however faulty, that prompted scholars to look again at the ancient sources, particularly the New Testament. One reason it was possible for Boswell to create what appeared to some a convincing reinterpretation of the sources is that passages in the Scriptures and in early Christian literature on homosexual practice are sketchy, scattered, fragmentary, and ad-hoc. In the Christian and Jewish traditions, homosexuality was usually discussed in relation to other things, idolatry, marriage, and childbearing. By contrast marriage received extensive treatment in moral and theological treatises as well in ecclesiastical legislation. The paucity of evidence makes it difficult to construct a comprehensive picture of how Christians thought or felt about homosexuality.

What this means is that the task of reinterpretation will turn less on what the texts say, since they say so little, than on general considerations about the nature of homosexual practices. Boswell had the wit and intelligence to urge a redefinition of the terms used in the ancient texts in light of contemporary understanding of homosexuality. He introduced into the discussion, and perforce imposed on the ancient texts, the idea of the homosexual person, that is, a person whose sexual inclination from birth was to persons of the same sex. His first book begins with a chapter on "definitions" (as does the second), a rather unusual approach for a historian. But Boswell realized that if he wished to make his view of the sources plausible, he had first to persuade the reader to accept his notion of homosexuality.

The opening chapter of *Christianity, Social Tolerance, and Homosexuality*, then, is key to Boswell's program, not because of what it tells us about the ancient sources, but because of what it tells us of how the sources will have to be understood. Boswell wants to use the term "gay" to designate "persons who are conscious of erotic *preference* for their own gender." That seems reasonable enough in the present intellectual climate, but it is anachronistic in dealing with classical antiquity and Christian history. For it is apparent in antiquity that those who engaged in homosexual acts *also* engaged in heterosexual acts. According to K. J. Dover, author of *Greek Homosexuality*, the fundamental work on homosexual practices in ancient Greece, Greek society "recognized alternation of homosexual and heterosexual preferences in the same individual." That is, those who engaged in homosexual acts were not persons who had a preference for persons of their own gender. By defining the subject of his inquiry in this way, Boswell is able to provide a scaffolding on which to construct a novel interpretation of a key biblical text from St. Paul's Epistle to the Romans:

> Ever since the creation of the world [God's] invisible nature, namely, his eternal power and deity, has been clearly perceived in the things that have been made. So they are without excuse; for although they knew God they did not honor him as God or give thanks to him, but they became futile in their thinking and their senseless minds were darkened. . . . [They served the Creator,] who is blessed forever! Amen. For this reason God gave them up to dishonorable passions. Their women exchanged natural relations for unnatural, and the men likewise gave up natural relations with women and were consumed with passion for one another, men committing shameless acts with men and receiving in their own persons the due penalty for their error (1:20-27).

The plain meaning of this passage, to which even the notes in the New Revised Standard Version attest, is that in turning from God those engaged in homosexual acts "violated their true nature, becoming involved in terrible and destructive perversions," that is, women by having sexual relations with women violated their nature as women, and men by having sexual relations with men violated their nature as men. In this sense their acts are "perversions," a turning away from what is good and proper, acting contrary to nature.

Using contemporary ideas about "gays," Boswell argues that in this passage St. Paul is speaking about the sexual behavior of heterosexual persons, that is, the class of persons whose sexual preference is for members of the opposite sex and for whom sexual relations with a member of the *same* sex is contrary to nature. St. Paul is not speaking about the class of persons known as "gay," those for whom sexual preference is for members of the same sex. As Boswell says, "the persons Paul condemns are manifestly not homosexual; what he derogates are homosexual acts committed by apparently heterosexual persons."

St. Paul is saying that it is contrary to nature for heterosexuals to engage in sexual relations with someone of the same sex. He says nothing about the behavior of gays. Hence, since it is the case that some people are "gay" by nature, that is, have an erotic preference for persons of the same sex, it is natural for such persons to engage in sexual activity with persons of the same sex.[5]

This is sophistry, pure and unadulterated. It rests on a contrived notion of homosexual as a class of persons that is a tertium quid, neither a male nor a female. By insisting on the use of the term "gay" and giving it a meaning that is alien to ancient society, Boswell not only misrepresents the sources, and hence the attitudes of ancient societies, but also creates historical realities that are self-contradictory—and hence not historical. This is apparent in his treatment of Roman as well as Christian sources. After arguing that the categories of "homosexual" and "heterosexual" did not intrude on the consciousness of the ancients, he goes on to speak of "gay literature" in antiquity or of social tolerance of "gayness." Yet in the same paragraph he says that Roman society assumed that adult males would be interested in sexual relations with both sexes. If that is so, one cannot speak of "gay" as a class of persons defined by "preference." He says that there were no prejudices directed "to homosexual relations as a class." The reason is obvious: the ancients did not think there was a class of people with sexual "preferences" for the same sex.

The notion that there is a "class" of people defined by sexual preference is a very recent idea that has no basis in earlier Western tradition. To use it as an interpretive category is confusing. Where there were laws or social attitudes against homosexuals, they had to do not with homosexuals as a class but with homosexual acts. Even where certain homosexual acts were tolerated by society (as in ancient Greece), there was no suggestion that sexual preference played a role or that certain people were thought to belong to a distinct group within society. In fact, even when tolerated (for instance, between an adult male and a youth), there was *no* social approbation given to an adult male who played the "passive" role (that is, the role of the boy) with another adult male.

Boswell's scholarship is no less tendentious in dealing with the patristic and medieval sources. He ignores those features of the texts that do not suit his argument and strings together a series of possible interpretations until the reader begins to think that the possible has become the historical. He regularly opts for a (just barely) plausible reading of a text while ignoring its more likely sense. Boswell is a master of scholarship by innuendo.

As for Boswell's discussion of the medieval period, scholars have been no less critical of his conclusions. In his interpretation of medieval statements of friendship and love between males, Boswell consistently chooses to read the texts as evidence of erotic interest, ignoring those scholarly views that give a different interpretation. Writing in the *Times Literary Supplement*, Peter Lineham observes that "it takes a very literal and insensitive reading to conclude that while 'erotic interest appears not to have been the primary component of most of Anselm's relations', some of his epistolary output appears erotic by any standards.' This is the leaden interpretation of the obsessive inquisitor rather than of the dispassionate inquirer. B. McGuire's study of Anselm's sexual nature. . . is cited, but not his conclusion that there is no evidence of Anselm's ever having given physical expression to his affections, nor his observations that he not uncommonly used physical imagery in writing to people he did not know."[6]

Boswell argues that there was a dramatic shift in attitudes and legal restrictions on homosexual acts from 1150 to 1350. This view is based less on the interpretation of the changing social situation in the Middle Ages than on his contention in the first part of the book that in the earlier centuries Christians were more accepting of homosexual behavior. But, as Keith Thomas observed in his review in the *New York Review of Books*, it is more likely that the changes that occurred at that time were not the result of a new moral outlook but the introduction of new ways to implement them in society as a result of other social and religious changes. Boswell has been misled, writes Thomas, because of his "desire to establish a long lineage for modern 'gay culture.' If he had had the chance to read Dover's *Greek Homosexuality* (where the evidence is overwhelming) he might have changed his mind. In general, Mr. Boswell seems to underrate the cumulative impact of the patristic tradition."[7] Boswell's assumption that homosexuality is a presocial biological constant throughout different periods of history and in different societies makes it difficult to assess the historical data fairly and judiciously.

In his second book, *Same-Sex Unions in Premodern Europe*, Boswell discusses the ritual of *adelphopoiia,* the rite of "making into a brother or adopting as a brother."[8] This practice, which has deep roots in ancient Greece, was a way of building alliances between cities by a ritual act of binding two men together in friendship. In the eastern Roman Empire and the Byzantine world, ritual friendship became a way of legally adopting someone who was not a member of one's family for purposes of inheritance or giving a person the benefits of association with a family different from one's own.

Boswell examined the language of these rituals in Greek and Slavonic liturgical books and argued that they were used by Christian clergy in medieval Eastern Christendom to bless "gay marriage." The rituals, notes Boswell, refer to the joining of two people in a lifelong relationship, they speak of a bond of peace and love, they include ritual actions that parallel those of marriage ceremonies, for instance, placing their right hands on the Gospel books, kissing of the book, the priest, and one another.

There were, however, differences between these rites and marriage rites. The relationship, as the texts make clear, was spiritual, not carnal. There is no mention of the marriage bed, the term marriage is not used, different biblical readings are assigned, and usually the relation is of an elder to a younger. Further, the persons who were bound by such friendship were usually married.

There is much of interest in the book and Boswell has alerted

western readers to a dimension of Eastern Christian life that is unknown in the West. Yet on the central question, whether medieval
Christendom blessed "gay marriages," Boswell has no argument. Indeed, his book is not really a work of historical scholarship. All the
laborious apparatus of scholarship is put at the service of a contemporary social agenda. Boswell wishes to legitimate the introduction
of "gay marriage" ceremonies in the contemporary Christian churches.
But the price Boswell exacts from readers is steep. To make his case
he must impose on the texts meanings they cannot bear and wrench
them out of their context in medieval Christian society.

His book also has an underside. In his view, Christian resistance
to homosexual activity and "gay marriages" is a result of prejudice
against gays. As in his earlier book, Boswell claims that Christian
prohibition of homosexual acts is a relatively late development in
Christian tradition. He does not allow that there may be biblical,
theological, and moral arguments undergirding the traditional Christian view. Using charged language ("rabid and obsessive negative pre-
occupation with homosexuality as the most horrible of sins"), he argues
that it is only "Western horror" and "visceral revulsion" over homosexual unions that led to the suppression of these rituals.

Boswell's books create a world that never existed in order to change
the world that does exist. He misrepresents Christian practice and
distorts the past. As Brent Shaw wrote in his review in the *New Republic*, "tinkering with the moral balance of the past is a disservice to
the study of history and to the reform of society. The past is dead.
We cannot change it. What we can change is the future; but the way
to a better future requires an unsentimental and accurate understanding of what happened in the past, and why. A more civil and humane
modernity will not be achieved by tendentious misreadings of antiquity."[9]

In any discussion of homosexuality and homosexual acts within
Christian tradition, one must begin with Christian attitudes toward
marriage and childbearing. Because Boswell treats homosexuality in

isolation from marriage as a distinctive form of love, the reader is given no context in which to interpret Christian attitudes toward homosexual acts, nor any tools to understand the moral dimension of Christian legislation on the subject. In Christian tradition, homosexuality cannot be discussed without reference to marriage and the purpose of sexual activity within marriage. Homosexual practice is not simply a matter of specific sexual acts; these acts have moral and social consequences. As St. Augustine of Hippo wrote, "the first natural union of human society is the husband and wife. God did not create even these as separate individuals and join them together as if they were alien to each other, but he created the one from the other. . . . The result is the bonding of society in children, who are the one honorable fruit, not of the union of male and female, but of sexual intercourse."[10]

13

Homosexuality and Judaism

Rabbi Barry Freundel

H OMOSEXUALITY, once a word whispered only with revulsion or derision, is now out in the open for all to see and hear. In fact, homosexuality and its attendant issues have become big news. Whether it is the rapidly spreading and evermore frightening AIDS epidemic, the increase in sympathetic "gay" characters in the theatre and in literature, or the widening legal battles over the status of homosexuals, one cannot go very far in contemporary society without confronting this once extremely closet-bound topic. Traditional Judaism has been forced to confront it as "gay" individuals and "synagogues" have appeared on the Jewish landscape, often appealing for support from liberal segments of the Jewish community.

An authentic Jewish response must begin with the biblical prohibition against homosexuality. The Bible unequivocally states that a homosexual act between two consenting adult males is a capital crime.[1] Therefore, homosexuality is an activity that no traditional Jew can engage in, endorse, accept, or approve of (recent televised statements to the contrary notwithstanding).[2]

Despite this initial biblical negative, there is much to discuss regarding our attitude to the homosexual, the issue of the homosexual's place in the community, the question of approach to and the treatment of the homosexual, and the problem of the homosexual's rights and acceptance in society. In addition, we must consider why the Bible and Jewish thought reject homosexuality, keeping in mind as we do that female homosexuality, though forbidden, is not nearly as serious a crime as its male counterpart.[3]

Drawing the Right Picture

Our analysis of Judaism's approach to homosexuality begins with the question, "What is Judaism's view of the Jewish homosexual?" I contend that the only appropriate answer to this question is that there is no such individual.[4]

To explain this rather radical statement, one must go back to the structure that halacha places upon Jewish society. In this structure there are certain legal personalities who constitute the dramatis personae of the Jewish community. A Cohen is such a personality, as is a Levi. A woman is such a personality, as is a slave or a king. Other "characters" populate the Jewish landscape. The *mamzer* and the *Cohen Gadol*, the *Katan* and the *gadol*, the *cheresh* and the *shoteh*—each has his place in the scheme of things.[5] Missing from this list is the homosexual, and one is hard put to find a halachic term used specifically for him.[6]

If one were, in fact, to apply a halachic category to this individual, it would be the general category of *mumar l'teiavon* (one whose desires put him in opposition to Torah law), specifically *mumar l'mishkav zachor* (one who because of his repeated involvement in homosexual activity is in opposition to Torah law). Such a category exists in halachic literature,[7] is clearly defined, and places the homosexual on an equal footing with other *mumarim* who violate other laws.

It seems clear from this that halacha never viewed the homosexual as a member of a distinct category or as different from the nonhomosexual. He has no greater or lesser rights or obligations. He deserves no special treatment or concessions or any special vilification. In fact, the term "homosexual" is an essentially inappropriate term for him. We should, rather, refer to this individual as a person engaged in homosexual activity. "Homosexual" is, therefore, not a noun that identifies and categorizes the individual but an adjective that describes his activity.

This approach has great intuitive appeal. It is hard to imagine Jewish thought accepting the premise that sexual desires and activities provide grounds by which to define an individual's place in the community. In addition, this picture of the individual as a person involved in homosexual activity and not as a homosexual has vast and important implications.

The first effect of this conceptualization is to alter and improve the individual's perception of himself. If one is labeled and defined by the term "homosexual," he is consequently different from the heterosexual. As such, he will struggle for minority status and for his rights as a member of that minority. He is, and should be, portrayed as a unique character type in movies, theater, and on television, and he should command an appropriate number of participants in any institution that constitutes itself along racial, ethnic, and religious lines. He agitates for gay pride and gay power, and if he is Jewish, he establishes gay synagogues and other gay institutions.

On the other hand, if "homosexual" is a term that is limited to the description of an activity, then the individual practicing this activity remains an undifferentiated member of society, and if Jewish he is part of Jewish society. He need not feel irreparably and irretrievably stigmatized. Above all, he need not feel excluded from the community. In the same way that the adulterer, the practitioner of premarital sex, the *mechallel Shabbat*[8], or the speaker of *lashon harah* all enter the synagogue and feel at home while individually dealing with whatever guilt they carry as a result of their sinful activities, so too the individual involved in homosexual activity can and should enter the synagogue and feel himself to be part of the community. He is most assuredly not part of a separate homosexual society or sub-society. Obviously, the adulterer, *mechallel Shabbat*, and the like are duty-bound to change their ways—to do *teshuva*—and the *mumar l'mishkav zachor* has the same obligation.[9]

The second implication of this approach concerns the community's dealings with the individual involved in homosexual activity. If the practitioner of homosexuality is considered a full-fledged Jew (albeit a *mumar*), the community should welcome him as such. This is particularly true in our post-holocaust era, in which our heightened awareness of the value of each Jewish soul has motivated many communities to make *kiruv rechokim* (attempts to bring non-observant Jews into the fold of Torah observance) a hallmark of their activities. This *kiruv* work should not and cannot be limited only to violators of halacha in ritual matters. Deviance from halachic norms in sexual matters is as much an area for concern, outreach, and proper education as anything else. Particularly in an area that is as difficult to control as sexual desire,[10] the support of the community for one who might want to bring his lifestyle in line with halacha may be crucial to success.

At this point something should be said about the term *toeivah*[11] as used by the Torah in connection with homosexuality. Some may feel that its appearance in this context precludes treating the practitioner of homosexuality in the same way that one would treat an individual who is guilty of a different sin. The problem with this suggestion is that to be consistent we would require similarly negative treatment of the person who eats non-kosher food,[12] the idolator,[13] the unethical business man,[14] and the individual who remarries a woman who, since her divorce from him, has entered and left (by death or divorce) another marriage to another man.[15] All of these individuals are guilty of committing a *toeivah*, according to the respective verses that prohibit the particular activity. If we are going to ostracize the individual who commits homosexual acts, then we must ostracize these individuals as well, but since we do not take this approach in the other cases, we should not do so in dealing with the individual involved in homosexual activity.

How then to understand the *toeivah* designation? In an article in the *Encyclopedia Judaica Yearbook*, Dr. Norman Lamm defines *toeivah* in aesthetic terms.[16] These actions are repulsive in and of themselves; no rationale or explanation is necessary. Rather, the divine aspect within the human being is automatically and instinctively repelled by these activities. The fact that any number of individuals are possessed of a deadened spiritual sensitivity that allows them to accept or even participate in the acts in question does not mean that the spiritually sensitive individual allows his revulsion to be diminished or that he apologizes for that revulsion.

Further, it is important to note that the wording of the verses in question indicates that this revulsion is directed only at the act and not at its perpetrator, who is not to be ostracized. One who commits a *toeivah* is halachically and societally no different from one who commits a transgression of a non-*toeivah* law of equal severity.

Although it may be true that a leopard cannot change its spots, Judaism holds that a human being can change or control his activities.[17] While we certainly recognize that many individuals have personality factors that promote certain sinful activities, our expectation is that these individuals will control these tendencies. We no more would accept the act of murder as legitimate because the perpetrator is prone to violence, than we should accept the act of homosexuality as inevitable because of the existence of biological, genetic, or environmental factors that contribute to an individual's preference for homosexual acts. A rational individual can control himself, and no amount of apologetics, explanations, or rationalizations can change this fundamental fact. Simply put, the individual engaged in homosexual activity is wrong in what he is doing and is held responsible for having done it.

It is on this issue that the approach presented here parts company most completely with Dr. Lamm's view. Whereas Dr. Lamm sees the homosexual as an *anuss* (an individual forced by heredity or environment into activity that the Bible forbids),[18] I see him as *mumar*. Whereas Dr. Lamm effectively relieves him of culpability,[19] I insist that creating a sense of culpability should be an integral part of Judaism's approach in confronting the individual involved in homosexual activity. This sense of culpability may be just the push necessary for the individual to begin the *teshuva* process.

The view presented here seems more in keeping with biblical,[20] talmudic,[21] and other halachic sources.[22] The consistent position taken by these sources is that the homosexual is ultimately subject to punishment for his actions. The halachic system fully expects that an individual properly warned, witnessed, and brought to trial for this act will be killed. There is no indication anywhere in the literature that such individuals have a prima facie defense as *anussim*.

Dr. Lamm supports his approach by arguing that present public policy and social reality preclude punishment of all offenders.[23] We must, therefore, maintain our condemnation of the act while refraining from dealing punitively with the offender. In his view, this can best be done by treating the offender as an *anuss*. Yet there is nothing in his argument that prevents our labeling the individual as a *mumar*. We do not punish Sabbath violators or those who eat *treif*. Environment and heredity are not enough to label the individual involved in homosexual activity an *anuss*. Rather, label him a *mumar*, indicating that he is responsible for his actions.

Further, a stance such as Dr. Lamm's seems to carry with it the possibility of pushing the individual presently questioning his own sexual orientation over the wrong edge. After all, if biology and upbringing are the causes, and the participant is only the victim of irresistible forces, he has a handy excuse and less reason not to succumb to his desires.

Labeling someone a *mumar* does not necessarily mean that the community should respond with public condemnation and rejection of the individual. In an era which lacks a Sanhedrin and adequate Jewish communal structures, we have long tolerated, worked with, and even welcomed and accepted violators of many halachot within our community. It is necessary, therefore, to couple our tolerance of the individual with disapproval of the activity. This must then be combined with an expectation and hope that the individual will change his behavior. Calling him a *mumar*, if handled correctly, strengthens the chances for change.

The subject of change brings us to our next point. Jewish thought would argue that homosexually oriented individuals can change their sexual orientation and can ultimately develop an interest in and derive pleasure from heterosexual activity. This conclusion is an obvious consequence of our discussion so far. If a homosexual act is punishable, and if we expect the individual who has homosexual desires to avoid giving in to them, what then is the life situation of such an individual? There seem to be two possibilities. First, such an individual cannot change his feelings. If this is the case, he is a prisoner trapped in a body which, while commanded to marry and procreate, has an emotional structure that finds such a concept at best unfulfilling and at worst a living purgatory. Second, he can change, and a normal, happy, fulfilled life, marriage and heterosexual union are possible for him.

We are told by the Talmud that G-d does not play tricks on His creations.[24] Particularly as the area of sexuality is an area of such deeply personal implications to any individual, it is difficult to imagine G-d creating a situation in which those who feel themselves to possess a homosexual orientation cannot change and are consequently locked in a living prison with no exit and no key. Therefore, some method or methods must exist to successfully change the sexual orientation of motivated individuals. It is heartening to note that a recent study indicates a 70 percent success rate among such individuals.[25] It is unfortunate that the mass media and most mental health professionals publicly portray the goal of "acceptance of one's orientation" as the ideal, while downplaying or denying the possibility of change. Our task must be to make known the possibility of change and the relevant statistics that now become statistics of hope. We also should encourage the mental health community to develop new and more effective methods to alter the sexual orientation of those striving to live a way of life true to the Torah.

Perhaps one further support for the idea that homosexual orientation is at least preventable, if not totally changeable, is the anomalous fact that the one community in which the percentage of homosexual preference is significantly lower than in the general population is the Orthodox Jewish community.[26] It is almost as if halacha rejects the notion of an individual called a homosexual, rejects the necessity of the homosexual act for any individual, rejects the idea of an irrevocable homosexual orientation, and then creates a society in which these ideals can, apparently quite successfully, be lived.

Judaism rejects the suggestions that homosexuality is either a form of mental illness or an "acceptable alternate lifestyle." Judaism's position would be a third and as yet unconsidered option. Homosexuality is a maladaptive and inappropriate activity entered into volitionally by individuals, who may be psychologically healthy. Depending on one's theory, it may indicate arrested development, poor family structure, early trauma, frustration of the purpose of creation, disruption of the basic family structure, unnatural behavior, and the like. But whatever the case, it constitutes activity that will diminish an individual's capacity to fulfill, in his own life, G-d's expressed plan for creation. As such, this individual cannot achieve his full potential as a human being. Therefore, our task is to treat and redirect this individual to more appropriate and fulfilling activity.

Why Condemn Homosexuality?

In discussions of the Jewish view of homosexuality, the question "Why does Judaism condemn a pleasurable, victimless act that takes place between two consenting adults?" often takes center stage. Although explanations are not lacking in the literature, a truly consistent approach should shed some light on why female homosexuality, though forbidden, is far less heinous a crime than male homosexuality.[27] In fact, a number of suggested answers suffer from a failure to adequately explain this last point.

One such approach centers around the primacy of family and children in our system of values. The practice of male homosexuality obviously frustrates the implementation of these values.[28] But so does the practice of female homosexuality. Yet the two are not treated with equal severity. A second approach argues that homosexuality is somehow unnatural. Our bodies are constructed to act in certain ways, and the practice of male homosexuality perverts these ways.[29] Once again, female homosexuality seems to be every bit as unnatural as the male variety, yet we do not react to it in the same way.

Often, those who advocate these two approaches resort to the *hashchatat zera* (destruction of seed) argument. Since male homosexuality involves *hashchatat zera* and female homosexuality does not, the prohibition as violated by the men is more stringent.[30] There are two problems with this response. First, it does not adequately explain the treatment of the male participant. *Hashchatat zera* in other contexts does not entail the death penalty.[31] However, males involved in homosexual activity (as opposed to females) are subject to capital punishment. *Hashchatat zera*, therefore, does not appear to be a significant enough factor to explain this severe reaction on the part of Torah law. Second, the biblical prohibition concerns the homosexual act and not *hashchatat zera*. In Jewish law, homosexual activity, if consummated, is a capital crime even if there is no *hotzaat zera*, yet male physical contact, even if it results in *hotzaat zera*, is not punishable in this way unless actual sexual consummation occurs.[32] For these reasons, the approaches cited seem unable to serve as complete explanations for the Torah view on this issue.

One variation on the "unnatural" theme seems to fare better in dealing with our question. This position takes its definition of the natural not from physiology and nature as studied in the laboratory but from nature as defined in the Torah, which says: "Therefore shall a man leave his father and his mother and cleave to his wife and they shall be as one flesh."[33]

The Torah has, in this verse, defined "natural" as man and woman united in heterosexual union. Any person engaged in homosexual activity acts against G-d's natural order of things, and is therefore culpable. Women involved in homosexuality are less in violation of the "natural" than men, as "he shall cleave . . . and they shall be as one flesh," can be accomplished by males in homosexual union but not by females. This explanation seems to deal neatly with the various facets of the problem.[34]

One other approach to the question of why Judaism has such antipathy to homosexuality deserves mention.[35] This approach expands on the previous argument, reintroduces the centrality of the family in Judaism to the discussion of homosexuality, and treats the halachic differences between male and female homosexuality in a rather interesting way. This explanation argues that homosexuality, when it did occur at all in the Jewish community, usually occurred in a bisexual context and not as an exclusively homosexual orientation on the part of the individual. Individuals raised in the Jewish community usually possessed a strong sense of family as part of their tradition and heritage. This, coupled with the desire to find personal continuity into the next generation and with communal pressure to marry, would naturally lead almost everyone to establish a conjugal relationship. Unfortunately, some individuals might seek additional companionship elsewhere. This extramarital companionship could possibly be homosexual in nature. Such an outside relationship might then be devastating to the special intimacy between husband and wife and to the family, the fundamental building block and most important religious institution in Jewish society.

Many rabbinic discussions allude to homosexuality in a strongly negative tone.[36] The Talmud discusses the meaning of the term *toeivah* as used in the context of homosexuality.[37] Says Bar Kapparah, *toeivah* means *to'eh ata ba*, "you have strayed from her." This phrase is explained by Tosafot as meaning "that they leave their wives to follow homosexuality." This statement seems to embody the essence of the proposed explanation. Whether because of different emotional needs on the part of women, their status in society, or because of the physiological impossibility of two women uniting in one flesh, male homosexuality is considered a far more serious danger in this context and is therefore treated with greater severity.

Our discussion leads to the following conclusions:

1. Homosexuality is an activity, not a state of being. Put another way, "homosexual" is an adjective, not a noun.
2. Homosexual activity is wrong.
3. Homosexuality may be a foreign incursion into Judaism.
4. The perpetrator of homosexual activity is held responsible for the activity.
5. We expect individuals involved in such activity to make every attempt to stop the activity and to alter their sexual orientation.
6. No greater halachic stigma attaches to the practitioner of homosexuality than to the Sabbath violator or the violator of many other divine commandments.

In light of these conclusions the traditional Jewish community should agree on the following goals:

1. The primary goal should be to create an environment that is most conducive to motivating the practitioner of homosexuality to want to change his orientation.

2. In the absence of this motivation or during a period when initial attempts to change are unsuccessful, our task is to keep this individual within the Torah community. We must create a situation which offers a positive alternative to the "gay synagogue" and to the even worse choice of complete abandonment and assimilation.

It would seem that these goals can best be realized by implementing the following agenda: All unnecessary negative stigma must be removed from the individual involved in homosexual activity. Such an individual must be encouraged to see himself as someone with a problem that he is responsible to overcome and not as a person who has been defined by his sexual orientation. At the same time that the individual is told of his responsibility to change, he must also be told, with great compassion, that we recognize the difficulty of his task and that we are willing to help in any way possible. This is similar, in general terms, to the way in which we treat others such as the alcoholic.

Specific programs of outreach to those participating in homosexual activities should be implemented so that those best able to respond to the questions of these individuals will have a chance to work with them. Contemporary Jewish organizations do *Kiruv* (outreach) work with individuals who violate many commandments. We must do the same with those whose failures are in sexual areas. This is particularly true because of the all-pervasive nature of sexual desire and because of the constant encounter with sexual imagery that pervades our society.

Mental health professionals must be encouraged to develop new and better therapeutic techniques to alter sexual orientation. Methods that are even partly successful must be highlighted and publicized to offer hope to those who would want to change.

The issue of homosexuality is an extremely sensitive, difficult, and emotional one. It is a topic that creates a sense of discomfort and even revulsion not only in those who may have been personally involved in such activity but also in many who have never had any personal contact with it at all. Stereotyping and personal doubts about one's sexuality tend to maintain and reinforce these reactions and the AIDS scare has given them new impetus. Our response as Jews faithful to the Torah must be to reject these prejudicial and counterproductive reactions. On the other hand, we cannot equivocate in our opposition to homosexual activity. This is particularly true in light of the media's continuing portrayal of homosexuals as positive role models and the increasing acceptance of the homosexual as a minority group with "legitimate" civil rights.

The program described above entails walking a difficult tightrope between condemnation of an act and acceptance of the perpetrator as a Jew worth saving. We cannot close our eyes and pretend that a problem of this magnitude will go away. It is our task to present a legitimate Jewish response, balancing our opposition to homosexual activity with our concern for the human beings involved.

14

Homosexuality and
Catholic Doctrine

Bishop Fabian Bruskewitz

T HE OFFICIAL DOCTRINE of the Catholic Church on the morality of homosexual acts is set out with brevity and clarity in the Catechism of the Catholic Church:

Homosexuality refers to relations between men or between women who experience an exclusive or predominant sexual attraction toward persons of the same sex. It has taken a great variety of forms throughout the centuries and in different cultures. Its psychological genesis remains largely unexplained. Basing itself on Sacred Scripture, which presents homosexual acts as acts of grave depravity, tradition has always declared that homosexual acts are intrinsically disordered. They are contrary to the natural law. They close the sexual act to the gift of life. They do not proceed from a genuine affective and sexual complementarity. Under no circumstances can they be approved.

The number of men and women who have deep seated homosexual tendencies is not negligible This inclination, which is objectively disordered, constitutes for most of them a trial. They must be accepted with respect, compassion, and sensitivity. Every sign of unjust discrimination in their regard should be avoided. These persons are called to fulfill God's will in their

lives and, if they are Christians, to unite to the sacrifice of the
Lord's Cross the difficulties they may encounter from their condition.

Homosexual persons are called to chastity. By the virtues of
self-mastery that teach them inner freedom, at times by the support of disinterested friendship by prayer and sacramental grace,
they can and should gradually and resolutely approach Christian
perfection.[1]

In an earlier document, issued in 1986, the Holy See had also spoken officially about the Catholic position in regard to homosexual acts.
This document, concerned with the pastoral care of homosexual persons, was the successor of a previous and even more important document issued in 1975, which was entitled "A Declaration on Certain
Questions Concerning Sexual Ethics." In the 1975 document, which
has validity for Catholic moral theology, the document stressed the
duty of trying to understand the homosexual condition and noted that
culpability for homosexual acts should be judged with prudence. At
the same time, there should be a distinction drawn between a homosexual condition or tendency and individual homosexual acts. These
acts, of course, are deprived of their essential and indispensable finality
and are intrinsically disordered and in no way can be approved.

Catholics, and many Christians with them, believe that the discussion of homosexuality should be based on a theology of creation,
particularly that which is found in the first book of the Bible, Genesis, in which God is seen in His infinite wisdom and love, bringing
into existence all of reality as a reflection of His own goodness. He
fashions the human race, male and female, in His likeness. Therefore, human beings are nothing less than the work of God Himself,
and this includes the complementarity of the sexes, which are called
to reflect the inner unity of the Creator. They do this in the most
striking way in the transmission of life by the mutual self-giving to
each other in the institution of marriage. We find further in Genesis
that the truth about human beings as God's image has been obscured

and smeared by original sin, with a concomitant loss of awareness of the covenantal character of the union of person with God. As Pope John Paul II says, the human body thus retains its "spousal significance," but now this is clouded by sin. Further, in Genesis 19, the deterioration due to sin is brought to a certain climax in the story of the men of Sodom. Although there may be other components to the sin of the Sodomites, it is quite clear that their sin consists in their homosexual relations, not simply the abuse of hospitality. This is further corroborated by the legislation set down in Leviticus 18:20, which describes the conditions necessary for belonging to the Chosen People, and excludes from God's family those who behave in a homosexual way. In the New Testament, this perspective is developed by St. Paul in the 1 Corinthians 6, where he proposes that those who behave in a homosexual fashion will not enter the kingdom of God. He also, in Romans 1, uses homosexual behavior as an example of the blindness which has overtaken all of the human race. And, finally, in the 1 Timothy 1:10, St. Paul explicitly names as sinners those who engage in homosexual acts.

In 1997, a series of monographs was published by the Vatican's semi-official newspaper, *L'Osservatore Romano*, under the general title "Christian Anthropology and Homosexuality." These fourteen studies by various authorities in psychology, psychiatry, family life, and moral theology are a treasure for those who seek to understand and deal with problems involving this phenomenon of homosexuality.

The moral tradition of the Catholic Church on this issue is based on the light of Divine Revelation and also on the light of natural reason. Under the glow of these two lights, the Church has always stressed univocally that the use of the sexual function has its true meaning and moral rectitude only within a legitimate marriage. Through the symbolism of the sexual difference which marks their bodily nature, man and woman are called to achieve two closely connected values: first, the gift of self and the acceptance of the other in an indissoluble union of one flesh, and second, an openness to the

transmission of life. Only in the context of legitimate marriage are
these values proper to sexuality adequately respected and achieved.

As Livio Melina, a professor of moral theology at the Pontifical
Lateran University in Rome, says very well,

> In the homosexual act, true reciprocity, which makes the gift of
> self and the acceptance of the other possible, cannot take place.
> By lacking complementarity, each one of the partners remains
> locked in himself and experiences contact with the other's body,
> merely as an opportunity for selfish enjoyment. At the same time,
> homosexual activity also involves the illusion of a false intimacy
> that is obsessively sought and constantly lacking. The other is
> not really other. He is like the self; in reality, he is only the mirror
> of the self which confirms it in its own solitude exactly when the
> encounter is sought. This pathological narcissism has been
> identified in the homosexual personality by the studies of many
> psychologists. Hence, great instability and promiscuity prevail in
> the most widespread model of homosexual life, which is why the
> view advanced by some, of encouraging stable and institutional-
> ized unions, seems completely unrealistic.

Professor Melina goes on to note that it is obvious that the homosexual act lacks openness to the procreative meaning of human
sexuality. In the sexual relationship of husband and wife, their bodily
act of mutual self-giving and acceptance is ordered to a further good,
which transcends both of them: the good of that new life which can
be born from their union, and to which they are called to dedicate
themselves. It is the logic of love itself which requires this further
dimension and transcendence, without which the sexual act risks turning in on itself by concentrating on the search for pleasure alone, and
literally sterilizing itself. Through its openness to procreation, the
intimate act of the spouses becomes part of time and history and is
woven into the fabric of society. The homosexual act, on the contrary,
has no roots in the past and does not extend to any future. It is not
grafted into the community or the succession of generations. It re-

mains locked in an unreal moment outside time and social responsibility. To speak of the spiritual fruitfulness of homosexuality is unduly to ascribe the positive aspect which is always involved in true friendship and of which homosexual persons are also capable, to homosexual practices which are psychologically marked by a frustrating sterility. In fact, psychologists with broad clinical experience state that often when an authentic personal friendship forms between male homosexuals, it frequently happens that they are then unable to continue having these homosexual relations. Because the unitive and procreative aspects of sexual activity which give a legitimacy to its practice can only be found in marriage, a loving and life-giving union of man and woman, the Catholic Church has always taught, and continues to teach, that a person engaging in homosexual behavior acts immorally. As the Congregation for the Doctrine of the Faith puts it,

> To choose someone of the same sex for one's sexual activity, is to annul the rich symbolism and meaning, not to mention the goals of the Creator's sexual design. Homosexual activity is not a complementary union able to transmit life. So it thwarts the call to a life of that form of self-giving which the Gospel says is the essence of Christian living. This does not mean that homosexual persons are not often generous in giving of themselves, but when they engage in homosexual activity they confirm within themselves a disordered sexual inclination which is essentially self-indulgent. As in every moral disorder, homosexual activity prevents one's own fulfillment and happiness by acting contrary to the creative wisdom of God. The Church in rejecting erroneous opinions regarding homosexuality, does not limit, but rather defends personal freedom and dignity, realistically and authentically understood.

The Catholic Church teaches that morality is a morality of human acts. To be fully human, an act first has to be done volitionally, that is, out of free will and without external coercion. Second, it must be done with due deliberation, that is, an understanding of what is happening and what is being done. The morality of an act is determined in the objective order by its conformity to law, the natural law, which God writes on the heart of every human being, as well as divinely revealed law. Law can also require obedience when it is enacted by lawful authority in the Church and, sometimes, even in the state. The supreme subjective norm of morality is conscience, which is reason judging the rightness and wrongness of an individual act. For conscience, however, to be followed, as it must be, it is necessary for conscience to be properly formed. As Pope John Paul II puts it in his encyclical *The Splendor of Truth*, "Acting is morally good when the choices of freedom are in conformity with man's true good, corresponding to the wise design of God, indicated by His commandments which are a path leading to life." The Second Vatican Council, speaking of the norms of conjugal morality, justified their value precisely as being directed to keeping the exercise of sexual acts within the context of true love by safeguarding the total meaning of mutual self-giving and human procreation. The fundamental moral requirement is simply this: to do good and to avoid evil. It is our duty as human beings, then, using reason and divine revelation, to discover what doing good is and what evil is.

The Church has through almost two thousand years of her history consistently made a distinction between the sin and the sinner. There must always be inflexible and flint-hard hatred of sin, while at the same time there must be compassion, understanding, and concern for the one who commits the sin, that is to say, the sinner. This theoretically is quite possible, but in practice it frequently is quite difficult to distinguish the sin from the sinner, since, as has been pointed out many times, we in a certain sense become what we do. In other words, if we lie, we become liars. If we fornicate, we become fornicators. If we do homosexual acts, we become homosexuals. Nonetheless, the door to mercy and forgiveness must never be closed. It should be pointed out, however, that in Christian theology, the conditions for mercy and forgiveness are repentance and recognition of sinfulness.

It is not possible for God, even in His infinite mercy, to pardon one who refuses to accept His pardon or even refuses to recognize a need for such pardon.

This, of course, leads to another important aspect of the moral evaluation of homosexuality from the ecclesiastical point of view, which is to say, the distinction between the homosexual condition or inclination and actual homosexual acts. Homosexual acts are intrinsically disordered. In Catholic terminology, when they are done with free will and deliberation, they are mortal and lethal sins which terminate one's friendship and relationship with the Creator. They are intrinsically disordered because they lack an essential and indispensable goal.

The Catholic Church has not made any official pronouncement about the problem of homosexual orientation, that is to say, whether it can be or is acquired, or whether it is congenital and may have some basis in psychosomatic or even physical factors. If this orientation is not the result of morally negative choice, then, obviously, it cannot be called a sin. Nevertheless, even in that instance, that is, even when it is present without being desired, or willed, or deliberated upon, and therefore is not a sin, it is intrinsically disordered. It must be seen as a more or less strong inclination to intrinsically evil behavior from the moral viewpoint, and therefore, cannot be thought of as neutral or good. In Catholic tradition, this corresponds to what the Council of Trent calls the meaning of concupiscence, which is not sin in the true and proper sense but is an effect of original sin, and can be called sin insofar as it comes from sin and inclines toward sin. There are many aspects of the human condition that are represented by such concupiscence, things such as excessive desire for power, selfishness, greed, and those kinds of perversions which we call kleptomania, sadism, and pyromania. Such disordered inclinations are not in themselves sins but are objectively disordered and lead to objective evil. And insofar as the acts that proceed from such inclinations are under the dominance of free will and have received due deliberation, they are sinful and culpable on the part of those who commit them.

Compassion for, and pastoral concern for and care for, those people who have these kinds of orientations should never be confused with the approval of any acts that may derive from these inclinations. At the same time, Christian charity, which is not an option but an obligation for those who follow the teachings of Jesus Christ, requires that there be constantly exercised compassion, mercy, concern, and care for all people, even those who are inclined toward evil actions, and this is particularly the case if these inclinations have not been caused by their own incorrect use of free will.

A word should also be spoken about the word "discrimination." There are two kinds of discrimination, unjust discrimination and just discrimination. Unfortunately, the discussion about this issue in our present American society leads to a great deal of confusion and ambiguity, which sometimes result in apparent contradictions in Catholic approaches to anti-discriminatory legislation in various state legislatures and various municipalities. Certainly there is such a thing as unjust discrimination. And to deprive someone unjustly of work or housing or other arrangements simply on the basis of past actions, or on the basis of announced inclination, could and would be unjust. At the same time there are certain measures of just discrimination which are not only morally neutral but are sometimes morally necessary. For instance, it would be a case of just discrimination to prevent a pyromaniac from having a job as a custodian in a gasoline storage facility. It would certainly be just discrimination to disallow employment as a bank teller to a person given to kleptomania. There are certain kinds of activities which, I believe one can say, should not be engaged in by homosexuals, particularly if the homosexuality has certain other phenomena associated with it, such as pedophilia. It would be morally reprehensible to hire a pedophile to take care of a children's daycare center. Because of the simplistic use of particular political slogans in our time, this kind of just discrimination is frequently lumped together under a general title of discrimination and declared unacceptable in modern American culture, which exalts tolerance at any cost as the supreme virtue.

Moreover, Christians have not only a right but a duty to avoid placing people in occasions of sin. Housing discrimination, for example, with regard to homosexual couples is, in my view, a very just and rightful form of discrimination which Christians not only can, but should, exercise. They should refuse, for instance, to rent apartments or rooms to persons (heterosexual or homosexual) who are obviously in an intrinsically disordered arrangement in regard to their sexual lives.

It is also a right and perhaps a duty of Christians to see that the civil laws of the country in which they live recognize that the promotion and defense of families, founded on monogamous heterosexual marriage, is an essential part of the common good. The state should not be allowed, with their acquiescence, to deprive itself of the healthy social fabric that it alone can make possible and which is necessary for harmonious society and the continuation of human civilization. In my view, as well, a Christian, and certainly a Catholic, has a right and a duty to oppose "gay culture," which does not simply mean a tragically homosexually oriented person but rather signifies a collection of persons who publicly adopt a homosexual lifestyle and are committed to having such a lifestyle accepted by society as fully legitimate in civil law. Professor Melina states quite correctly that "justifiable opposition to offenses and discrimination which violate a person's rights cannot be confused with this demand. In fact a systematic plan for the public justification and glorification of homosexuality is taking place, starting with the attempt to make it fully accepted in the minds of society. It aims through increasing pressure at a change in legislation so that homosexual unions may enjoy the same rights as marriage including that of adoption."

Jesus promised, "You shall know the truth, and the truth shall set you free" (John 8:32). We are also told in Sacred Scripture that we are to "speak the truth in love" (Ephesians 4:15). So God, who is at once truth and love, calls us to minister in the Church to all people, including those people with homosexual inclinations or homosexual acts in their past. It does not serve the cause of either truth or love, however, if they do not interpenetrate one another. Truth is not truth unless it is accompanied by love, just as love is not genuine love unless it is accompanied by truth.

Obviously, there is much more that could be said about this issue, particularly in refutation of various and serious misinterpretations of Sacred Scripture, such as the relationship of David and Jonathan, or even more blasphemously, those who would misunderstand or misinterpret the relationship of Jesus Christ and the "disciple whom He loved," which from the Greek text tells us very clearly is a disinterested, pure, and dispassionate love and has absolutely nothing to do with any homosexual relationship or inclination. The Fathers of the Church have always considered with undeviating consistency homosexuality as an intolerable sin for Christians. And although it was a cultural fact in ancient times, just as it is in our own, the general norms of Christian ethics, from the first days of the Catholic Church's existence to the present, have been unvarying in their understanding that human sexual activity is permissible only in the context of Christian marriage.

I would like to conclude this very brief presentation of the teaching of the Catholic Church on homosexuality with a paraphrase from the poet John Donne, who said quite eloquently: Human beings are never really free unless they are chained by God's commandments, just as they are never really pure until they are ravished by God's love.

V

The Homosexual Experience

15

Courage

Father John Harvey

M Y TASK is to show how the spiritual support system known as Courage provides an opportunity for persons with homosexual orientation to live an interior life of chastity. Before describing Courage, however, it is necessary to describe its theological and ethical foundations.

The Argument from Scripture

In using both the Old and New Testaments it is understood in Catholic moral theology that they are to be evaluated in light of the divine oral Tradition operative in the living teaching office of the Church, that is to say, the pope and the body of bishops throughout the world.[1]

In Genesis 1:26-28, God says: "Let us make man in our own image—in the likeness of ourselves. . . . God created man in the image of himself, in the image of God He created him, male and female he created them. . . . God blessed them, saying to them, be fruitful, multiply, fill the earth, and conquer it." In Genesis 2:22-24, we read the more poetic Yahwist account of the creation of Eve from Adam's rib. When God presents Eve to Adam, he responds: "This, at last, is bone from my bones, and flesh from my flesh. This is to be called woman, for this was taken from man. This is why a man leaves his father and mother and joins himself to his wife, and they become one body."

From these primordial texts one may conclude that human sexual activity has two purposes: the permanent commitment of a man and a woman in a two-in-one-flesh union; and the procreation of children. Genesis 4:1 further underlines the procreative purpose of sexual intercourse when it says that Adam knew his wife Eve, and she conceived and bore him a son, Cain. The norm of heterosexual union leading to children and family persisted throughout the Old Testament despite violations of the norm by sinful humans.[2]

In the New Testament Jesus confirms the two purposes of human sexual activity in marriage (in Matthew 19:1-9, as well as in Mark 10:9-12). Jesus is challenged by the scribes and pharisees for not granting a bill of divorce, as Moses had done. He responds that Moses granted a bill of divorce because of the hardness of their hearts, and then he adds: "Have you not read that the Creator from the *beginning made them male and female*, and that he said: *This is why a man must leave father and mother, and cling to his wife, and the two become one body*? They are no longer two, therefore, but one body. So then what God has united man must not divide" (Matthew 19:3-8).

In all the passages where Paul discusses the relationship between man and woman he is really confirming the norm of marriage found in Genesis. Indeed the classic text on marriage in the New Testament, Ephesians, 5:21-33, also confirms the sexual norms of Genesis: "As Christ loves His Church, so a man ought to love his wife. . . . *For this reason a man must leave his father and mother and be joined to his wife, and the two will become one body*" (Ephesians 5:25, 30-32). Thus Paul stresses the two-in-one-flesh union of marriage. Again, in 1 Corinthians 7:9, Paul teaches that if one does not desire to be celibate, he should marry, "since it is better to be married than to be tortured." Please note he does *not* say that it is better to be in a committed homosexual relationship than to be promiscuous.

I have not quoted the specific biblical passages of both Testaments in which homosexual acts are condemned. (Genesis 19:4-11; Leviticus 18:20-22 and 20:13; Romans 1:26-27; 1 Corinthians 6:9; 1 Timothy 1:9; Jude 7). This omission does not mean that these texts lack probative value; on the contrary, they strengthen the argument already presented, which is based upon the nature of marriage. Heterosexual marriage is the proper place for the sexual-genital expression of human sexuality, and so homosexual activity is not an acceptable moral alternative to marriage. This conclusion is valid whether one argues from the divine authority of Sacred Scripture and Tradition or from natural moral reasoning, as it is exemplified in Michael Pakaluk's article, "Why is Homosexual Activity Morally Wrong?"[3]

Pakaluk argues that sexual intercourse between a man and a woman has a special status that makes it different from other human activities. If it did not have a special status, rape would be no different from mere assault and battery. Sex is special because it is a sign of the union of the *persons* who engage in sex. The sign is the union of bodies, and the sign signifies the union of persons. Thus, it is correct to say that "when a man and a woman engage in sex, the union of their bodies signifies the union of their selves."[4] One cannot minimize or take away this meaning of sexual intercourse. In heterosexual intercourse, moreover, there is a complete physical union, something not attainable in homosexual intercourse. Again, sexual intercourse between a man and a woman has a reproductive character, the act tending to produce offspring, who combine the characteristics of husband and wife and in so doing promote the unity of the spouses. Homosexual intercourse has no such power. Pakaluk goes on to say that homosexual intercourse is not a natural sign at all, lacking the two components that make sexual intercourse a natural sign, namely, reciprocal containment, and the power of procreation. He concludes that the "most that can be achieved in homosexual intercourse is mutual masturbation."[5]

The entire argument against homosexual acts can be summed up in a syllogism: From Sacred Scripture and Sacred Tradition as well as from natural moral law it is clear that the two purposes of human sexuality are the permanent commitment of a man and woman in a two-in-one-flesh union, and the procreation of children. But homosexual activity does not fulfill either purpose. Therefore, it is always immoral.[6]

While homosexual activity is objectively immoral, it does not follow that the person involved in such activity is fully responsible. There are many obstacles to human freedom, including the very seductive culture in which we live.

Now, I will describe a program to help persons of homosexual orientation to live chastely in the world. This is why the spiritual support system called Courage came into existence in 1980 in New York City, under the inspiration of the late Terence Cardinal Cooke.

The Five Goals of Courage

"The Five Goals of Courage," written by its early members, are really a summary of this spiritual strategy. They are:

1. To live chaste lives in accordance with the Roman Catholic Church's teaching on homosexuality.

2. To dedicate our entire lives to Christ through service to others, spiritual reading, prayer, meditation, individual spiritual direction, frequent attendance at Mass, and the frequent reception of the sacraments of Reconciliation and of the Holy Eucharist.

3. To foster a spirit of fellowship in which we may share with one another our thoughts and experiences, and so ensure that none of us will have to face the problems of homosexuality alone.

4. To be mindful of the truth that chaste friendships are not only possible but necessary in chaste Christian life and to encourage one another in forming and sustaining them.

5. To live lives that may serve as good examples to others.

What makes Courage different from some other ministries to persons with homosexual tendencies within the Catholic Church is its insistence on a radical change in one's way of thinking, willing, and acting. On the level of thinking, Courage members accept completely the teaching of the Catholic Church that all homosexual acts are immoral and that one should follow a plan of life that takes the person as far away as possible from the gay milieu.

On the level of willing, Courage members are asked to make a commitment to a life of chastity, and to use the means provided by the Catholic faith for the practice of interior chastity. Goals two, three, and four all are concerned with the development of an interior life of prayer and of fostering chaste friendships. Goal two is concerned with prayer of the heart, what is sometimes called meditation. Such prayer helps one to have a closer relationship with God. Goal three helps the individual to learn to trust members of his own sex through weekly discussions in which he talks only about himself.

The flexible use of the Twelve Steps of Alcoholics Anonymous is a great aid in keeping the conversation focused on the subject under discussion. Each person is allowed to speak about himself for a limited amount of time, so that all have a chance to express their feelings during the course of the hour or so session. As the group works together from week to week, they learn to accept and trust each other. This is one place where each person realizes that he is accepted by the other members. There is no need to hide oneself, but there is also no need to "come out of the closet" to gain acceptance and love.

On the level of behavior, Courage members develop good friendships with other members of the group and also with persons who are heterosexual. In this respect they fulfill a human need that is deeper than the desire for physical-genital sex. There are, then, two elements in the chastity of the individual with homosexual tendencies who has made a commitment to Christ: the need for prayer of the heart and solid friendships with persons of both sexes. Beginning with same-sex friendships, one moves to making friendships with the other sex.[7]

The Desire to Escape Homosexuality

Since Courage is primarily concerned with helping individuals to live a life of interior chastity, it does not require that its members strive to get out of the condition itself. There is a basic moral principle that one may not be required to do something that he cannot do, and since at the present moment of research we do not know any reparative therapy that guarantees the restoration of one's heterosexual orientation, we cannot impose an obligation upon a member to seek to get out of the condition. Courage, however, does encourage members who want to do so to seek counsel and group therapy in a context of prayer. In fact, Courage has both a male and a female group whose members go to additional meetings for this purpose. It is also true that the guided effort to rediscover one's heterosexual state will lead the one away from homosexual temptations, making it easier to be chaste.

On the one hand, Courage does not agree with those holding that it is practically impossible to get out of the homosexual condition, or that it is even harmful to the person to make such an attempt.[8] On the other hand, Courage does not believe that one is guaranteed freedom from the orientation, provided one follows a particular program over a period of time. Nevertheless, the younger the person is, particularly teenagers and young adults, the higher the probability that one may rediscover his heterosexual state. The truth is that some do regain their heterosexual orientation, and some are not able to do so, while continuing to lead chaste lives.

Does Courage Work?

At this point one may ask the question whether the spiritual strategy of Courage has worked, or is it just an impossible dream? Courage works for those who work the program, as many individual testimonials indicate. Courage is in seventy-five dioceses of the United States, and just beginning in several others in the United States. It exists in six dioceses of Canada, Toronto being the largest; it has been established for several years in London, the Philippines, Belfast, Dublin, Cork, and most recently in New Zealand, Australia, and Poland.

Courage has a sister group called EnCourage for parents who are concerned with adult sons and daughters seduced into the gay lifestyle. We have a newsletter, days of recollection beyond the weekly meetings, and annual meetings in a city of the United States or Canada. Our New York office is now an international network, communicating by e-mail, the Internet, and fax with Europe, Asia, South America, and Australia.[9]

The most frequent objection to Courage is that its many groups are small in numbers attending a meeting, averaging about eight people, while other organizations in the Catholic Church ministering to people with homosexual orientation have more members at individual meetings. But so far these organizations have no program for chaste living. Courage, however, provides its members with the opportunity to develop a prayer life with Christ and to form chaste friendships with other men and women, whether they are homosexual or heterosexual.

I believe that Courage continues to spread, because it teaches the truth about the immorality of homosexual activity and because it encourages everyone to try to get as far away from the condition as possible. Courage will continue to grow, because the Catholic laity wants its message. Recently, near Kracow, Poland, two Polish women counselors decided to start a support group to help men and women with homosexual tendencies to live chastely. They set goals similar to those of Courage, and they decided to call the group Courage—without knowing that Courage already exists in America. Truth has a way of making itself known.

16

Freed from Lesbianism

Jane Boyer

I AM FOUNDER AND DIRECTOR of Amazing Grace Ministries, a Christ-centered organization in Portland, Maine, reaching those who desire freedom from sexual brokenness such as homosexuality, cross-dressing, transsexuality, pedophilia, and sex addiction. I am a former lesbian.

I accepted Jesus into my heart when I was five years old. I worshipped God, attended church. I've been married for nineteen years and have two adopted children from India. But for about five years of my marriage, I lived a double life, one as Christian and one as homosexual. I kept this hidden from my family and the body of Christ for fear of rejection and condemnation.

I was raised by two alcoholic parents. My father was a violent and abusive man. As I got older, I developed fear and hatred towards men and determined in my heart I would never allow a man to get close to me emotionally. My mother was emotionally unavailable to meet my needs as a child. She was a victim of my father's violence. I was her caretaker, her protector. I felt resentful of her, for I perceived her as weak, clingy, passive, and ineffective. If being a woman meant being a victim, if it meant helplessness, being vulnerable to abuse, if the feminine meant being used as a sex object by men, I didn't want any part of it. I developed a hardened, masculine shell for self-protection.

I hated the feminine and yet still needed to bond with it. As far back as I can remember, I had intense emotional attachments with other women. They were mainly my teachers. I seemed always to have a crush on some woman, not in a sexual way, but craving their attention and validation. I had a sense that even this was not normal, that I was different. I felt there was something really wrong with me. Looking back on this and knowing now what I know about homo-sexuality, this was symptomatic that my needs for love and acceptance were not being met at home.

I was raised French Catholic. In those days one never heard or talked about homosexuality. All I knew was "good Catholic girls" were not allowed to have these feelings. I was twelve years old when I began to drink alcohol and do drugs in order to numb my emotional pain. My teenage years were unhappy, lonely, and empty.

I thought that perhaps marriage would fix this. Soon after I married, however, I went to my first gay bar. That gay bar and the gay community became my haven for the next five years. For the first time in my life I had friends; I belonged and felt accepted. I realize now the reason why the gay community had such a pull on my life. My background being full of rejection, I wanted acceptance very badly, at whatever cost.

I made a lot of friends; I was popular in the gay community. A double life emerged. I was involved in lesbian relationships and keep-ing this hidden from my husband and the body of Christ. Time and time again I vowed never to return to the bar only to go back because my desire for love and acceptance was so strong. But as time went on I saw my gay friends in deep emotional pain from their past, and many were in conflict over their homosexuality. We were all looking for the perfect love, the perfect relationship, and never seeming to find it.

For years I wondered if I was born gay. And if not, why was I not able to be free from this condition? I sought counsel with a pastor and a therapist, who both called themselves Christians. Now mind you, there is a difference between Christian and born-again believer: II Timothy 3:7 speaks of those "always learning but never able to acknowledge the truth"; II Timothy 3:5 says "there will be terrible times in the last days . . . those having a form of godliness but denying its power." They told me I was born gay, that homosexuality was acceptable to God, that once I accepted my "true identity" as a homosexual that only then would I find peace. I was encouraged to leave my husband and my family and to "celebrate homosexuality."

I encountered pro-gay theology, which is a theology that either takes the Bible out of context, giving it a personal interpretation, or ignores the Bible altogether to support the view that homosexuality is acceptable to God. There are many denominations that embrace pro-gay theology. There are many books written promoting pro-gay theology and the authors are the theologians themselves. Pro-gay proponents say the law of the Old Testament no longer applies. The reasoning behind this is, for instance, that though eating pork was condemned in the Old Testament, it is acceptable today, and we can assume the law no longer applies. Homosexual behavior, condemned in the Old Testament, is now acceptable according to pro-gay proponents.

Of course, there is a difference between dietary law (which is temporary, having to do with culture at the time) and moral law (which is permanent and universal and when violated in serious cases was punishable by death). Incest, rape, murder, and homosexual behavior are all part of the moral law. So if homosexual behavior is acceptable, according to pro-gay proponents, then we'd also have to conclude that rape, incest, and murder are also acceptable, under this reasoning. We must remember that Jesus came not to abolish but to fulfill the moral law. Jesus took the punishment of death for us. God, who is extremely merciful, provides ample opportunity to repent and receive the free gift of salvation. The purpose of the moral law is to direct those who violate it to Christ. But there are consequences to sin and consequences to not receiving the free gift of salvation because "the wages of sin is death." Is God willing to act in love at the expense of His Holiness? In Jeremiah 6 we read of "priests and prophets alike, they all practice deceit, they dress the wounds of my people as though they were not serious."

Are there some of you that accept the theory that homosexuality is inborn? Do you believe everything you hear or read from the media? Homosexuality has become a politicized issue of gay rights, which has tilted the debate over the biological causes of homosexuality. We are also dealing with a liberal and biased media. Over 80 percent of media representatives do not think there is anything wrong with homosexuality, over 90 percent favor abortion rights, and only 20 percent attend church. So the truth about homosexuality will not be heard from the media. I do media appearances for Exodus International and was once on the *Geraldo* show. When it was aired, I was appalled to see that 90 percent of what I had said on the show had been cut. The media will not tell you that most of the widely accepted authorities in the area of human sexuality, both Christian and secular, conclude that homosexuality is caused by emotional wounding as a child, that it is not inborn. And you are not going to hear from the media about a global, ex-gay movement called Exodus International where thousands are being set free from the gay identity and the gay lifestyle by the power of Jesus Christ.

And what if homosexuality is found to be inborn? The greatest error being promoted is the assumption that homosexuality can be normalized by proving it is inborn. There are many conditions that are inborn that aren't normal. Take for example the research that concludes alcoholics are born with a chemical in the brain predisposing them to alcoholism. I was born predisposed to alcoholism and for many years lived as a drunk. But twelve years ago, while in detox, I was persuaded that I could live sober. What if the medical and scientific community decided that, because alcoholism is inborn, it's normal, and they refused to treat it? If there are no moral absolutes, then Christ died for nothing. God's law and truth are absolute and not contingent on the latest research. God's grace and power is available to overcome any number of sinful tendencies, homosexuality included. The moment we allow science to redefine our lives above the Word of God, we are guilty of idolatry.

For many years I was in turmoil. I came to believe the lie: that there was no hope for change, no hope for my marriage. But there came a time when I had to decide between the man I married (who is a fine Christian man, but for whom I had no desire at that time) and my lesbian relationship (which I felt I could not live without); I had to choose between what God said about homosexuality and what appealed to my flesh; and finally I had to choose between the gay community which gave me much support and acceptance and the church which I felt was cold and detached. The conflict seemed unbearable. I turned to alcohol and drugs, and I contemplated suicide, because there seemed to be no hope.

It was then that with all my heart I cried out to Jesus. God allowed me to get to the bottom, to the end of self. The only place left to go was to the cross. And how He is faithful! How He longs for us to go to Him with the brokenness of our hearts, our wounds and disappointments—and how we go here and there, to and fro looking for answers, for comfort—so that when we seek Him, and Him only, then we will know the truth and the truth will make us free. It's been a process, a difficult process. But today I am no longer struggling with homosexuality. I've been set free, my marriage healed.

When I cried out to God, He intervened and I found myself at my first conference with Exodus International. Most of the four hundred Christians there were former homosexuals. I saw worship with a love for Jesus I had never seen before because, you see, they had been redeemed from the pit; they were forgiven much, therefore they loved much. It was the former homosexuals that showed me how to have an intimate relationship with Jesus. I could see their passion for Jesus and I wanted that.

Jesus showed me the truth about homosexuality. The homosexual act is sin, but the homosexual orientation comes from emotional wounding as a child, and He can heal those wounds. But Jesus was also clearly telling me to give up my lesbian relationship. Now, as a child in my home, I felt hurt and rejection and not a whole lot of love. This lesbian relationship was to me the best love I'd ever known and I wasn't sure I wanted to give it up. But God was calling me to a radical obedience—radical for the day in which we live, radical, committed, determined, and unwavering obedience. Why? Because God will never reveal more truth about Himself until you have obeyed what you know already. In order to have an intimate relationship with Jesus we must obey. If unwilling, are we willing to be made willing? We begin by realigning our will with His, and then He will empower us to go further in our obedience. It's in obedience to God that we have an intimate relationship with Jesus and it's in our relationship with Him that we are healed. And I wanted an intimate relationship with Jesus, like the ones I saw in those former homosexuals, so in faith I made the decision that I would break off the lesbian relationship I had waiting for me back home. I wondered, though, if Jesus could fill the void, the emptiness and longing I carried in my heart. Perhaps it was too late for me. I was guilty of idolatry, adultery, and homosexual behavior. I wondered if I had crossed the line with God, used up His grace and mercy. Perhaps I was irredeemable.

And there was anger in my heart. "God, if you love me, then where were you when my father abandoned me, when my mother was beaten, where were you when I was sexually abused, alone and rejected, where were you, God?" He was on two pieces of wood, a hole in His side, nails in His hands and feet, face and head bleeding from the crown of thorns, taking unto Himself all the pain of the world, all of my pain. In Isaiah 53 we read "surely He took our infirmities, carried our sorrows . . . and by His wounds we are healed." Jesus transcends all time, He can go back, touch and heal those hurts that happened years ago. Jesus knew how much I longed for the arms of a daddy. And as I pondered, there came a picture that I could see with the eyes of my heart. I was a little girl about three years old and there was Jesus. I couldn't see His face very clearly but I knew it was He, for there was so much love radiating from Him. His arms outstretched reached for me, picked me up, and held me. At that moment His love poured into the deepest place in my heart to overflowing. When one has an encounter with the glory of God, one will never be the same.

Lesbian love is a counterfeit, a lie. It never satisfied, it never filled. It only left me craving. The love of Jesus satisfies. This man Jesus I could trust. I felt He was taking from me when He was calling me to a radical obedience, but what He was doing was giving me a love and joy far better than anything I'd ever known. "Purity is the condition for a higher love, for a possession superior to all possessions, God Himself."

In closing, I ask you to look with me at 1 Corinthians 6:9-11 as this passage has given a profound hope in my freedom from homosexuality. Paul is writing to the church in Corinth, some of whose members were former homosexuals. He begins by saying "Do you not know that the wicked will not inherit the kingdom of God? Do not be deceived. Neither the sexually immoral, nor idolaters, adulterers, male prostitutes, homosexual offenders, thieves, greedy, drunks . . . will inherit the kingdom of God." I noticed the following:

1. The homosexual offender was placed alongside thieves, the greedy, drunks, which said to me that my sin was neither the least nor was it the greatest. That set me free from shame.

2. In verse 11 "and that is what some of you were," meaning past tense—they had been homosexual, but were no longer. That meant I could be changed. That meant there was hope for me. It didn't matter what the supposed research said; Jesus said I could be changed!

3. It also meant the church was populated by former homosexuals, that not only could I change, but I could be forgiven.

4. Paul goes on to say "but you were washed"—when I repented of my sin, I was made clean from sin and guilt.

5. "But you were sanctified. . . ." I've been set apart for God. I belong to Him; I am redeemable.

6. "But you were justified. . . ." I could come before God possessing His righteousness as a gift of His love.

Paul ends by saying "In the name of our Lord Jesus Christ in the Spirit of our God."

The homosexual act, shame, guilt, and bondage are all dealt with in the redemptive work of Jesus Christ. The power to change and be healed is in the person of Jesus Christ. Jesus loved me when I did things I vowed I would never do. He in no way condoned my sin, but He was more concerned with healing my heart. When I longed to be held, He wrapped His arms around me. When I'd known rejection, He accepted and affirmed me. He bound up my wounds and healed my hurts. When I've known fear, He gave me courage. When I've known shame and self-hatred, He gave me a new name, a new identity. I am a new creature, the old things are passed away, behold all things are become new. The love and acceptance I so desperately needed I found in Jesus Christ, thereby setting me free from homosexuality.

And so, as Christ is to us, so must we be to the homosexual. Compassionate without compromising the word of God. If you are reading this and struggle with homosexuality, know that Jesus loves you and He can set you free. Amazing Grace, how sweet the sound, that saved a wretch like me. I once was lost but now I'm found; I once was blind but now I see.

Hatred, Bigotry, and Intolerance

Christopher Wolfe

T HIS BOOK, LIKE ITS PREDECESSOR, *Homosexuality and American Public Life,* has put forward a view that both reflects the understanding of past generations that homosexual acts are wrong and that society should not legitimize active homosexuality, and takes advantage of modern research that has improved our understanding of the causes of homosexuality and of ways to provide support for those who struggle with same-sex attractions. We hope that it will be a valuable contribution to public debate on this important subject. At the same time, we are aware of a major obstacle, namely, the growing intolerance that makes public debate on this issue very difficult.

The popular radio talk show personality Dr. Laura Schlessinger was scheduled to host a new television program in the fall of 2000. Enormous pressure has been brought on the sponsoring studio (Paramount) and on advertisers to suppress this show. Why? Because its host has publicly taken stances on homosexuality that parallel those of the contributors to this book; that is, because she believes that homosexuality is a disorder and that "reparative therapy" to achieve a heterosexual orientation is often possible. Gay activists do not want to debate her. They just want to silence her.

246

Consider some recent examples of intolerance. Dr. Robert Spitzer, former American Psychiatric Association (APA) president, who took a leading role in the APA's decision to remove homosexuality from its list of psychological disorders in 1973, became intrigued by the claims that reparative therapy could sometimes lead to a genuine reversal of sexual orientation. He organized a panel to debate the issue of reparative therapy for the 2000 annual meeting of the APA. But shortly before the meeting, the opponents of reparative therapy dropped out of the debate, which then had to be canceled. Again, preventing debate, rather than engaging their critics, appeared to be the goal of gay activists.[1]

The conference on which this book is based was held at the Georgetown University Conference Center in the summer of 1997. An official of the Human Rights Campaign, a major gay rights organization, wrote her alma mater, Georgetown, complaining that the university would permit such a conference and asking it to cancel the conference—again, an effort to shut down debate.[2] It is worth noting that, while the *Washington Post* found this protest by a gay rights group newsworthy, it chose not to print a single word about the three-day conference, which included presentations by thirty-five noted scholars and activists on the other side of the issue. The overwhelming media bias in the coverage of this issue is extraordinary.

On various campuses throughout the country, Christian groups (many of them associated with the InterVarsity Christian Fellowship) have been denied official student organization status, funding, and use of campus facilities because of their opposition to homosexual activity. In some of these cases, the groups were content to have active homosexuals as members but did deny them the possibility of holding leadership positions. For this they were pilloried in meetings and publications and deprived of official recognition.[3]

What is the rationale for these attempts to suppress debate? Debate, the argument appears to go, is fine where there are legitimate differences of opinion. But there is no legitimate difference of opinion here. The opinions of those opposed to the legitimization of homosexual conduct are not merely "wrong opinions." They are acts of "hatred, bigotry, and intolerance," and therefore they should not be tolerated. But is there any plausibility to this contention?

It is essential to begin with a simple distinction between people who believe that homosexual activity is morally wrong and those who genuinely hate homosexuals. The former distinguish between the act and the person (opposing the former, but respecting and caring for the latter), while the latter do not. It is certainly the case that there are pockets of real "hatred, bigotry, and intolerance" in our society, exemplified by those for whom people with same-sex attractions are "disgusting" and deserve society's contempt and opprobrium. But much of the rhetoric of gay activism attempts to blur, or rather to eradicate completely, the line between those who make reasoned moral arguments against homosexual activity and those who have irrational hatred for men and women who experience same-sex attractions.

I want to examine the accusations of "hatred, bigotry, and intolerance" when they are directed against those—like the contributors to this volume—who believe that homosexual activity is wrong and that legitimization of homosexual activity would be contrary to both the common good and the good of homosexuals themselves.

Hatred

Hatred, by its nature, involves an animus against certain people—an intention to do them harm or a desire to see them harmed. Those who oppose the legitimization of active homosexuality, who promote reparative therapy for those willing to pursue it, and who believe that the place of sex is within marriage clearly argue that these principles will make life *better* for individuals—be they homosexual or not—as well as for society at large. Not only do they make a reasoned case for these positions, but many of these people have dedicated their lives to helping homosexually oriented individuals through counseling or support groups. This is the very opposite of "hatred."

The reaction to a speech I gave at Boston College in April 2000 illustrates this point. First, let me quote from a letter to *The Heights* (the Boston College student newspaper):

> In Dr. Wolfe's own words, the following assertions were made concerning his recent lecture at Boston College:
>
> "Homosexual acts are immoral."
> "I did say [homosexuality] was an affliction that can be reversed in some cases."
> "One of the contributing causes to homosexuality in many cases has to do with abusive relationships with parents."
> "The ideal conditions for raising a family are in family with an intact mother and father."
> "To consummate a marriage you have to engage in a reproduction [*sic*] kind of act."
> "Marriage is invalid if at least one partner is not open to children."
> "The only appropriate or moral form of complete sexual activity is between a man and a woman who are married."[4]
>
> As members of the Boston College community who advocate social justice issues and the promotion of equal rights, we are angered and profoundly saddened by the recent hate speech at Boston College. We deplore the recent admonishments and denigrating charges Dr. Wolfe made. As people who value human dignity and acceptance, we seriously ask the student body if you want your tuition dollars to sponsor Christopher Wolfe's hate speech or others who would promote bigotry on your campus.[5]

What are the grounds for the letter's charge that the statements quoted constitute "hate speech"? The authors of the letter may judge the statements to be false: people frequently disagree on moral issues.

But how does disagreement *in itself* entitle people to characterize another's moral opinions as hate speech or bigotry? None of my statements in any way indicates an attitude of hatred, or denigration, or dislike *of people* who act in ways that seem to me to be wrong—they simply indicate opposition to the acts themselves.

Bigotry

An allied charge is that cases against legitimization of homosexual activity constitute "bigotry." It might be instructive to begin with an example of how we use the term in another area, namely religion. What do we mean by "religious bigotry"? Whatever else we might mean, it cannot be the simple fact that we disagree with someone's religious views and believe them to be false. If that were the case, then *anyone* who sincerely believed his own religion (and disbelieved significant elements of others) would be a "bigot." But that is not how we use the word. We normally reserve it for those who are so closed-minded that they are not willing to engage in respectful discussion.

But those of us who defend views of sexuality according to which homosexual acts are wrong, and who believe that it is important for society to take that stance—men and women like the contributors to *Homosexuality and American Public Life* and to this volume—sincerely pursue respectful discussion of the issue of homosexuality. Their arguments are parts of well-developed philosophical and theological arguments that focus on moral valuations of particular human conduct, not on morally irrelevant facts such as a person's color. (Again, their arguments may be wrong or right—but they are arguments, not unreasoned prejudices.) The charges of hatred and bigotry seem to come down simply to this: those who make the charge disagree with the moral arguments of those they criticize.

In the public sphere, it is precisely the homosexual activists who typically refuse to engage in respectful discussion, confining themselves to unsupported—and unsupportable—accusations that their opponents act out of "hatred, bigotry, and intolerance."[6]

Intolerance

With regard to accusations of "intolerance," we have to begin by asking what tolerance means, and by noting, again, that it cannot mean simply that there is no true opinion about the matter. Any nonself-defeating notion of tolerance must be compatible with the belief that there are some right answers and wrong answers. In fact, it might be said that tolerance is precisely a position adopted by someone who believes that other people are *wrong* on some important issue—if you believe either that others are not wrong or that their opinion is as likely to be right as your own, then the issue of whether to suppress or tolerate them never comes up. So it is possible to believe that a certain opinion is correct but to tolerate those who express different opinions.

Intolerance, as it is understood in ordinary language, I think, typically involves someone denying someone else's legal or political right to have or express a different opinion. It is not as clear whether private refusal to countenance certain opinions constitutes "intolerance," or whether this is a bad thing. For example, we might hear someone say "I won't tolerate anti-Semitic remarks in my presence" and consider this kind of "intolerance" perfectly compatible with the kind of tolerance that a good person ought to manifest.

Acting on an opinion is more complicated. Some cases of refusing permission to act on an opinion seem fairly described as intolerance. Societies that deny people the right to practice their religion—as long as the practice does not harm others—would be regarded as intolerant. But that qualification ("as long as the practice does not harm others") suggests that there are limits to tolerating actions inspired by conscience. For example, if a society prohibits human sacrifice or racial discrimination (even when it is based on religious beliefs), such a prohibition would generally be considered perfectly compatible with the kind of tolerance we consider praiseworthy.

In other words, we all tolerate certain forms of intolerance. But what kind of intolerance is intolerable? Is intolerance "an unreasonable unwillingness to permit others to hold, express, and act on beliefs different from one's own?" The qualifier "unreasonable" has to be included, since otherwise, any prohibition of action (even murder, theft, rape, and the like) would be per se intolerant, no matter how reasonable. The problem, of course, is this: since questions of toleration involve precisely important areas where people disagree about what is reasonable, does intolerance simply become understood as "the quality of those who disagree with me about what is reasonable?" That definition obviously will not work: it is too intolerant a definition of intolerance.

Somehow, "reasonable" has to be understood as something different from "being right" about a matter. That is why we tend to gravitate toward an emphasis on "open-mindedness" and willingness to listen to and discuss different opinions. As with "bigotry," what we condemn is some form of closed-mindedness, an unwillingness to discuss issues respectfully with others.

But understood in this way, there are no grounds to accuse many who oppose the legitimization of homosexual activity and lifestyles based on it of being intolerant. In fact, it is not they who are trying to shut off discussion—it is their opponents.

An Instigation to Violence?

A particularly appalling accusation is that those who oppose the gay rights agenda are responsible for violence against homosexuals because *by their very opposition* they create an atmosphere of hatred. "Heterosexist attitudes," it is said, "deprive non-heterosexuals of their civil rights and create an unsafe environment which instigates violence."[7]

This allegation—directed at those who attempt to make reasoned arguments in the public square about homosexuality—is ridiculous. The kinds of people who beat up homosexuals are not notably the kind that engage in, or even listen to, public debates about the nature and causes of homosexuality and the proper stance of law and society toward homosexual acts. They are simply thugs, and the sources of their violence lie elsewhere.

The fallacy of the argument can be easily seen by applying it to a hypothetical case involving gay activists themselves. If someone listened to a gay activist arguing that those who are opposed to the gay rights agenda create an atmosphere that instigates violence, and the listener subsequently went out and beat up a "heterosexist," could it fairly be said that the gay activist was guilty of "creating an unsafe environment" which "instigated" that violence? Such a charge would be absurd. Disagreeing with other people on important moral issues is not in itself an invitation to anyone to harm those people.

The irony of these overwrought reactions—their self-contradiction—is sometimes so blatant as to be perplexing, as the following e-mail message to me after the speech at Boston College suggests:

> You disgust me. I hope with all of my heart that you are fired and live a horrible life. You are nothing but a hate monger, attempting to spread homophobia and sexism wherever you go. No one believes in you. Your ignorance is astounding. Indeed you are a professor, not one of knowledge, but of bigotry and idiocy.

The message condemns hatred, it is aghast at hate-mongering—and it is delivered in tones of deep hatred, without any apparent awareness of the contradiction.

I confess that I did not initially find persuasive Justice Antonin Scalia's argument in *R.A.V. v. St. Paul* that the hate speech law in that case was not "viewpoint-neutral" because it forbade hate speech to racists, sexists, religious bigots, and the like, but allowed *opponents* of hate speech to engage in hate speech. My experience has suggested that he might be right.[8]

Conclusion

The accusations of hatred, bigotry, and intolerance deployed as rhetorical weapons by gay activists, then, are regrettable. At the same time, it should be said that these accusations are not surprising. When people have come to believe that their very identity is tied up with a certain way of behaving sexually, it should not surprise us that they consider a critique of that way of behaving as an attack on themselves, and that they react, or rather overreact, accordingly.

In this respect, again, homosexuality has some strong parallels with alcoholism. Alcoholics often react very sharply and angrily to those who try to help them by convincing them that they have a problem and by encouraging them to go through very difficult and distressing efforts to change their way of life. That reaction is magnified by the fact that alcoholism typically is rooted in deep personal wounds of various sorts. Touching a wound can hurt, no matter how good someone's intentions are.

If the analysis of homosexuality as primarily a developmental disorder is correct, and if that disorder is seen as frequently resting on deep (though often unrecognized) personal wounds that arise, for example, from poor relationships with parents or peers, it would not be surprising if these underlying wounds had the effect of magnifying resentment against those who question what certain homosexuals have come to consider their self-definition, their identity.

For many homosexuals, grappling with same-sex attractions in youth has been a profoundly unsettling and unhappy experience. These attractions are often accompanied by a painful sense of being different from others and can be experienced initially with a kind of horror or self-loathing even as homosexual experimentation begins. The discovery that others have similar feelings and the claim that this is just the way nature made them and that homosexual activity is a positive good, in these circumstances, can be experienced as a profound liberation—an enormous relief from a deeply painful state of being. Once someone is integrated into this culture and belief system, those who question homosexual activity become terrible threats to what is experienced as a newfound and liberating equilibrium.[9]

This extreme reaction to those who oppose legitimizing homosexual activity is reinforced by other strands of current American culture: a society-wide growth of (selective) moral relativism masked as "non-judgmentalism," the widespread acceptance of very broad theories of personal "autonomy," the propagation of ideologically driven "science" that provides specious intellectual justification for political agendas, and the post-1960s search for new "liberation movements" that give meaning to life and often serve as substitute religions. These factors encourage a dramatic escalation in the rhetoric of those who attack those they view as reactionaries and obscurantists.

Under these circumstances, cries of "hatred, bigotry, and intolerance" in response to reasoned efforts to understand the disorder of homosexuality and to articulate a positive and hopeful response to it are understandable, though not justifiable. Intelligent, fair, and open-minded citizens should see them for what they are—that is, fundamentally irrational. Only by removing the obstacles to fair and reasoned discussion and debate can our society make progress in dealing with this difficult issue.

Notes

1   I do not mean to imply by this observation that it would be wrong or inappro-
     priate for religious believers to make arguments in the public sphere on the ba-
     sis of their religious commitments. I merely observe that, because many
     Americans do not share those commitments, or are reluctant to bring them to
     bear on public issues, religiously-based appeals alone are inadequate to the task
     of forming public opinion on the issue of homosexuality.

2   Throughout the chapter I will be using "homosexual" as the generic term that
     includes both male and female homosexuality. I do not mean by this usage to
     deny that there are significant differences between male and female homosexu-
     ality, but I do not believe that these differences justify differences in the broad
     outlines of public policy on the homosexuality issue.

3   I will sometimes use the term "active homosexuality" in order to describe those
     homosexuals who live according to the belief that homosexual acts by those who
     experience same-sex attractions are intrinsically good, or at least are morally licit.
     I use this term to distinguish between them and those homosexuals who expe-
     rience same-sex attractions but understand it to be a disorder or affliction.

4   While I will occasionally use the term "homosexual orientation," as convenient
     shorthand for "the state of having attractions to people of one's own gender," I
     want to be clear about something I do *not* mean by that phrase. Some people
     interpret the phrase "homosexual orientation" as meaning a determined and in-
     variable homosexual "nature," probably established by genes or other biological
     causes. For reasons given in Part 1 of *Homosexuality and American Public Life*

(Spence Publishing Company, 1999), especially in Dr. Jeffrey Satinover's discussion (chapter 1, "The Biology of Homosexuality: Science or Politics?") I do not believe that there is such a "determined" homosexual orientation.

5   See the essays by Satinover, Rekers, Fitzgibbons, and Nicolosi in *Homosexuality and American Public Life* and the essays in Part v of this volume.

6   In particular, there is the difference that moderate drinking is morally unobjectionable, but there is no morally unobjectionable "moderate indulgence in homosexual acts." Also, alcoholics counter efforts to constrain them with "denial," but unlike homosexuals they have not constructed a whole social ideology to justify themselves.

7   George Rekers "The Formation of a Homosexual Orientation" in *Hope for Homosexuality*, Patrick Fagan, ed. (Free Congress Research and Educational Foundation, 1988); Jeffrey Satinover *Homosexuality and the Politics of Truth* (Baker Books, 1996); Elizabeth Moberly, *Psychogenesis: The Early Formation of Gender Identity* (Routledge and Keegan Paul, 1983); Joseph Nicolosi, *Reparative Treatment of Male Homosexuality* (Jason Aronson, 1991); John F. Harvey, *The Truth About Homosexuality* (Ignatius Press, 1996).

8   While homosexuality is involuntary, as a general rule, this is not to deny the existence of some cases of "ideological" homosexuality, where ideas lead to active homosexuality, rather than being an after-the-fact rationalization of prior same-sex attractions.

9   See Michael Pakaluk's argument in chapter 9 of *Homosexuality and American Public Life* for more on this point.

10   On the alcoholism analogy, see also Jeffrey Satinover *Homosexuality and the Politics of Truth* (Baker Books, 1996), 49-50.

11   This list is found in Satinover, op. cit., 51, and discussed at length in chapter 3 of that book.

12   The Court has created the category of "mature minors" especially in its abortion jurisprudence (see, for example, *Planned Parenthood of Missouri v. Danforth* 428 L Ed 2d 52 [1976], at 73-75), which makes it seem likely that such a category might be recognized in the area of homosexuality as well, since, if the law's approbation and protection is extended to homosexual activity, this is likely to occur through some variation of a "privacy" right.

13   See Mary Eberstadt "Pedophilia Chic: A Sex Crime and Its Apologists" in *Weekly Standard*, June 17, 1996

14   See Satinover, *Homosexuality and the Politics of Truth*, where he speaks to a number of these issues. On homosexual promiscuity, see 54ff.; on higher levels of homosexual pedophilia, see 64-65; on childhood abuse of homosexuals, see 44.

15   See especially George Rekers' work in this regard.

16   This is the title of a well-known article by Barbara Dafoe Whitehead in *Atlantic Monthly*, April 1993.

17 See Christopher Wolfe, ed., *The Family, Civil Society, and the State* (Rowman and Littlefield, 1998).

18 In most public discussions, the debate tends to be formulated as the morality of heterosexual sex versus the morality of monogamous, faithful homosexual sex. As I discuss below, there is strong reason to doubt that most homosexual relationships involve genuine fidelity. And, in fact, homosexual "theorists" often tend to be radical in their understanding of sex and in their positive aversion to conventional heterosexual morality. But public advocates of the homosexual cause know that "conventional" homosexuality is much more likely to attract public sympathy, and so the arguments are typically framed to justify that form of homosexual conduct. Despite the realities of homosexual sex, defenders of traditional morality should give answers to defenders of homosexual monogamy, even if their numbers are few.

19 I have been assuming throughout this argument that consent is accepted by everyone as a kind of rock bottom moral norm governing sex. But, of course, there might be some people who would challenge even that norm. They too would have to be given some explanation about why non-consensual sex is immoral. Those who reject arguments that legitimate sex is confined to heterosexual sex, and that traditionalists are just "imposing their prejudices" on homosexuals, might find it surprising and discomfiting to be confronted with the arguments that they are just "imposing their preferences" for consensual sex.

20 See *Homosexuality and American Public Life*, Part II. This account of homosexuality accords with the argument that Patrick Fagan makes in this volume, that widespread acceptance of contraception entails a view of sex that makes it difficult to oppose homosexuality. I think that Fagan's view is correct, despite the contention of others that sex apart from children must be validated because certain forms of married sex accepted by all—for example, post-menopausal sex and sex between married persons where one of them is infertile or sterile—are not essentially different. (See, for example, Lawrence Burtoft's contribution to this volume and Stephen Macedo's use of this argument in his defense of homosexual acts in the "Homosexuality and the Conservative Mind," *Georgetown Law Journal*, 84:2 (1995): 261-300.) That contention, I think, overlooks a key distinction between human sexual acts in which the the nature of the act is deliberately changed, rendering it something less than a full one-flesh communion (the partners thereby not forming a single reproductive unit), and acts (such as sex where one spouse is infertile or sterile) where the act engaged in is fully a one-flesh communion (that of the ordinary human reproductive unit), but where an obstacle in the human "matter" (due either to ordinary deterioration of bodily capacities, or to some special defect) prevents the act from achieving reproduction. See Robert P. George and Gerard Bradley, "Marriage and the Liberal Imagination," *Georgetown Law Journal* 84:2 (December 1995): 301-20.

21 Even if this argument is not a strictly consistent logical argument—that is, even if valid arguments against homosexual acts logically require rejecting contemporary morality regarding a variety of heterosexual issues—it may still be rhetorically effective in persuading most people to adopt a proper stance on homosexual acts, even if they are unwilling to carry the logic through completely for heterosexual morality. This inconsistency in moral logic regarding the morality of certain heterosexual and homosexual acts is not attractive on its own terms, but I would argue that it is better than being *consistent but wrong* about both sets of issues.

22 There is no way, of course, to prove "empirically" that homosexuals would be just as promiscuous in a society that completely tolerated homosexual activity, there having been no such societies. But the plausible psychological explanations of homosexuality suggest that the promiscuity is not simply a function of homosexuals living in a society that refuses to legitimize homosexual activity, as is sometimes claimed.

23 See especially the chapters by George Rekers, Richard Fitzgibbons, and Joseph Nicolosi in Part 1 of *Homosexuality and American Public Life*.

24 For a powerful argument against legitimizing same-sex marriages, see George and Bradley "Marriage and the Liberal Imagination."

2   *The Inversion of Heterosexual Sex*

1 With acknowledgments to Judge Robert Bork, *Slouching Toward Gomorrah* (New York: ReganBooks, 1996).

2 *Griswold v. Conn.* 381 U.S. 479 (1965).

3 From: Ismond Rosen: "Psycho-Analysis and Homosexuality: A Critical Appraisal of Helpful Attitudes," quoting Bernice Krikler, Senior Clinician at the Portman Clinic, London, England, in Fagan, Patrick, ed., *Hope For Homosexuality* (Washington D.C.: Free Congress Foundation, 1988), 29-30.

4 Ismond Rosen, "Psycho-Analysis and Homosexuality," 33.

5 Sigmund Freud, "The Sexual Life of Human Beings" in *The Complete Psychological Works of Sigmund Freud* , James Strachey, ed., Volume 16, 303-19.

6 Mahatma Gandhi, quoted in Father A.S. Antonisamy, *Wisdom for All Times: Mahatma Gandhi and Pope Paul VI on Birth Regulation* (Family Life Service Centre, Archbishop's House, Pondicherry 605001 India, June 1978). Quotes are taken from D.G. Tendulkar, ed. *The Collected Works of Mahatma Gandhi*, Volumes 2 and 4, published by the Ministry of Information and Broadcasting, Government of India.

7 The aggregated figure assumes that there is only one sterilization per couple.

8

9 Charles Murray, commenting on the sharp rise in crime in the African-American community when out-of-wedlock births reached 30 percent.

10 Margaret Sanger, *Woman and the New Race* (New York: Eugenics Publishing Company, 1923), 25.

11 Vicki Z. Kaplan, "Organizing for Action" (New York: National Abortion Rights Action League, no date).

12 Lasch, Christopher; "The Quest for Community" (San Francisco: Institute for Contemporary Studies edition, 1990).

13 C. K. Millard in "The Modern Churchman," May 1919, quoted in Halliday G. Sutherland *Birth Control: A Statement of Christian Doctrine against the Neo-Malthusians* (New York: P. J. Kennedy and Sons, 1922).

14 Report of the Lambeth Conference, 1920, 44.

15 Dr. Walter A. Maier, Concordia Lutheran Theological Seminary, St. Louis, Missouri. Cited at www.all.org/encyclopedia/plae098.htm.

16 Bishop Warren Chandler, *Methodist Episcopal Church South*, April 13, 1931. Cited at www.all.org/encyclopedia/plae098.htm.

17 *The Presbyterian*, April 2, 1931. Cited at www.all.org/encyclopedia/plae098.htm.

18 Cited at www.all.org/encyclopedia/plae098.htm.

19 *Washington Post*, March 22, 1931. Cited at www.all.org/encyclopedia/plae098.htm.

20 *Washington Post*, March 24, 1931. Cited at www.all.org/encyclopedia/plae098.htm.

21 Pope Pius XI, *Casti Connubi*, December 31, 1930, Section 4, Paragraph 4.

22 1988 National Survey of Family Growth, National Center for Health Statistics/Center for Disease Control/U.S. Department of Health and Human Services

23 See Rabbi Barry Freundel, chapter 13, *infra*.

3 A Rhetoric of Hope

1 Patrick Fagan, 45, *supra*.

2 Norman Podhoretz, "How the Gay-Rights Movement Won," *Commentary* 102:5 (November 1996): 32-40.

3 Harry V. Jaffa, "Homosexuality and Natural Law"(Claremont, California: The Claremont Institute, 1989).

4 Fagan, loc. cit.

5 Christopher Wolfe, 3, *supra*.

6 R. W. Jensen, "How the World Lost Its Story," *First Things* 36 (1993): 19-24.

7 Wolfe, 15, *supra*.

8 Information supplied by Tom W. Smith, Director, General Social Surveys, 1972-1996, National Opinion Research Center, University of Chicago.

9 Podhoretz, op. cit.

10 William H. Masters and Virginia Johnson, *Homosexuality in Perspective* (Boston: Little, Brown, 1979).

11 M. Wood, Reuters Ltd., 21 April 1981.

12 P. McCormack, "Homosexuals: Born, Not Made, by Domineering Moms or Weakling Dads," United Press International, 24 August 1981.

13   V. Cohn, "Homosexuality Tied to Biology, New Study Says," *Washington Post*, 25 August 1981, AI.

14   J. Seligmann and M. Gosnell, "Gays are Born, Not Made," *Newsweek*, 7 September 1981, 42.

15   A. Bell, M. Weinberg, and S. Hammersmith, *Sexual Preferences: Its Development in Men and Women* (Bloomington, Ind.: Indiana University Press, 1981).

16   A. Rossiter Jr., "A Biological Link to Homosexuality?" United Press International, 7 September 1984.

17   M. Kelly, "Nudity in the Home," *Washington Post*, 7 June 1984, D5.

18   Sandra Blakesee, "Panelists Cite Biological Roots of Homosexuality," *New York Times*, 26 August 1985, AII

19   N. Sherman, Press Release, PR Newswire, 31 July 1986.

20   R. Pillard and J. Weinrich, "Evidence of Familial Nature of Male Homosexuality," *Archives of General Psychiatry* 43 (1986): 808-812.

21   D. Bjorklund and B. Bjorklund, "Straight or Gay?" *Parents* (October 1988): 93-98.

22   J. Marmor, ed. *Homosexual Behavior: A Modern Reappraisal* (New York: Basic Books, 1980).

23   J. Marmor, "Shrunk to Fit," *Los Angeles Times Book Review*, 19 February 1989, 1.

24   K. Painter, "A Biological Theory for Sexual Preference," *USA Today*, 1 March 1989, 4D.

25   The search parameters used were: "homosexual! w/20 biolog! OR genetic OR inherit! AND date is bef 1990 AND born AND NOT aids."

26   S. LeVay, "A Difference in Hypothalmic Structure Between Heterosexual and Homosexual Men," *Science* 253 (August 30, 1991): 1034-1037.

27   D. Gelman, "Born or Bred?" *Newsweek* (February 4, 1992): 46-53.

28   M. Elias, "Difference Seen in Brains of Gay Men," *USA Today*, 3 August 1992, 8D.

29   L.S. Allen and R.A. Gorski, "Sexual Orientation and the Size of the Anterior Commisure in the Human Brain," *Proceedings of the National Academy of Science —USA* 89 (1992): 7199-7202.

30   T. H. Maugh II, "New Homosexuality Study Lingk Found in Brain," *Los Angeles Times*, 1 August 1992, BI.

31   Associated Press, "Study Shows Brain Differ in Gay, Heterosexual Men," *Washington Times*, 1 August 1991, BI.

32   D. Hamer, "A linkage between DNA markers on the x chromosome and male sexual orientation," *Science* 261 (July 16, 1983): 321-27.

33   K. Painter, "Key Evidence More Maternal Kin are Gay," *USA Today*, 16 July 1993, AI.

34   J.E. Bishop, "Research Points Toward a 'Gay Gene'," *Wall Street Journal*, 16 July 1993, BI.

35   W.A. Henry III, "Born Gay?" *Time* (July 26, 1993): 36-39.

36 C. J. Lee, "Biologist Reassures Gays About His Research.," *Pittsburgh Post-Gazette*, 24 January 1994, B1. See also T. Radford, *Guardian* (February 1994) Home Page, 2.

37 K. E. Enulf and S. M. Innala, "Biological Explanation, Psychological Explanation, and Tolerance of Homosexuals: A Cross-National Analysis of Beliefs and Attitudes," *Psychological Reports* 65 (1989): 1003-10.

38 J. Pickur and D. Degelman, "Effect of Reading a Summary of Research about Biological Bases of Homosexual Orientation on Attitudes Toward Homosexuals," *Psychological Reports* 71 (1992): 1219-25.

39 P. Stanton and R. DeGrandpre, "My Genes Made Me Do It," *Psychology Today* 28:4 (July/August 1985):50-53, 62, 64, 66, 68.

40 For an excellent discussion of the current state of scientific literature regarding genetic and biological causes for homosexuality, see Jeffrey Satinover, "The Biology of Homosexuality: Science or Politics?" in *Homosexuality and American Public Life* (Dallas: Spence Publishing Company, 1999), 3-61.

41 For information regarding the status of the American Psychiatric Association's attitude toward reparative therapy for homosexuals seeking help, see *NARTH Bulletin* 8:2 (August 2000).

42 National Association of Research and Therapy of Homosexuality, "Survey of Sexual-Orientation Change" (Encino, Calif.: NARTH, 1997).

43 Fagan, loc. cit.

4   *Homosexuality and the Principle of Nondiscrimination*

1 See Nan D. Hunter, "Life after Hardwick," *Harvard Civil Rights-Civil Liberties Review* 27: 537-8.

2 Ibid., 533, n.9, which refers to John D'Emilio and Estelle B. Freedman, *Intimate Matters: A History of Sexuality in America* (New York: Harper and Row, 1988), 16, n.6.

3 *Poe v. Ullman*

4

5 I develop this point at some length in "Why is Homosexual Activity Morally Wrong?", my contribution to *Homosexuality: Challenges for Change and Reorientation*, edited by Fr. John Harvey, a special issue of the *Journal of Pastoral Counseling* 28 (1993).

6 I take this objection from an earlier, unpublished paper by Christopher Wolfe, "The Rhetoric and Politics of Homosexuality in America Today."

7 For example, the Department of Defense's "Summary Report of the Military Working Group," 1 July 1993, on the question of homosexuals in the military, several times observes that it would be inconsistent to require the military not to discriminate on the basis of homosexuality, when homosexual conduct is ruled out by the Uniform Code of Military Justice.

8   Overlooked Opinions, a gay market research company, reports that 54 percent
    of gay men have household incomes of fifty thousand dollars a year or more,
    and 30 percet have advanced degrees or graduate degrees.

9   Jonathan Rauch writes: "As more and more homosexuals come out of hiding,
    the reality of gay economic and political and educational achievement becomes
    more evident. And as that happens, gay people who insist they are oppressed
    will increasingly, and not always unfairly, come off as yuppie whiners, 'victims'
    with $50,000 incomes and vacations in Europe. They may feel they are op-
    pressed, but they will have a harder and harder time convincing the public."
    Jonathan Rauch, "Beyond Oppression, *"New Republic*, May 10, 1993.

10 See Richard Duncan, "Who Wants to Stop the Church: Homosexual Rights
    Legislation, Public Policy, and Religious Freedom," *Notre Dame Law Review*,
    69:3 : 395. Duncan presents a similar case and says it is based upon *Donahue v.
    Fair Employment & Housing Comm'n*, 2 Cal Rptr. 2nd 32 (Cal. App. 2nd Dist.
    1991), review granted, 825 P.2nd 766 (Cal. 1992); review dismissed and cause re-
    manded, 859 P.2nd 671 (Cal. 1993).

    Duncan argues that "the issue our society faces is one of bedrock principle—
    we must choose between inconsistent value systems, between the values of moral
    relativism and the sexual revolution on the one hand, and the traditional values
    of family and religious freedom on the other. And in making this decision we
    must never forget the high stakes involved." Ibid., 415.

11 On gay marriage, see *Homosexuality and American Public Life* (Dallas: Spence
    Publishing Company, 1999), especially chapters 7, 10, and 11. Mary Beth Style
    discusses adoption in length in her article in this volume.

12 I do not discuss here the question of whether homosexual couples should be
    permitted to acquire a child through artificial insemination (for lesbians) or sur-
    rogate motherhood (for male homosexuals), since it can be argued on other
    grounds that these practices should be illegal across the board.

5   *Romer, DOMA, and ENDA*

1   *Romer v. Evans* 517 U. S. 620 (1996).

2   Codified as 28 U.S.C. 1738C.

3   Reintroduced with modifications as S. 869/H.R. 1858.

4   DOMA provides definitions for the terms "marriage" and "spouse," to be ap-
    plied in interpreting the over one thousand federal laws that refer to marriage.
    It states that a "marriage" for federal purposes only consists of a union of one
    man and one woman and that a "spouse" is a partner of the opposite. The act
    further permits states to refuse to acknowledge same-sex marriages from other
    jurisdictions.

5   Robert H. Knight and Daniel Garcia, "Homosexuality is not a Civil Right," *In
    Focus*, Family Research Council (1993). See Michael Nava and Robert Davidoff,

Created Equal: Why Gay Rights Matter to America (New York: St. Martin's Press, 1994). For discussion of reaction in the African-American community: Lena Williams, "Blacks Reject Gay Rights Fight as Equal to Theirs," *New York Times,* 28 June 1993, A-1 and Andrea Neal, "Group to Protest NAACP's Stand on Gay Rights," *Indianapolis Star,* 8 July 1993, B-1.

6 See Cass R. Sunstein, "Sexual Orientation and the Constitution: A Note on the Relationship Between Due Process and Equal Protection," *University of Chicago Law Review* 55 (1988): 1161 and Robert Bork, *Slouching Towards Gomorrah* (New York: ReganBooks, 1996). See also the statement of Hadley Arkes, published in DOMA.

7 Mitchell S. Muncy, ed., *The End of Democracy? The Judicial Usurpation of Politics,* (Dallas: Spence Publishing Company, 1997) and Mitchell S. Muncy, ed., *The End of Democracy? II: A Crisis of Legitimacy* (Dallas: Spence Publishing Company, 1999).

8 478 U.S. 186 (1986).

9 Due Process has historically been limited because its tasks were to prevent innovation by the government and insure stability for both liberty and property for the people. See Sunstein, *supra.*

10 Sunstein, 1163. It is popular among elites to discuss the due process clause in terms of majorities. The governing power, however, is the subject of the clause and this group may itself be a controlling minority the clause is intended to restrain.

11 Sunstein, 1163.

12 Amendment XIV, section 1, passed in 1868 following the Civil War provided the protection of due process and equal protection of law against state actions. The Fifth Amendment, a part of the original Bill of Rights provided protection against federal government action.

13 *Dred Scott v. Sanford,* 60 U.S. (19 How.) 393 (1857).

14 852 P.2d 44 (Ha. 1993).

15 *Baker v. Nelson,* Minnesota (1971); *Jones v. Hallahan,* 501 S.W. 2d 588 (Ky.Ct.App.1973); *Singer v. Hara,* 11 Wash.App. 247.522 P.2d 1187 (1974); For federal principles see *Maynard v. Hill,* 125 U.S. 180 (1888). Federal courts have generally linked marriage with procreation and family. See Bruce C. Hafen, "The Constitutional Status of Marriage, Kinship, and Sexual Privacy—Balancing the Individual and Social Interests," *Michigan Law Review* 91 (1983): 463. See *Baehr* for the state courts recognition of the limits of federal precedents. See *Baker v. Nelson,* Minnesota court refuses to engage in social engineering, finds traditions and values a limit on judicial authority.

16 Sadler, "The Gay Rights Lobby," *Crisis* (July-August 1996). p. 21 at 25.

17 Prior to the passage of DOMA, fifteen states had passed legislation to prevent recognition of out-of-state same-sex marriage. Legislation was pending in many other states. In some instances, however, the progress of legislation had been

slowed because of Full Faith and Credit concerns. DOMA was intended not only to secure past legislation but to permit confidence in the ongoing process.

18   Article IV, section 1, clause 1.

19   Article IV, section 1, clause 1, provides in relevant part: "Full Faith and Credit shall be given in each State to the public Acts, Records, and judicial Proceedings of every other State. And Congress may by general Laws prescribe the Manner in which such Acts, Records and Proceedings shall be proved, and the Effect thereof."

20   Laurence Tribe, *American Constitutional Law* (Foundation Press, 1978), 944-47. Tribe presented himself as the defender of swinging America. Adults' right to sexual experience were too fundamental, he argued, to be limited to something as narrow as a state sanctioned relationship (marriage); rather a breathtaking list of activities were sure fire candidates for protection. Tribe wrote states might be hard pressed to defend laws against "polygamy, adultery, and bestiality, as well as variations such as group sex which are generally dealt with under sodomy and fornication laws," Ibid.

      Later, during the DOMA debate, Tribe wrote, "Who but a scoundrel could oppose the defense of marriage?" (See *Congressional Record*, Senate, June 6, 1996, S5932). Tribe had apparently forgotten his earlier position, or hoped Congress would.

21   Hadley Arkes, in Charles A. Donovan, ed., "In Defense of Marriage: Why Same-Sex Unions Miss the Mark," (Washington, D.C.: Family Research Council, 1996).

22   President Clinton endorsed the 1995 version of the bill and the White House continues its support.

23   Section 2 (1), and 3 (9)

24   The coverage would be significantly expanded in certain key areas, as in application to religious institutions, and with the new language on coercion. Proponents claim ENDA does not provide for quotas or preferences but see below for proof it does.

25   See statement and press release of Senator Jeffords on introducing ENDA, June 10, 1997.

26   Ibid.

27   See Hewitt, "Socioeconomic Position of Gay Men: A Review of the Evidence," *The American Journal of Economics and Sociology* 54:4 (1995): 461.

28   Jeffords' statement, *supra*.

29   "The Other Side of Tolerance," 3.

30   See Breast, "Forward in Defense of the Anti-Discrimination Principle," *Harvard Law Review* 90 (1976): 1.

31   ENDA would ban employer consideration of any aspect of sex-related inclination or practice except for a small range of "non-private" acts where the employers treat all orientations equally. The term "non-private" may apply only to

a very narrow range of commercial acts intended for broad distribution, as in pornographic films.

32 This effect results from the bill's sweeping protection which broadly defines sexual orientation and limits exclusions to a vaguely worded group of non-private acts, which appear to be commercial acts intended for broad distribution. Other ENDA sections declare sexual behavior irrelevant to employment, including as teachers in schools.

33 Duncan, supra. Richard Duncan of the University of Nebraska asserts in his article "Who Wants to Stop the Church?"

34 Hadley Arkes "Homosexuality and the Law," in Christopher Wolfe, ed., *Homosexuality and American Public Life* (Dallas: Spence Publishing, 1999), .

35 ENDA sections 9 (a) and (b).

6 *Homosexuality and the Military*

1 Professor Robert Doughty's *Seeds of Disaster: The Development of French Army Doctrine, 1919–1939* (Hamden, Conn.: Archon Books, 1985) is a seminal work on this point.

2 Robert Bork, *Slouching Towards Gomorrah: Modern Liberalism and American Decline* (New York: ReganBooks, 1996).

3 *Planned Parenthood v. Casey* 505 U.S. 833 (1992), joint opinion.

7 *Homosexuality and Adoption*

1 405 U.S. 645 (1972).

2 Lynn Wardle, "The Potential Impact of Homosexual Parenting on Children," *Illinois Law Review,*

3 463 U.S. 248 (1983).

4 The Uniform Adoption Act, the UAA, proposed by the National Conference of Commissioners on Uniform State Law recommends making a change to allow two unmarried individuals to adopt the same child. The provision is extremely controversial, with many ardent supporters of the UAA opposing this fundamental change of law.

5 Wardle, 1997.

9 *Homosexuality and the Entertainment Media*

1 Michelangelo Signorile, *Outing Yourself.*

2 Michelangelo Signorile, *Queer in America*: Sex, the Media, and the Closets of Power (New York: Random House, 1993).

3 Michael Medved, *Hollywood versus America.*

4 Ibid.

5   See Michael Medved "Television as a Medium Undermining the Family", in *The Family, Civil Society, and the State* (Rowman and Littlefield, 1998).
6   See Robert Knight, "Opposing Homosexual Advocacy," chapter 10, *infra*.

10   *Opposing Homosexual Advocacy*

1   *Romer v. Evans* 517 U.S. 620 (1996).
2   Hunter Madsen and Marshall Kirk, *After the Ball: How America Will Conquer Its Fear and Hatred of Gays in the 90s* (New York: Doubleday, 1989).
3   See Jeffrey Satinover, "The Biology of Homosexuality: Science or Politics?" in Christopher Wolfe, ed., *Homosexuality and American Public Life* (Spence Publishing Company, 1999), 3–61.
4   July 22, 1997, 52
6   See chapter 16 in this volume by Jane Boyer.

11   *Churches, Schools, and Libraries*

1   Joe Dallas, *A Strong Delusion: Confronting the "Gay Christian" Movement* (Eugene, OR: Harvest House, 1996), 65.
2   http://www.qrd.org/qrd/religion/orgs/.
3   See Dallas, *A Strong Delusion*, 29, citing Paul Varnell, "Learning from Catholic's Change," *OutNOW!* 3:13 (June 27, 1995): 15.
4   Bernadette J. Brooten, *Love Between Women: Early Christian Responses to Female Homoeroticism* (University of Chicago, 1996), 194.
5   Quoted in Dallas, *A Strong Delusion*, 34.
6   http://www.glstn/respect/letter from a rabbi, p.2.
7   Quoted in F. LaGard Smith, *Sodom's Second Coming* (Eugene: Harvest House Publishers, 1993), 130.
8   See Joe Dallas, *A Strong Delusion*, 62.
9   Ramsay MacMullen, *Changes in the Roman Empire* (Princeton: Princeton University Press, 1990), 177-189.
10   Personal interview with Prof. MacMullen.
11   Brooten, *Love Between Women*, 302.
12   Tom Hanks, "Sleeping with the Enemy: A Political Necessity for All of us?," *More Light Update* 17:4 (March-April 1997); http://www.epp.cmu.edu/~riley/PLGC.html.
13   Ibid. Bracketed material in original.
14   Ibid.
15   Dallas, *A Strong Delusion*, 22.
16   "Gay-Straight Alliances: A Student Guide," Massachusetts Department of Education, July 1995 (hereinafter "Student Guide").
17   Ibid., 5.

18 Ibid., 8.
19 Dallas says the term "homophobe" was coined in 1972 by psychologist George Weinberg. Dallas, *A Strong Delusion*, 135. His cite is to Richard Isay, *Being Homosexual* (New York: Farrar, Strauss & Giroux, 1989), 145.
20 Student Guide, 8.
21 Ibid, 12.
22 Associated Press, "Utah Lawmakers Pass Ban on Gay Clubs at Schools"; see *Washington Times* 19 April 1996, A-11.
23 A third, emerging issue is use of Internet facilities at libraries.
24 Personal Interview, June 11, 1997.
25 Ibid.
26 See, e.g., C.S. Lewis, *Mere Christianity* (New York: Collier Books, 1943), 75.

12   *Historical Scholarship on Homosexuality*

1 Chicago: University of Chicago Press, 1980.
2 *New York Times Book Review*, August 10, 1980: 12.
3 D. F. Wright, "Early Christian Attitudes to Homosexuality," *Studia Patristica* 18 (1989): 333. See also his article "Homosexuality," in *Encyclopedia of Early Christianity*, 2 ed. (1997), 1:542-3 (with bibliography).
4 New York: Villiard Books, 1994.
5 For criticism of Boswell's interpretation of Romans see R. B. Hays, "Relations Natural and Unnatural: A Response to Boswell's Exegesis of Romans 1," *Journal of Religious Ethics* 14 (1986): 184-215.
6 January 23, 1981, 73ff.
7 December 4, 1980, 438-46.
8 For reviews, see Robert L. Wilken in *Commonweal* 9 (September 1994): 24-26 and Robin Darling Young in *First Things* 47 (November 1994): 43-48.
9 July 18-25, 1994, 33-41.
10 *The Good of Marriage*, 1.

13   *Homosexuality and Judaism*

1 Levit. 18:22 and 20:13.
2 On WNBC TV's *Donahue* show during a discussion of the controversial Harvey Milk High School for homosexual students, June 12, 1985.
3 See below for sources.
4 Spero, M.H., in (a) "Homosexuality: Clinical and Ethical Challenges," in *Judaism and Psychology Halakhic Perspectives*, Yeshiva University, New York, 1980 and (b) "Further Examinations of the Halakhic Status of Homosexuality", *Proceedings of the Association of Orthodox Jewish Scientists*, vol. 7, 1983, disagrees with this position and claims that a homosexual personality, as defined by desires,

orientation and lifestyle does exist, and that this state is intrinsically prohibited. In addition to the philosophical problems discussed in the article that arise from this position, there is an even more serious problem with his approach. The sources that Spero uses to support his position, *Torah Temimah* to Gen. 2:24, T. J. *Kiddushin* 1:1, all deal with Gentiles. Although anything forbidden to Gentiles is forbidden to Jews, the prohibition against engaging in a homosexual state cannot apply to Jews if the state does not exist for Jews. At best Spero has supported the idea of a homosexual subgroup in Gentile society. See below for discussion.

5   See the *Mishnayot* in the third chapter of Tractate *Horiyot* and the *Mishnayot* in the eighth chapter of *Yevamot*. The categories of individuals mentioned here are *Cohen*—priest, *Levi, mamzer*—product of an adulterous or incestuous marriage, *Cohen Gadol*—high priest, *katan*—child, *gadol*—adult, *cheresh*—deaf-mute, *shoteh*—mental incompetent. This list is by no means complete.

6   *Roveia* (c.f. *Sanhedrin* 9b) refers to only one aspect of the homosexual act and is also used for other sexual acts, e.g. bestiality (Levit. 18:23 and Mishna *Sanhedrin*, 1:4), and intercourse between animals (Levit. 18:23 and *T.J. Avodah Zarah* 40a). A. Even-Shoshan, *HaMilon Hehadash*, s.v. ___, sees this first meaning as the primary and original meaning of the term. Interestingly R. Ishmael (*Sanhedrin* 54b) requires a different verse (Deut. 23:18) to warn the "female" participant in the homosexual act from the verse (Levit. 18:22) which warns the "male" participant. As a result if an individual plays both roles at one time he is punishable for two sins. R. Akiba disagrees and allows an alternate reading of the verse in Levit. to serve as warning for the "female" participant, and consequently holds that an individual who plays both roles at once is punishable only once. It seems that R. Ishmael, certainly, and R. Akiba, probably, saw the two types of activity as being different. This strikes another blow against "*Roveia*" being a term for a homosexual and another blow against one who would want to suggest that the rabbis did recognize a homosexual personality. If there are two types of actions involved and two different verses or readings needed to cover them, there can not be a homosexual in Jewish law. If there were such an individual one verse should be sufficient. Other possible terms such as *Shochev Im Zecharim* or *Shochev Mishkivei Isha* are awkward and do not appear in colloquial usage. The modern transliteration of homosexual in Hebrew only proves the point that no term exists.

7   See *Avodah Zarah* 26b, *Hulin* 5a, *Horiyot* 11a, Rambam *Yad, Hilchot Teshuva* 3:9 and *Kesef Mishneh* ad. loc., *Shulchan Aruch, Yoreh Deah* 2, and *Choshen Mishpat*, 266:2. Some might argue that homosexuals who are exclusively homosexual are actually *Mumarim L'hachis* (following Rashi A.Z., ad. loc., sv. *L'Teiavon*). Although some militant homosexuals may come close to this definition, the emotional conflicts and extenuating circumstances involved make it difficult to describe most, if any, homosexuals as having actively chosen to reject permis-

sible sexual relations for forbidden ones in the same way that Rashi describes the *Mumar L'hachis'* behavior regarding non-kosher meat. Even if one could define some or all homosexually oriented individuals as *Mumarim L'hachis* the comment of the *Chazon Ish* quoted in the next footnote would allow us to treat such an individual in the same way that we would treat a *Mumar L'Teiavon*, i.e. like any other Jew (see *Kesef Mishneh* loc. cit.).

8   It is well known that if one violates the Sabbath in public there is a serious stigma attached (see *Hulin* 5a-6b and *Eruvin* 69a.). However, the equating of the Sabbath desecrator and the idolator is rarely applied in any more than a pedagogic sense in contemporary halachic literature (see R. Moshe Feinstein, *Iggerot Moshe, Orach Chaim*, 1, No. 23 and especially 1, No. 33). In addition to R. Feinstein's lenient stance on *Mechallelei Shabbat*, the *Chazon Ish, Yoreh Deah* 2:16, says that the stringent treatment of transgressors described in the Talmud does not apply today, as such treatment will cause greater abandonment of Judaism. Since our task is to improve the situation and not to make it worse, the only approach to take with sinners is "to bring them back with ropes of love." This statement from the *Chazon Ish* could serve as the central message of this article.

9   Rambam, *Sefer Hamitzvot* Positive Commandment, No. 73.

10 "There is no guardian against unchastity" (*Ketubot* 13b and *Hulin* 11b), or the even more dramatic, "Even the most pious of the pious is not appointed guardian over unchastity" (TJ *Ketubot* 1,8). See also Rambam, *Issurel Biah*, 2:19, that inappropriate sexual behavior will occur from time to time, in all communities because of man's extreme desire for sexual matters.

11 Levit. 18:22 and 20:13.

12 Deut. 14:3.

13 Deut. 7:25-26 and 27:15.

14 Deut. 25:16. Parenthetically, it would be interesting to see the stigma presently attached to homosexuality placed on anyone guilty of unethical business practices—at least for a brief time.

15 Deut. 24:4.

16 "Judaism and the Modern Attitude to Homosexuality," *Encyclopedia Judaica Yearbook* 1974, (Jerusalem: Keter, 1974), 198.

17 The concept of *Teshuva* makes no sense without this premise.

18 Ibid., 202. See also Matt, H.J., "Sin, Crime, Sickness or Alternative Lifestyle: A Jewish Approach to Homosexuality", *Judaism*, vol. 27 No. 1 Winter 1978. and Bleich, J.D., *Judaism and Healing, Halakhic Perspectives*, Ktav, New York, 1981. Bleich comes closest to the view presented in this article on the homosexual as *anuss* (forced). However, *"mumar"* (sinner) as opposed to *"anuss"* is the term to be used in the discussion of homosexuality. Introducing *"oness"* (compulsion) in a discussion of homosexuality is as appropriate as introducing it to a discussion of murder. There are murderers who are *anussim* (psychopathological murderers), but a discussion of these individuals is not a discussion of murder or the

Jewish attitude to that crime. Yet we continue to speak of *anussim* (psycho-pathological murderers), who may make up only a small portion of those involved in that activity, in regard to Judaism's general view on the subject.

19 *Bava Kama* 28b, *Avodah Zarah* 54a, *Nedarim* 27a. Spero op. cit., (b) also rejects the *anuss* position on these and other grounds.

20 Levit. 20:13.

21 e.g., *Sanhedrin* 9b and 54a.

22 Rambam, *Yad., Hilchot Issurel Biah* 1:14.

23 Ibid., 203-204.

24 *Avodah Zarah* 3a.

25 Schwartz, M.F. and Masters, W.H., "The Masters and Johnson Treatment Program for Dissatisfied Homosexual Men", *American Journal of Psychiatry* 141:2, February, 1984, 173-181. This study shows a remarkable success rate. After 1 year the success rate was 79.1 percent and after 5 years it was 71.6 percent.

26 ". . . except that the (frequency of the) homosexual among Orthodox Jewish groups appears to be phenomenally low", Kinsey, A.C., Pomeroy, W.B., Marx, C.E., *Sexual Behaviour in the Human Male*, W.B. Saunders, Phila., 1948, p. 4. See also Rosenheim, E., "Sexual Attitudes and Regulations in Judaism", Money, J. and Musaph, J., ed., *Handbook of Sexology, Excerpta Medi* (Amsterdam, 1977), 1321-22.

27 *Yevamot* 76a, *Shabbat* 65a. Female homosexuality is punished by *"Makot Mardut"* which is a rabbinic and not a biblical punishment, *Yad, Issurei Biah* 21;8. On the other hand male homosexuality is a capital crime as has been indicated. For a more complete discussion of female homosexuality see Spero, op. cit., (b).

28 *Sefer HaChinuch* No. 209.

29 *Torah Temimah* to Levit. 18:22, No. 70.

30 *Sefer HaChinuch*, loc. cit.

31 *Nidah* 13a, Rambam, *Yad, Hilchot Issurei Biah* 21;18, *Shulchan Aruch*, E.H. 23;1-2. There is no question of the seriousness of this sin, but it is not a capital crime to be tried in a human court of law as is homosexuality. See also Feldman, D.M., *Birth Control and Jewish Law* (New York University, 1968), chs. 6 and 8, and the debate between him and M. Tendler in *Tradition*, vol. 9, No.'s 1-2 and 4. Even if we accept the view that Er and Onan (Gen. 38) died for the sin of *haschatat zera*, their punishment came at G-d's hands and not in a court of law.

32 *Sanhedrin* 55a, Rambam, *Yad, Hilchot Issurei Biah* 1;10, and 1;14. *Shulchan Aruch, Even Ha'Ezer*, 20;2.

33 Gen. 2:24.

34 This approach is suggested by the *Beraita, Sanhedrin* 58a, which derives prohibitions for various immoral sexual activities for Gentiles from this verse.

35 This approach was suggested to me by Mr. Mat Hoffman, national director of *The Flame*, Jewish College Student's Organization. It is also suggested, in brief terms, by Dr. Lamm, op. cit., pp. 197-198.

36   *Gen. Rab.*, 26;5 (commenting on Gen. 6:2).
37   *Nedarim* 51a.

14   *Homosexuality and Catholic Doctrine*

1   *Catechism of the Catholic Church*, #2357-59. The second sentence of the second paragraph (#2358) in the original edition was subsequently modified, and now reads as presented here. "Promulgation of Catechism's Latin Typical Edition" September 8, 1997.

15   *Courage*

1   Letter to the Roman Catholic Bishops of the World, PCHP, October 1, 1986, #5; also *Dei Verbum*, #10: "It is clear, therefore, that in the supremely wise arrangement of God, Sacred Tradition, Sacred Scripture, and the Magisterium of the Church are so connected and associated that once of them cannot stand without the others."

2   Pierre Grelot's *Man and Wife in Scripture* (London: Burns and Oates, 1964) provides many more details on this issue.

3   "Homosexuality: Challenges for Change and Reorientation," *Journal of Pastoral Counseling*, 28, 1993.

4   Ibid. 53.

5   Ibid. 56.

6   See my books, *The Homosexual Person* (San Francisco: Ignatius Press, 1987) and *The Truth About Homosexuality* (San Francisco: Ignatius Press, 1996).

7   See Elizabeth Moberly, *Homosexuality: A New Christian Ethic?* (Cambridge: James Clarke, 1983)

8   For example, Richard Isay, *Becoming Gay: The Journey to Self-Acceptance* (Pantheon Books, 1996).

9   Our New York office phone is 212-268-1010. Our address is Courage, c/o St. John the Baptist Church, 210 W. 31 St. N.Y., N.Y., 10001. Our website is http://world.std.com/~courage.

Afterword: Hatred, Bigotry, and Intolerance

1   Psychiatric Association Schedules Debate on Reorientation Therapy: Gay-Affirming Psychiatrists Refuse to Participate," on the NARTH website, at www.narth.com.

2   See "Gay Activists Protest Plans for Conference: Georgetown U. Gets Letter of Complaint," *Washington Post*, May 31, 1997, B3.

3   Ethics and Public Policy Center "Gay Rights v. Religious Freedom Fact Sheet," with various citations to other sources.

4 For the record, I should make these observations on the statements attributed to me: The first two and the last are accurate. The third statement runs together two distinct points: that the causes of homosexuality often are found in a homosexual's relation with his parents and that a significant number of homosexuals experienced sexual abuse in their youth. The fourth statement is substantially accurate though grammatically mangled (the family is intact, not the mother and father). In the fifth statement "reproduction" should be "reproductive." It should be noted that a "reproductive act" is not necessarily an act that actually reproduces, but an act of the kind that is in principle capable of reproduction. The sixth statement is accurate if it is understood to refer to a marriage in which one person deliberately and permanently excludes the possibility of ever having children.

5 *The Heights,* May 2, 2000.

6 There are notable exceptions such as Stephen Macedo of Princeton University, who has engaged in debate at the highest levels of sophistication with leading critics of homosexual conduct. See Stephen Macedo, "Homosexuality and the Conservative Mind," Robert P. George and Gerard V. Bradley, "Marriage and the Liberal Imagination," Hadley Arkes, "Questions of Principle, not Predictions: A Reply to Macedo," and Stephen Macedo, "Reply to Critics" in the *Georgetown Law Journal* 84:2 (December 1995).

7 This quotation is from a flyer circulated on the Boston College campus after the speech on gay marriage referred to earlier in the text.

8 *R.A.V. v. St. Paul* 120 L.Ed.2d 305, at 323 (1992).

9 See Jeffrey Satinover, *Homosexuality and the Politics of Truth,* and Joseph Nicolosi "The Gay Deception," in *Homosexuality and American Public Life.*

Index

This book was designed and set into type
by Mitchell S. Muncy,
with cover art by Stephen J. Ott,
and printed and bound
by Edwards Brothers, Inc.,
Ann Arbor, Michigan.

The text face is Caslon,
designed by Carol Twombly,
based on faces cut by William Caslon, London, in the 1730s
and issued in digital form by Adobe Systems,
Mountain View, California, in 1989.

The index is by IndExpert,
Fort Worth, Texas.

The paper is acid-free and is of archival quality.

27